Imagery in Psychotherapy

Imagery in Psychotherapy

Jerome L. Singer

AMERICAN PSYCHOLOGICAL ASSOCIATION

WASHINGTON, DC

Published by
American Psychological Association
750 First Street, NE
Washington, DC 20002
www.apa.org

To order
APA Order Department
P.O. Box 92984
Washington, DC 20090-2984
Tel: (800) 374-2721
Direct: (202) 336-5510
Fax: (202) 336-5502
TDD/TTY: (202) 336-6123
Online: www.apa.org/books/
E-mail: order@apa.org

In the U.K., Europe, Africa, and the Middle East, copies may be ordered from
American Psychological Association
3 Henrietta Street
Covent Garden, London
WC2E 8LU England

Typeset in Goudy by World Composition Services, Inc., Sterling, VA

Printer: Data Reproductions, Auburn Hills, MI
Cover Designer: Berg Design, Albany, NY
Technical/Production Editor: Harriet Kaplan

The opinions and statements published are the responsibility of the authors, and such opinions and statements do not necessarily represent the policies of the American Psychological Association.

Library of Congress Cataloging-in-Publication Data

Singer, Jerome L.
  Imagery in psychotherapy / Jerome L. Singer.— 1st ed.
    p. cm.
  Includes bibliographical references and index.
  ISBN 1-59147-333-0
  1. Imagery (Psychology) Therapeutic use. 2. Visualization—Therapeutic use. I. Title.

RC489.F35S576 2006
616.89′14—dc22   2005014099

British Library Cataloguing-in-Publication Data
A CIP record is available from the British Library.

Printed in the United States of America
First Edition

For Dorothy

CONTENTS

ACKNOWLEDGMENTS

Although I must take full responsibility for the opinions and content of this book, I wish to acknowledge the many intellectual contributions I have received from students in my graduate courses in psychotherapy at Yale, the City University of New York, and Teachers College, Columbia University. Many of these students in their classroom comments, conversations with me, and their course papers have broadened my awareness and understanding of the psychotherapy process immeasurably. My instructors and colleagues at the William Alanson White Institute of Psychiatry, Psychology, and Psychoanalysis have also enriched my consciousness of the nature of interpersonal transactions. I very much want to thank my many clients in my more than 50-year career as a psychotherapist. I believe I helped many of them, and I hope my efforts on their behalf afforded some recompense for the important things I learned from our interactions.

I must also acknowledge specific help in preparation of this manuscript from Lisa Pagliaro and from my research assistants Lauren Ng, Sarah Treem, Brittania Weatherspoon, Jane Erickson, and Julia Hayden. Scott Barry Kaufman collaborated with me in developing the work on successful intelligence and its link to psychotherapy. My long-term colleague and early collaborator, Kenneth Pope, also encouraged me recently to write this book for the American Psychological Association. Needless to say, my wife, Dorothy Singer, was a valuable contributor, not only for case material on child therapy but also in terms of morale and the nitty-gritty of solving computer glitches.

Imagery in Psychotherapy

1

WHY IMAGERY, PERSONAL MEMORIES, AND DAYDREAMS MATTER

Two people confront each other in what is by now the universally acknowledged practice we call psychotherapy, whether behavior modification or some related form of psychological counseling. The client or patient must communicate to the professional therapist a list of symptoms or troubling interpersonal and social dilemmas, and do so not only in a common language but also in a fashion that permits the listener to enter into the settings, contexts, and cast of characters of the speaker's world in some meaningful fashion. Just a few weeks ago, I was presenting to a group of students an old example, from my psychotherapy practice in New York City, of a woman who began her interview by saying, "Do you know what it's like to grow up in a town called What Cheer, Iowa?" To my utter amazement a student in this class called out, "I know that place!" This was the first person I had encountered in almost 50 years who could connect immediately with that opening statement without the further explanation and details I had required at the time. And how can the therapist faced with a "stranger from a strange land" begin to make sense of the patient's communication without that person drawing on her stream of event memories to create a narrative sufficiently vivid so that the therapist can begin to form some mental representations? These may involve pictorial, auditory, or even olfactory sensory-like images, which can then lead to meaningful schemas that permit a reasonable approximation of the other person's private experience.

Human evolution has afforded us a fundamental capacity to reconstruct sensations and perceptions that are ongoing or long past into fairly specific images. These may lack the clarity of a television instant replay, but they seem nevertheless, as we dwell on them, to allow us at least temporarily to inhabit a setting in time or space other than the immediate processing of the client's face or the feel of an easy chair. Just in the past decade, computer technology has begun allowing us to "Google" up a description, perhaps even a photograph, of the town of What Cheer with a few finger taps. We would still need to draw on the client's evocation of her experiences and daily encounters to grasp to some degree why she began her search for psychotherapeutic help by mentioning this little-known town.

Mental imagery is a critical feature of all effective human communication, but it also has a special role to play in the psychotherapeutic process. I propose in the present volume to examine that special role in a variety of therapeutic approaches. By no means do I intend to cover all of the potentially effective methods by which we can strive to relieve psychological symptoms, overcome interpersonal difficulties, change self-defeating habits, or ease emotional distress. My emphasis in this volume is to suggest how both the patient's and the therapist's imagery capacities can be sharpened and focused so that they can play critical roles in improving the therapeutic alliance.

More than 30 years ago, I was among the first clinicians and personality researchers to call attention to the ways in which our imagery system was used in a great variety of psychotherapies ranging from forms of psychoanalysis through the newer behavioral and emerging American cognitive–behavioral approaches as well as in the so-called "humanistic" or the guided imagery orientations then more prominent in Europe (J. L. Singer, 1974). My goal in the present volume is to focus more directly on the research-based understanding of our imagery system, its links to cognition and emotion, and its practical usefulness to the working clinician and to students of psychotherapy, cognitive–behavioral therapy, and counseling. I use some of my personal experiences as a means of encouraging awareness of the reader's own memories and fantasies as guides to effective professional employment of imagery.

A PERSONAL NOTE TO THE READER

After 50 years of psychotherapy practice, I retired from that intriguing line of work. As I continue, however, with other university activities as a professor emeritus and supervisor of research, I am attempting in this book to summarize for clinicians and students my experience in the clinical applications of the human imagination. I began my career as a psychologist in late 1946, having just completed a tour of duty as a special agent in the U.S. Army Counter-Intelligence Corps in the Pacific Theater in the late phases of World War II and the beginnings of the occupation of Japan. On my first day as a clinical psychology trainee from the University of Pennsylvania at the Philadelphia Veterans Administration Mental Hygiene Clinic, I was assigned patients for assessment and psychotherapy. As a member of a small cohort of clinical psychologists in the immediate postwar period, I experienced the excitement and challenges of the emergence of this new field of endeavor. Thousands of war veterans were being referred to the clinics and mental hospitals being developed all over the United States.

Our task was to find ways of assessing their psychological difficulties and then deciding on courses of treatment. The psychology departments that were offering clinical training programs were themselves trying at that time to determine methods of assessment and treatment as well as seeking to establish formal academic criteria in what had been a relatively small field of graduate study before the 1940s. With only limited guidance from the university departments, most of us relied most heavily on our reading of the psychoanalytic literature and of the early works of Carl Rogers. We sought help in the assessment process by teaching each other the new Minnesota Multiphasic Personality Inventory, the Wechsler Intelligence Scales, and the projective techniques then just gaining popularity—the Rorschach inkblot and thematic apperception tests, among others.

It seemed to many students in those days that the basic science of psychology had little to offer someone confronted with the reality of evaluating and treating an individual with neurosis or psychosis. Learning theory was largely relegated to the study of rats, and although sophisticated models were apparently being generated in the laboratories of Clark Hull and Edward Chase Tolman, this information was hard to transfer to the realities of daily clinical confrontations. In the next 15 or 20 years, literally dozens of psychotherapeutic and behavior modification approaches emerged and even became the focus of "schools." It seemed as if psychology as a scientific discipline had been left behind in the rush of efforts to generate new total approaches, many of which in effect incorporated their own psychological systems. Seeing the limitations of the formal doctoral training available, psychologists looked wherever possible for postdoctoral training opportunities. For political reasons not germane to this volume, the doors to the psychoanalytic institutes that were the main avenues for further training were limited to physicians and shut to psychologists and social workers. I was one of a very small number of psychologists who managed to attain psychoanalytic training in the 1950s at a formal institute, in this case the William Alanson White Institute in New York City, which focused primarily on the interpersonal psychoanalysis developed by Harry Stack Sullivan and others. Even while I was undertaking courses and the clinical training of the institute, I was also carrying out an extended research program, begun in my graduate student days, on the psychology of the human imagination. I believe that I was one of the first psychologists to seek formal research methods for studying various facets of human conscious experience such as daydreams and the nature of spontaneous imagery. At the start, my research activities seemed quite separate from my clinical work, influenced as it had been by my postdoctoral training in psychoanalysis, but the experience of actively conducting empirical research and the concomitant scholarship it entailed led me to explore the emerging area of cognitive psychology. The link between cognition and emotion proposed in the great two volumes of Silvan S. Tomkins (1962, 1963) pointed toward an increased opportunity to build clinical practice from basic psychological science rather than from the separate quasi-psychologies of the burgeoning psychotherapy schools.

My own research on human imagination provided me, I believe, with an integrative opportunity. I recognized how much of what seemed to be necessary and also effective in clinical treatment depended on the patient's ability to produce vivid and concrete memory and fantasy images. I surveyed the various psychodynamic therapies and how they operated in practice. I also trained myself in the use of the new forms of behavior therapy. It was increasingly clear that all of these approaches relied heavily on the human capacity for producing images in the various sensory modalities. As it turned out, most of the behavior therapies, labeled as such to emphasize their "objective" properties, still relied heavily on the ability of the patients to generate private images, whether of phobic situations or of successful achievements by imagined models. This realization suggested an opportunity for drawing on the scientific knowledge in cognition and emotion and thereby linking together the various seemingly disparate schools of therapeutic practice. I attempted this in some articles and subsequently in a scholarly book, *Imagery and Daydream Methods in Psychotherapy and Behavior Modification* (J. L. Singer, 1974). Kenneth Pope and I edited two volumes, *The Stream of Consciousness* (Pope & Singer, 1978) and *The Power of Human Imagination* (J. L. Singer & Pope, 1978), in which we brought together experts on research in these areas and sought to point the way toward further establishment of scientifically based applications of imaginative consciousness and the imagery processes. The establishment of the American Association for the Study of Mental Imagery in the late 1970s offered an organizational basis for assembling practitioners and researchers around the study of conscious experience and imagination. Psychology more generally, despite the cognitive revolution that could be dated from the 1960s, was still not dealing directly with consciousness. Kenneth Pope and I introduced a journal in this area in the early 1980s, *Imagination, Cognition and Personality: Con-*

sciousness in Theory, Research and Clinical Practice, with the support of the Baywood Publishing Company. This company also undertook to publish a series of volumes on imagery and its various applications in health, psychotherapy, and even sports.

It was only in the 1990s that we began to witness a revival of psychology's early interest in conscious experience. Indeed, with the emergence of neuroscience and great developments in computer simulation of thought, philosophers, psychologists, cognitive scientists, and neurophysiologists are now increasingly talking and writing about conscious experience, of which, of course, imagery and imagination are critical components. A new journal, *Consciousness and Cognition*, has also appeared. William James, the great proponent of conscious experience as a central issue in human psychology, is increasingly cited not only as a historical figure but as the instigator of current research efforts (J. L. Singer, 1995). This seems an especially propitious time for a practically oriented book designed for clinicians that can reflect the current state of scientific knowledge in the uses of imagery and related conscious phenomena.

OBJECTIVES AND ORGANIZATION OF THIS BOOK

I have two major objectives in this book. The first is to provide the practicing clinician with an indication of the scientific research-based evidence on the nature of the human imagery capacity and its relationship to fundamental processes such as information processing, cognition more generally, emotionality, and motivation as applicable to what we know of relevant social processes and psychobiology. Rather than working within the framework of a particular school, whether classical Freudian or some other variant of psychoanalysis, object relations, self psychology, the interpersonal psychoanalytic school, or cognitive–behavioral therapies, I intend to link the uses of imagery to the basic psychological processes and the research evidence currently available. I propose that the interesting ideas one can derive from the various theories that have prevailed as separate systems can be integrated within the framework of what is currently known in basic psychology. It is true that important suggestions about the role of early childhood relationships came originally from psychoanalysis. These include, for example, the importance of child–parent attachment or, from Adler, the significance of the lifelong struggle between the individual's needs for power versus the desire for social involvement or intimacy.

As we shall see, the various "schools" of psychotherapy and personality theory in many cases have suggested important avenues for research that have increasingly been incorporated into the development of basic psychological science. Some of the schools have perhaps contributed more to technique (as is the case for Gestalt therapy) rather than useful theoretical areas for exploration. My emphasis in this book is specifically on the ways in which the imagery system can be used in a variety of psychotherapeutic interventions. Many of the other aspects of how basic psychological science integrates the various schools and can be applied to the general psychotherapeutic process will not necessarily be covered here. It is my hope, however, that clinicians can begin to recognize from the example of this book how their work can be increasingly derived from and related to more general psychological research.

My second major objective is to provide practical suggestions to working clinicians on how to make use of their patients' and, as a matter of fact, their own imagery abilities in treating clients using a variety of approaches. I personally value the potential use of the human imagery capacity and all of consciousness more generally. The empirically demonstrated success of the various behavior therapies or of combined behavior and cognitive therapies forces us to recognize that many features of the therapeutic process can be carried out without a specific focus by the therapist on the individual patient's ability to produce imagery. It is my belief, however, that many therapists do not fully appreciate the particular ways in which the imagery system operates and the various applications of that system to their work even in the more behaviorally oriented treatments.

This book is not a psychotherapy manual. In the course of presenting the various uses of psychotherapy I refer to manualized treatments for particular conditions that incorporate imagery and that have, to some degree, been "validated." However, my goal is instead to arm the clinician with a broader, scientifically based understanding of the wealth of opportunities afforded by a knowledge of the way in which imagery may be applied in a variety of treatment or other practical situations.

The role of consciousness (and imagery as one of its major facets) has been to some degree minimized in many of the theories of cognition and of psychodynamic therapies. What I would prefer to show is the special advantages that consciousness as a narrowly focused but broadly implicative system has to offer to adaptive functioning and mental health. William James (1890/1950) perhaps went too far in arguing that evidence of thought and complex processes must always be conscious and that other operations of the organism that were not in focal or marginal awareness must be essentially biological or physical. The psychodynamic theories that prevailed in personality research for most of the 20th century took as their challenge the demonstration of how much of our affective and ultimately behavioral processes may be derived from unconscious thoughts or fantasies. In the past 20 years, the fields of cognitive and social psychology have demonstrated through systematic research that a considerable amount of human activity is traceable to processes that are at least temporarily outside cognitive awareness or in some cases (as in grammatical usage) never conscious at all (Hassin, Uleman, & Bargh, 2005).

My own work on daydreaming and the stream of thought (along with the contributions of John Antrobus, Eric Klinger, Mihaly Csikszentmihalyi, Leonard Giambra, the late Nicholas Spanos, and many others) has increasingly suggested the critical role of conscious processes in the human endeavor (J. A. Singer & Salovey, 1999). Recent debates concerning the significance of consciousness have involved philosophers like John Searle, Daniel Dennett, and Max Velmans; physiologists like Francis Crick, Joseph Bogen, and Michael Gazzaniga; and experimental psychologists such as Stephen Kosslyn, John Kihlstrom, and Anthony Marcel (Ciba Foundation, 1993). Bernard Baars (1997) has been perhaps the most systematic of all of these in his attempt to lay out both a theoretical place for consciousness in organismic functioning and also in pointing to potential research areas that require exploration. My plan in this volume is to incorporate some of the latest findings on the significance of conscious thought in relation to unconscious processes as a tool for the practicing clinical psychotherapist or the student of behavioral medicine.

The initial chapters describe the current status of knowledge about the imagery processes in relation to ongoing consciousness, fantasy, and daydreaming. I then move on to the specific role that imagery may have in defining personality variations and its special potential for effective human communication in the formation of life narratives. In the course of this discussion, I also point out some varieties of imagery for the assessment of personality differences and psychopathological tendencies. I next move to what I consider an extremely important feature of imagery: the ability to expand one's own self-awareness through attention to one's fantasies, memories, and dreams, whether these appear to occur spontaneously or whether they are guided in a more deliberate fashion. Through this discussion, I hope to stimulate clinicians not only to think about uses of this process with clients but also to expand their own self-awareness and consciousness as tools for both personal self-improvement and more effective work with others. Next, I review the current status of the literature on self-representations not only as critical determinants of individuals' goals and strivings but also as guides to the arousal of various emotions or as effective means of self-development and self-direction. The next sequence of chapters deals specifically with how imagery can be used in a variety of psychotherapeutic interventions ranging from psychodynamic and interpersonal approaches through the more symptom-focused cognitive–behavioral therapies and in health psychology situations. I also deal with the special issues relating to the role of imagery and the experience of self, an area that is the subject of some misunderstanding and much controversy. Finally, my concluding section explores more broadly the significance of human imagery in relation to our development of culture, aesthetics, and personal creativity, whether in the interests of art, science, or business or more directly in effective daily living with those around us.

I cite important relevant research literature, particularly in the earlier phases of presentation. My goal, however, is to talk directly to clinicians and not to attempt a critical analysis of the research literature. I believe the bibliography provided will be of considerable use to the reader who wishes to follow up in specific areas, whether for further potential research or for greater in-depth discussion of some of the technical literature.

SOME FINAL PERSONAL COMMENTS

I began these introductory remarks with a brief autobiographical statement relevant to my professional career as a psychologist. I should like to conclude by calling attention to some instances of my own self-awareness that may well have initially drawn me to studying the nature of human fantasy and daydreaming processes but may also have played a broader role in the formation of my personality as a son, husband, father, and grandfather as well as a professional colleague for many practicing psychologists and teachers of graduate and undergraduate students. In doing so I hope I can encourage my readers to use their own introspective capabilities as guides not only to general self-awareness but also as signposts toward new research and clinical approaches.

From my earliest years, I seemed to have been introspective and aware of events around me and the bearing they had on my imagination. When I used to read as an adult about the notion of childhood repression, I was somewhat puzzled because I did not seem to have ever been aware of significant gaps in my memory since the age of about 3. Whether my memories from those early days were fantasies, screen memories, or perhaps considerably reworked thoughts remains unknown. I seemed early in my childhood to be able to make a distinction between an actual memory and something that had been told to me. For example, as a toddler I was reported to have walked out of a New York City subway car onto the platform at a station stop. Before my parents could reach me the doors shut and I was left standing there as the train moved on. My father of course at the next stop took a train back and fortunately found me held by the hand of a kindly bystander. I can picture that scene even though I realize that I never actually remembered it; I had been told about it by my parents when I was perhaps 4 or 5 years of age. I reconstructed the image early on, including the sight (which I could never have seen) of my frantic father running up the station steps to cross over to the other side of the tracks and catch a returning train.

Other scenes from childhood, however, which were even more vivid found verification subsequently. For example, in the period between ages 3 and 4, I often seemed to have a fearful fantasy about a "creeping baby" that might appear to torment me if I didn't stay carefully covered under my blankets at bedtime. For many years I couldn't understand why this fantasy should have stayed with me and seemed to inspire such fear. I had other memories from that same period that as an adult did help me to formulate a connection, even though for me as a child the situations were not associated. During that same stage of my life, my family shared a large apartment with a cousin who was a practicing physician and whose office and waiting room were also located in the apartment. I had always remembered him showing me a jar in which there was a seemingly well-formed little infant. As a teenager I came to realize that what he was showing me was a human fetus that had been preserved. Because he never really seemed to have explained much to me about it, it is quite easy to see how it became a symbol of mystery and fright that I incorporated into my bedtime fantasies when left alone in the dark. These two relatively clear memories were not connected consciously during my earlier childhood; the possible linkage came to me much later.

Another example is an early memory between ages 4 and 5 (when we had already moved to a different apartment) in which my mother, to punish me for some misdeed, shut me up in one of the clothes closets of the apartment. She threatened that if I didn't change my behavior the "Bogey Man" would come for me. I remember this event rather clearly along with my weeping as I went into the closet. Because nothing happened while I was in there, I calmed down, and when I was let out somewhat later by my mother I seemed perfectly calm. I never believed that this event was especially traumatic with respect to my personality to any significant degree. I always believed that my mother and father were loving individuals who always showed great concern for and interest in me and who punished me only very slightly throughout my childhood. I had no reason to tell this story to anybody, although I did recount it at one point to my wife early in our marriage. When visiting my mother once during her stay in a nursing home a few years before her death at the age of 96, we were talking about various events in the past. She suddenly brought up this incident, which I had never heard her mention before. She remembered that she had punished me by locking me in a closet but that I had emerged perfectly calm. She told the story with some pride as an example of how I had always been "a good boy."

As an only child until almost age 7, although I played with other children from time to time, I engaged in many make-believe and fantasy games and sustained these, apparently with the tacit encouragement of my parents, through middle childhood. I believe these experiences sensitized me early on to the role of human imagination. However, I never in any way believed in the reality of such activities but viewed them primarily as resources for self-entertainment and enjoyment. In various subtle ways I am sure that these forms of play prepared me for an interest in psychology. This was manifest first of all in a great love of reading and, in particular, of stories that involved imaginative events (e.g., Edgar Rice Burroughs's many novels, including *The Adventures of Tarzan, John Carter of Mars*, and *Tanar of Pellucidar* [an underground region]). Such reading also heightened my interest in specific personality relationships within stories and novels.

I was in college when I first heard the term *psychology* used in the sense of its being a formal scientific discipline. Indeed, although Sigmund Freud had died just 2 years before this time, I had never even heard his name and knew nothing about the field of psychoanalysis. Once I was exposed to psychology in formal courses and through discussions among my circle of friends, there seemed no question but that this field that studied human imagination and the processes of fantasies and dreams was the one I would want to pursue even though at that time it did not seem to have any practical possibilities for "making a living," a term very critical to someone like myself who had grown up during the Great Depression.

Psychologists who appealed to me as an undergraduate were those who took the human imagination seriously. Besides Freud, they of course included Kurt Lewin, Henry Murray, and Hermann Rorschach. My greatest direct influence in those 3 years of college was Professor Gardner Murphy, whose work in the area of the psychology of personality, although reflecting all of the available formal scientific research of the period, also paid considerable attention to the nature of the human imagination.

After my military service in World War II, when I returned to begin graduate school at the University of Pennsylvania in 1946, I saw Rorschach's *Psychodiagnostics* (Rorschach, 1942) on the desk of the chief psychologist at the Veterans Administration Clinic where I began my practicum work. I borrowed it and stayed up all night reading it. The great emphasis that book placed on human imagery as a means of learning more about personality and psychopathology in general excited me. The special properties of the human movement (or M) response (e.g., describing the random inkblot as resembling "two people playing patty cake") as a feature of the inkblot test itself seemed clearly to connect with my long-standing interest in imagination. As a graduate student, although there were no mentors available who focused in any significant way on this area within the university itself, I pursued the possibility of finding ways of studying the nature of the human imagination. I was encouraged greatly by direct contact with Silvan S. Tomkins, who, as a consultant to the Veterans Administration clinic where I worked, gave an annual series of lectures on the Thematic Apperception Test, on which he was then the widely acknowledged expert. He certainly encouraged my further exploration of the imaginative realm.

I began my work as a researcher studying the Rorschach inkblot method itself and seeking to determine the reliability and validity of the M response as a measure of imaginativeness on the one hand and of self-control and motor inhibition on the other. I eventually came to believe that relying solely on the properties of a single test was not a satisfactory approach. This led me within the next years, once I was an established professional, to move more actively into studying daydreaming and fantasy processes by more direct techniques of inquiry as well as through a variety of laboratory research methods.

I was fortunate in meeting and marrying a young woman who, as it turned out, shared my interest in the imagination as well as my aesthetic tastes. She decided later to enter the field of psychology and quickly established her own independent career and professional status. We eventually tried collaborating on an issue that had always intrigued us both on the basis of our own childhood imaginative experiences. This was the development of imaginative play in children and its implications. That initiated what has now been 35 years of work in the areas of children's play and the role of imagination in early development as well as the special influences of the television medium, which introduces a "packaged" form of imagination into the daily life of every growing child who watches it.

I have presented some personal experiences in an attempt to indicate the continuity across my life of the role of imagination not only as a feature of personal introspection but also as a research focus that emerges throughout my many publications in books and professional journals. A significant goal of this book is to stimulate in my readers this kind of introspective awareness of one's own images and their personal, social, and professional implications. I believe that all too often, as Wordsworth suggested in the poem that follows (Hartman, 1980, p. 172), we ignore the great resources given to us for creating alternative scenes, settings, and, indeed, worlds through the resources of our imagination. I hope to encourage my readers to increase their sensitivity to the potential power of their own imagery capacities not only for enhanced self-entertainment and aesthetic enjoyment but also as a practical means for dealing more effectively with their troubled clients.

The World Is Too Much With Us

The world is too much with us; late and soon,
Getting and spending, we lay waste our powers:
Little we see in Nature that is ours;
We have given our hearts away, a sordid boon!
This Sea that bares her bosom to the moon;

The winds that will be howling at all hours,
And are up-gathered now like sleeping flowers;
For this, for everything, we are out of tune;
It moves us not.—Great God! I'd rather be
A Pagan suckled in a creed outworn;
So might I, standing on this pleasant lea,
Have glimpses that would make me less forlorn;
Have sight of Proteus rising from the sea;
Or hear old Triton blow his wreathéd horn.

2

EXPERIENCING AND COMMUNICATING PRIVATE IMAGERY: A SIGNIFICANT HUMAN CAPABILITY

To illustrate one way in which the human imagination is experienced and expressed, let me admit you for a brief time into my own consulting room as I meet with a patient. This woman, a middle-class "homemaker" in her early 50s, had sought psychotherapy because of persistent feelings of anxiety and episodes of depression. After some weeks of reviewing her life history and coming to grips with some of the difficulties she experienced in early relationships with her parents and siblings, she had begun talking more about her current relationship with her husband, to whom she had been married for more than 25 years. Mrs. Vogel, as I shall call her, was an articulate, voluble woman who showed both a broad cultural background and a clever wit. Although she described herself as a devoted wife and a mother of a grown son, she also conveyed a certain mild cynicism about the human race and life in general.

Her early years of childhood and adolescence had been spent in a troubled family in which quarreling and deceit mixed with near-criminal activities by various members of her nuclear family. She had escaped all this through marriage, devotion to her husband and her son, and concern for her husband's business career. She now lived in physically comfortable circumstances and devoted herself to providing "a good home" for her family and to some small amounts of community volunteering.

Mrs. Vogel seemed puzzled and troubled by the fact that she had been increasingly experiencing periods of anxiety and days when she had difficulty getting out of bed and felt depressed throughout the day. It should be stressed that these symptoms were not related to menopause, because she had passed through that stage of life earlier and emerged with a strong positive sexual relationship with her husband.

For our purposes here we can begin with Mrs. Vogel's arrival in the office for her session with her usual comment, "Well, here I am." What followed, however, was atypical. Instead of immediately beginning to talk about some episode in her life in the past or some recent interaction with a shopkeeper or relative that was troubling and linked to her difficult childhood years, in this session the patient seemed unable to get started. She talked about the fact that I seemed to have acquired new drapes, talked about some recent news events and a recent visit to the Metropolitan Opera, but she seemed unable to move into any extended personal material. It soon became apparent that Mrs. Vogel was showing a mixture of anxiety and resistance that seemed to be blocking her from her usual ease of communication. I proposed to her that she might lean back in her chair, shut her eyes if she liked, and let an image of some kind come to her mind as fully and vividly as possible. She complied and was quiet for a minute or so.

"You know, I just had the strangest picture come to my mind," she then remarked. "It was an image of Siamese twins, you know those infants who are born attached together. But this image was of two grown men attached at the hip. The weird part of it was that one was a much older man and one was a younger man."

We both smiled at the apparent absurdity of this image for, after all, how could two twins attached at birth be of such different ages? At the same time I had a series of thoughts myself about topics that she had been discussing in a largely factual manner in recent sessions. The "meaning" of this image quickly seemed apparent to me on the basis of what she had been saying in recent sessions, but at least at first she seemed to have no insight about it. The events she had been describing recently had involved the fact that her much-doted-on son had finished college and some further technical training and had now joined the father's manufacturing business. Father and son would now often come home from work together and become involved in business talk at dinner, apparently ignoring Mrs. Vogel except for appropriately complimenting her on the cooking. The men occasionally also went off by themselves to baseball games after work and also talked together a great deal about sports.

Rather than comment on my own associations to her image, I urged the patient to produce a few more images and then to see if any connections occurred to her. Before long she experienced a kind of "aha!" phenomenon and began to talk about her increasing sense that the dynamics of the family had changed. She had often pictured the family structure as involving a closeness between herself and her son, with the father and his work life largely isolated. The situation was now one in which it was she who felt increasingly isolated and was more and more envious of the rapprochement and rapport between father and son. Mrs. Vogel began describing a classic "empty nest" phenomenon. She gave examples of how her previously fulfilling roles as an attentive and loving mother and a proper wife and homemaker were no longer as relevant in this new family structure. She began then to confront more fully the fact that for many years she had been neglecting certain important interests and skills that she had developed during her college years but had submerged voluntarily in the interests of her view of what was expected in her marriage. She started to reexamine a variety of her options in light of her own views about herself and her sense of what lay ahead in her life.

From this reexamination in the next months came a determination to obtain further education to develop specific skills she had in art and art history. Eventually (and we therapists have to pray from time to time for happy endings), she developed a modest but fulfilling career as a docent and lecturer on art in several nearby museums and at a local community college. She found some new friends. Her relationship with husband and son remained good, and she no longer experienced the anxiety and depression that had come from having been increasingly left out of their conversations. If anything, the overall family situation was enriched further by her development in this new direction.

You cannot always be quite so fortunate in the outcome of a single imagery exercise. Nevertheless, my experience has been that many individuals have underestimated the range and variety or the intriguing quality of their own imagery capacities. Patients can gain this awareness through the vividness of a single image, as in this case, or in a series of guided imagery trips, or even through the use of imagery in the course of a specific behavior therapy practice session. It has been impressive to watch how individual clients become aware that their conscious experiences, built not only from personal encounters in the past but also from reading, the movies or television, theater, or aesthetic experience suddenly can recur and become sources of delight. The therapists confronted with such situations can often find a new sense of excitement in relation to work with patients who had first seemed stodgy, dull, or overly defensive. This is a theme I will return to again and again in this volume.

Mrs. Vogel's image as she described it would fit what is generally characterized as an *imagination image* in contrast to the kind of image that we might report if we simply looked at a flower arrangement and then looked away at a blank wall and reported our image of that specific experience. The imagination image is more like what we recall when we awaken from a dream. It involves combinations of what must certainly be remembered images reconstructed into something novel that seems at least initially unfamiliar to us. It is indeed fundamentally a creative mental performance. In this patient's report, the older and younger man tied at the hip by a piece of flesh did not specifically resemble her husband and her son. She may have at one time or another seen other older and younger men standing together and somehow fused them. It is even possible, although she couldn't specifically remember, that she had seen some images of grown twins attached at birth, because pictures of the original historical "Siamese" twins as adults have been published from time to time. My responsibility as a psychotherapist precluded my exploring in more detail in a fashion that would meet reasonable scientific standards why this particular image seemed to encapsulate so much personal meaning for this woman. If Mrs. Vogel had been a volunteer research participant, one could indeed have gone into some detail in asking her about her waking thoughts during the previous days or weeks. I would have asked her to carry around a paging device that would beep periodically during the day to remind her to record her ongoing thoughts to determine whether in some way an image of this kind might have been prepared in passing fantasies and metaphoric internal monologues. As a clinician, my ethical obligation was to help her to explore for herself the significance of this image and to experience the sense of autonomy and personal control that characterized her eventual ability to link this image to recent issues in her life.

Although we are not yet at the stage in our discussion here where we can make sharp distinctions between the various manifestations of imagery, we may be able to draw some rough distinctions assuming, at least to some degree, a continuity in the process that begins with the *sensory image* (which evidence increasingly indicates follows the same pathways as a conscious perception of an immediately presented object in the brain) as a conscious response to an immediately presented object. Next would come the longer term *memory image*, whose vividness, clarity, and measurable veridicality may vary depending on recency of the sensory image—for example, a vase of flowers. Further removed from "objective" external events would be the *planful* or *anticipated image*, which may involve a juxtaposition of relatively well-established mental scenes. The imagination image would be even further removed in time from actual percepts, which may now be recombined or reassembled whatever the original stimuli. As I have suggested, the imagination image often has the qualities of a night dream.

In this volume I provide a more systematic listing of some of the forms that human imagining takes. Before we go further, however, it seems reasonable to set the study of the human imagination within a historical context.

WHEN DID WE BECOME SELF-CONSCIOUS ABOUT THE HUMAN IMAGINATION?

We know from the cave drawings that have been discovered in southern France and Spain that people many thousands of years ago were sufficiently capable of mental imagery to draw remarkably vivid pictures of animals they encountered. It is unlikely that they could have brought these animals into the caves or could have had sufficient light to copy them even if they could occasionally have introduced a carcass or two; thus, it is much more likely that they used their own mental imagery to reproduce these animals on the cave walls for ritualistic or purely aesthetic reasons. Because it is even more unlikely that they could have directly observed the animals in motion within the caves, the vivid action depicted in the drawings certainly reflects the fact that the powers of human imagery were already well developed 20,000 years before we have any evidence of human literacy. Of course, we cannot know how conscious these cave dwellers were of their imagery capacities when they drew these beautiful reproductions.

Among the first known written documents, those in hieroglyphics on papyrus in Egypt of 2000 BC and scratched in cuneiform on clay tablets in Babylonia–Assyria of roughly the same time, 2 millennia before the Christian era (Lewis, 1996), are books of dream interpretation. These manuals, presumably used by the priestly castes of these cultures, are presented in a form in which there are lists of specific dream contents on one side and potential positive or negative outcomes, presumably predictions, on the other. One assumes that when a citizen had such a dream he or she turned to the priests, who examined their manuals and provided the individual with a prediction and perhaps also advice as to how to prevent an anticipated negative outcome through an animal sacrifice or a monetary contribution.

Dreams as a form of human imagery were taken very seriously, as is apparent from the Hebrew Bible written sometime after 1000 BC. We find references to dreams, such as Jacob's image of the ladder to heaven, as well as Joseph's personal dreams and the dreams of others that he interprets in what is perhaps the single most famous story of the Old Testament. These dream instances are all presented in the form of anticipations of future events, as are accounts of the dreams of Nebuchadnezzar and Astyages in the Babylonian and early Persian traditions during the time from 600 to about 500 BC. Compilations of dreams from the pre-Christian era by Hill (1968) and Lewis (1996) make it clear that most recorded dreams reflected the belief of the period (and one that continues among many people to the present day) that dreams are specific messages from the gods (as in the Greek *Iliad*) or are portents of future events.

A more scientific view of dreaming and waking imagination emerges in the writings of Plato and Aristotle. Plato himself was leery of the value of imagination, except in the case of the kind of poetic frenzy that leads to artistic creation. He seemed willing to ban such experiences from his Republic in favor of a more logical, orderly linguistic or mathematical form of thinking that characterizes philosophers rather than poets. Aristotle's views on dreams (Lewis, 1996) and on imagining, like his work on memory (Sorabji, 1972), seem very close to our current scientific view of these processes. He discounted the likelihood of prophecy or divine messages in dreams, proposing instead that because people all have a great variety of wishes, some will indeed come true in dreams but many will not, and those latter instances are conveniently forgotten. Imagination is closely associated with memory, both being also linked ultimately to the perceptual process. He actually described memory and imagination as associated—one, however, focused more on the past and the other pointed more toward potential futures. Aristotle thus anticipated the self-conscious examination of cognition as an ongoing process that emerged much later in Europe during the period of the Enlightenment from the late 17th through the 18th centuries.

There have been numerous references to night dreams, daydreams, and fantasies or "fancies" in the literary or artistic works of the past 3,000 years. Shakespeare, whom many would see as perhaps one of the most imaginatively resourceful writers in world literature, was often ambivalent about the values of imagination, mocking it and pointing to its self-deluding quality in many passages in his writing. At the same time careful analyses and statistical accounts have attested to Shakespeare's use of concrete and vivid images in all of the sensory modalities from touch, taste, and smell to the more common auditory and visual images in his plays and poems, images that lend a richness and excitement to his prose and poetry. His extensive recourse to what has been called "town imagery" or what we would now characterize as images involving the full range of the senses, stands in sharp contrast to the literary efforts of his contemporaries like Marlowe, Greene, and Kyd. They may have used some visual imagery but relied much less on the other sensory images in their poetry and prose (Spurgeon, 1935).

Although Shakespeare excelled in his wide-ranging use of imagery that grips us to this day, it remained for the philosophers and emerging scientific thinkers almost a century later to try to formulate conceptions of the nature of the human capacity for imaginative thought. The first of what might be called self-conscious efforts at providing systematic examinations of the nature of imagination can be found in the works of Thomas Hobbes, his *Leviathan* and *Elements of Philosophy* written in the mid-1600s (Hobbes, 1651/1968, 1642/1972). Hobbes moved from first defining *imagination* as an integrated summation of externally derived sensory experience to pointing to a more constructive role for the process. He stressed imagination's capacity for engendering desires or appetites (what psychoanalysts would call *drives*) as well as strong emotion. He also called attention to the directional force of imagination as a means by which human beings can explore future events through extrapolating from memories. This orientation toward the future puts humans into the position of being able to consider the moral implications of various forms of action. Hobbes was also sensitive to the importance of imagination in literary, artistic, and scientific creativity.

Gottfried Wilhelm Leibniz, the great mathematician (an inventor, along with Newton, of the mathematics of calculus), in his *Nouveaux Essaix*, written at the beginning of the 1700s, outlined a view of imagination designed to show what intrinsic qualities of mind were necessary for a broad understanding of human experience (Leibniz, 1705/1981). He suggested that people's thoughts are not only shaped by stimulation from the outside world but also reflect memories and anticipations. Imagination operates in what we might today call a "feedback loop" so that one's thoughts on the one hand provide a sense of separateness or uniqueness with respect to other people but on the other hand offer new ways of looking at relationships with others or, more broadly, with society. According to Leibniz's analysis, thought cannot be attributed only to externally generated stimulation; rather, one must recognize that imagination is a bipolar system, one that is related to external stimulation but also makes connections between oneself and others. The process also serves to distinguish oneself from others and to create a private awareness. Self-consciousness is thus an act of imagination. This particular view seems to anticipate not only Carl Jung's (1921/1971) views of introversion and extraversion but also David Bakan's (1966) polarity of community and agency, the striving to be part of a larger whole and also to experience oneself as a unique individual.

Leibniz (1705/1981) also proposed that consciousness may lead to the active production of a specific image of oneself, an early statement of our current concept of *identity*. This identity that unites one's experiences with one's intended actions or wishes about the future can also be seen as a way of shifting passive receptivity of external stimulation toward actions engendered by intentions directed toward the future. This is a view that seems in keeping with modern cognitive psychology. From Leibniz's argument one might also consider the possibility that we may first suffer in memory the pains and insults or "slings and arrows of outrageous fortune" and then try to reshape these memories, whether through a desire for vengeance or recompense, to eventual constructive actions. In this sense, one can even argue that Leibniz was anticipating an existential philosophical view that linked suffering to becoming. From Leibniz's standpoint, the self-aware, imaginative person not only explores nature, which represents the externally generated pole of experience, but also through imagination may come to know more about the world by recasting and reshaping such externally generated experiences. Through imagination, one constructs experiences in many different ways that can add considerably to one's sources of knowledge (Leibniz, 1705/1981).

An example of how the Enlightenment notion of imagination was organized can be found in a mid-18th century poem by Walter Harte, *An Essay on Reason* (Engell, 1981). Although the poet's presentation seems at first to reflect a purely cognitive approach, notice how toward the end of the sequence the imagination is linked to emotion, desire, and creativity, much as Hobbes's discussion had already suggested.

> Sensation first, the ground-work of the whole
> Deals ray by ray each image to the soul:
> Perception true to every nerve, receives
> The various impulse, now exults, now grieves:
> Thought works and ends, and dares afresh begin
> So Whirlpools pour out streams and suck them in;
> That thought romantic Memory detains
> In unknown cells, and in Aerial chains:
> Imagination thence her flow'rs translates;
> And Fancy, emulous of God, creates. (Engell, 1981, p. 21)

Although the philosophers of the Age of Reason continued to attribute importance to an imaginative dimension, their focus was primarily on orderly and logical thought. It was only with the shift toward what has been called the Romantic generation beginning in the late 1700s that we see an increasing emphasis, indeed perhaps an overemphasis, on the human capacity for imagery and for wide-ranging, fantasy-like thought. In 1788, the great German poet and playwright Friedrich Schiller (as cited by Freud, 1908/1962a) wrote to a friend about the considerable importance of allowing one's free-floating thoughts to come to consciousness and to develop fully, at first without any critical scrutiny by the more rational facet of the intellect, and how this flood of ideas "pell-mell" characterizes all truly creative minds. He appeared to be arguing for two kinds of thinking: one constrained by principles of orderliness and logic, the other characterized by possibilities, fantastic or realistic, and potential absurdities and serving a purpose in generating novel and original thought.

Similar positions emerged among the English poets of the turn of the 19th century such as Wordsworth and Coleridge. Wordsworth was perhaps one of the first writers to try to develop a sense of the origin of imagination in childhood and to stress the key role of human imagining as a consolation for loneliness as well as a stimulant for transcendental experience. In an early poem, *The Peddler*, Wordsworth appeared to reflect on his own childhood experience in his effort to explain how imaginative thought served an adaptive human purpose:

> From deep analogies by thought supplied,
> For consciousness not to be subdued,
> To every natural form, rock, fruit, and flower
> Even the least stones that cover the highway
> He gave a moral life;
> He saw them feel
> Or linked them to some feeling. In all shapes
> He found a secret and mysterious soul,
> A fragrance and a Spirit of strange meaning.
> Though poor in outward shew, he was most rich;
> He had a world about him—'twas his own,
> He made it—for it only lived to him,
> And to the God who looked into his mind. (Hartman, 1980, pp. 68–69)

One can sense in this description of the boy's attribution of life or of special meaning to his natural surroundings the kind of childhood "as-if" or pretend thinking that modern research links to the emergence of imagination and normal creativity. The make-believe play of an individual child or of small groups described by Mark Twain in *Tom Sawyer* (Twain, 1876) and examined in the research of the 20th century was already anticipated by Wordsworth (Piaget, 1962; D. G. Singer & Singer, 1990; J. L. Singer, 1973; Vygotsky, 1966).

Wordsworth's friend Coleridge provided one of the most extensive and detailed formulations of imagination written in that period. He argued strongly that imagination should not be separated from "reality." If one passively accepts one's thoughts as well as reorganizing them in a more active fashion one can influence all human activities. Such free-floating ideas, when acknowledged, can become sources of new forms of language and social communication. Coleridge believed that "without our imagination-created language, we are defeated and lost—bereft as Hobbes said, of civilization" (Engell, 1981, pp. 128–129).

The imaginative dimension of human experience, although already manifested through music in powerful works called "fantasies" written for solo keyboard instruments by J. S. Bach and Mozart, came to fullest flower in the 1800s and largely dominated the music, art, and literature of that century. Romanticism was characterized by the willingness to emphasize fragments of experience: in visual art, for example, artistic depictions of vine-covered ruins or decaying castles, and in music, short, seemingly improvised works that were often called "fantasies," "nocturnes," "rhapsodies," or "tone poems" (C. Rosen, 1995). Even more classically structured symphonies, such as Tchaikovsky's Symphony Number 1, first bore titles like "Winter

Daydreams." Some of Schubert's finest works for piano, written in the last years of his short life, were called "Fantasies." Beethoven, who represented the great transition between classicism and Romanticism in music, used as a subtitle for one of his most famous piano works (later called by many the "Moonlight Sonata") *"Quasi una Fantasia"* ("much like a fantasy").

In literature, German-language writers such as Goethe, Novalis, and E. T. A. Hoffmann represented the Romantic approach in poetry and literature. The Romantic style of literature has persisted through the 19th and the 20th centuries, influencing not only novels but also film.

Toward the end of the 19th century, a formal discipline of psychology began to appear in Europe and in the United States. There was increasing emphasis on human introspection as a source of data and on the importance of the study of imagery. Near the very beginning of William James's monumental *Principles of Psychology* (James 1890/1950) is a chapter entitled "The Stream of Thought" that lays out an agenda for intensive research on private human experience and the changing facets of the human imagination as expressed in one's ongoing thought processes. This research program, however, lay fallow until well into the last years of the next century largely because of psychology's great detour in search of a scientific basis through behaviorism. Meanwhile, James's ideas were taken up by fiction writers such as Dorothy Richardson, Virginia Woolf, James Joyce, and Marcel Proust, who used various stream of consciousness techniques in the early part of the 20th century. Use of these techniques was continued in the work of William Faulkner, Saul Bellow, and many other writers, continuing to the present time. Extensive use of such attempts to capture ongoing imaginative thought in the interior monologues, flashbacks, and anticipatory fantasies also can be seen in the theater, cinema, and television.

THE MOVE TOWARD THE 21ST CENTURY

Not only artists but also formal researchers in the behavioral sciences seem increasingly ready to examine systematically the structure and content of human conscious experience as it emerges in the form of interior monologues or imagery sequences. The kind of imagery reflected in my opening vignette of Mrs. Vogel and her "Siamese twins" may now be more readily understood not just on the basis of the somewhat scientifically limited reports of clinicians but as a human phenomenon subject to systematic scientific examination. In the next chapter, we will consider where the imagery process fits within current developments in the study of human consciousness on the basis of systematic research approaches.

3

CONSCIOUSNESS, THINKING MODALITIES, AND IMAGINATION: THEORY AND RESEARCH

When an adult patient and psychotherapist confront each other, they are primed with an expectation that researchers in the past 2 decades have labeled as a "theory of mind." As dozens of studies of children have shown, somewhere between ages 4 and 6 or 7, youngsters come to recognize that the thoughts and beliefs of other people are different from their own. A child watches with a companion as a candy bar is placed inside Box A. The companion leaves the room. As the remaining child watches, the experimenter moves the candy bar inside Box B. The child indicates an awareness that the candy is now in Box B. When the companion (or adult) is called back into the room, the experimenter asks the knowledgeable child, "Where will your friend look for the candy?" A child below about 4 years of age will very likely point to Box B, demonstrating the assumption that because he or she personally knows the candy is now in B, the other participant will likely be "of the same mind." In effect, the capacity for distinguishing one's own thoughts from those of another person is generally not developed in children until somewhere after the 4th year. Some degree of cognitive maturation and social experience, such as those a child acquires in playing games of make-believe, seems essential for the emergence of an awareness that one's own thoughts are truly private and that others may not think along the same lines (Harris, 2000; Leslie, 1987; Schwebel, Rosen, & Singer, 1999).

We may reasonably assume that the average client we confront has developed a theory of the separation of minds. At the same time, the research evidence suggests considerable variability not only in children's but very likely in adults' grasp of the complexity of mental differentiation and of effective means of conveying the richness of one's thoughts to another (Harris, 2000). We value poets and novelists because such artists can express in words many events and personal characteristics we may have experienced in our own thoughts but lack the vocabulary to convey to others.

In the therapeutic encounter, one can scarcely ever expect both parties to be "of one mind." The therapist cannot be sure initially of how well developed the patient's theory of mind may be. An important feature of almost all treatment is assisting patients to find ways of communicating their individual memories, fears, and expectations to the professionals in a fashion that can yield an effective dialogue. I am proposing that the use of specific language, of vivid enough imagery, can increase the chances that some degree of shared experience will emerge in the treatment dyad. Perhaps therapists can then help patients toward more effective understandings and communications with the significant persons in their lives. To assist therapists in this major task that confronts them, I believe it is necessary to understand more about the nature of ongoing human consciousness, the relationship between abstract and specific thought, and the special role of imagery.

SETTING IMAGINAL PROCESSES IN THE FRAMEWORK OF MODERN PSYCHOLOGICAL SCIENCE

Those psychologists who were dismayed a generation ago by the difficulties they were finding in relating reported attitudes to overt behavior (McGuire, 1973) have now recognized that more extensive samplings of individuals' conscious beliefs and expectations can lead to rather good predictions of their overt behavior in specific settings or in response to naturally occurring events (Fishbein & Ajzen, 1975; Kreitler & Kreitler, 1976, 1990). Social psychology has increasingly moved toward the study of social cognition and various representations of self. Research in that sphere has also depended on exploring processes of imagery and other phenomena of consciousness (Cantor & Kihlstrom, 1987; Hart, Field, Garfinkle, & Singer, 1997; Markus, 1977, 1983; J. L. Singer & Salovey, 1991). In the field of personality and social psychology there has been new acceptance of the significant role of processes out of awareness, the "cognitive unconscious" or "new unconsciousness" (Hassin, Uleman, & Bargh, 2005; Kihlstrom, 1990). We also have more research indications of the extent to which variations in what might be called the "private personality" depend to a considerable extent on assessments of ongoing conscious processes (Baars, 1997; J. L. Singer & Bonanno, 1990).

For those of us who felt somewhat "out of it" in our efforts 50 years ago to study the contents and structure of thought or of imaginative processes, these are truly exciting times. As I once wrote, "William James would be delighted to know that consciousness is (dare I say it) now the mainstream!" (J. L. Singer, 1984, p. 7). We see all around us a surge of interest in conscious thought by philosophers (Leahey, 1992, 1994), psychologists, neuroscientists (Baars, 1988, 1997; Bogen, 1995a, 1995b; Edelman, 1989; Kinsbourne, 1993; Shallice, 1978), and experimental psychologists (Kosslyn, 1995; Posner, 1994; Tulving, 1998). Researchers in learning and memory are paying more attention to prior processes of expectation and rehearsal that are part of an often conscious activity essential to learning (Estes, 1975). Researchers of artificial intelligence, psychophysiologists, and investigators of the neural and autonomic concomitants of sleep are increasingly intrigued by the necessity for studying personal "scripts," ongoing images, fantasies, and interior monologues (Ellman & Antrobus, 1991; Schank & Abelson, 1977; Sperry, 1976).

A major system of bodily regulation and human variation in motivation and experience involves the specific emotions as manifested through (a) differentiated psychophysiological patterns in the brain, autonomic nervous system, and musculature (Ahern, 1981; Schwartz, Weinberger, & Singer, 1981) and (b) differentiated facial or bodily manifestations (Ekman & Davidson, 1994; Izard, 1991; Tomkins, 1995) and differentiated private experiences or self-reports (Izard, 1991; J. L. Singer, 1984). It is increasingly clear that the affect system may well be regarded as a major source of human motivation and, as Silvan Tomkins has repeatedly proposed, it is also closely linked to the cognitive system, that highly developed set of operations by means of which we organize and assign meaning to the events outside our skins (Tomkins, 1962, 1963, 1995). Human emotions are aroused not only by externally generated events but by the continuously reverberating rehearsals of memories, appraisals of current situations, and fantasies of future situations that make up our ongoing stream of thought. They are manifest through interior monologues as well as imaginings (J. L. Singer & Bonanno, 1990).

We cannot neglect the significance of social processes and cognitions in formulating a view of imagining behavior. It is increasingly clear that humans are, whether in public or in private, continuously engaged in some form of interpersonal relatedness, as Kiesler's (1996) mammoth review of research on interpersonal behavior suggests. Much of our thought and private imagery takes the form of mental representations of scenes of interpersonal

intercourse or of communications verbally or in letters or e-mails to significant others or even to historical figures, deceased relatives, or even fantasy
characters from films or fiction.

We must also consider a developmental perspective. Early theories
and researchers of child growth were sensitive to the origins of imagination
(K. Lewin, 1935; Piaget, 1962; Vygotsky, 1978). There was, however, a
period of time in the 1930s through the 1970s when there was little systematic exploration of how adult imagination might be related to the symbolic
or fantasy play of children. This situation has now been remedied with a
surge of research on spontaneous play behavior in childhood and its links
on the one hand to the child's development of a "theory of mind" and also
to the significant role of attachment to parents or other adults as a key facet
of secure development (D. G. Singer & Singer, 1990).

The more recent interest in cultural variations that reflect ethnic or
national differences must also be taken into consideration. I do not personally
believe in separate psychologies for different cultural groups. Still, the traditions and values associated with the uses of mental storytelling, imagination,
legend, and myth in different subcultures must be taken into account when
considering not only the content of imagery but also the values it reflects.
A fuller exploration of the intriguing area of cultural and ethnic diversity
in imaginal processes will take us too far afield from the practical objectives
for this volume.

In summary, I do not propose that we need new theories of imagery
and fantasy, setting them apart as phenomena from the systems of cognition,
emotion, and motivation and the social or developmental processes that
are currently the subject of tremendous study in psychology. Although
advances in brain imaging are beginning to show us that certain areas are
essential to produce conscious experience, they also point to widespread
variations at the cortical level in the way groups of neurons become active
during different types of conscious activity (Baars, 1997). It is likely that
we will see in the first decade of the 21st century an enormous increase in
our sensitivity to brain functioning in relation to where and how imagery
may be produced at the cortical level. It is unlikely, however, as philosophers
like John Searle (1995) and Max Velmans (1996) have demonstrated, that
such research can sweep away the tremendous amount of continued study
we need at the more purely psychological level in the area of consciousness.
It is possible through positron-emission tomography (PET) and functional
magnetic resonance imaging (MRI) to identify areas of the brain that become
active when individuals are engaging in various forms of imagery. Studies
by Chen (1991) have shown that use of electroencephalograph (EEG)
measurement is able to differentiate individual differences in patterns of
"cortical power spectra" when individuals engage in either imagination
imagery or more logical sequential scientific thought imagery. Partiot, Graf-

man, Sadato, Wachs, and Hallett (1995) were able to demonstrate using PET that the dorsolateral prefrontal cortex and posterior temporal cortex prove to be more highly activated during nonemotional planful thought whereas the medial prefrontal cortex and interior temporal cortex were activated more during private thought about an emotional situation. Such brain demonstrations are undoubtedly valuable, but they can become more precise at the level of brain study only when we also provide more differentiated psychological demonstrations of individual variations in patterns of thought as well as in the range of phenomena that characterize private consciousness.

A COGNITIVE–AFFECTIVE FORMULATION OF THE HUMAN CONDITION

For nearly two thirds of the 20th century, the model of the human being emerging from both psychoanalysis as a presumed clinical science and from behaviorism in psychology was that of an individual largely motivated to satisfy basic drives such as sex and aggression as well as, of course, the needs to quench hunger and thirst and to manage the avoidance of pain. Such approaches were valuable in a variety of ways. They linked humans to other animal species in the best Darwinian tradition. Behaviorism made important advances by seeking to establish measurable, operationalized, and replicable situations for determining how learning occurs.

The exciting developments in cognitive psychology swept away the simplistic, reductionist stimulus–response, drive-reduction views of human learning and memory. At the same time the developments in clinical psychoanalysis emphasized broader autonomous ego functions and placed greater emphasis on the development of self-images and on object relations, or what I would prefer to call representations of self and others. Formal research in the clinical process stimulated originally by Carl Rogers also opened the way for studies of the importance of self-representation and ongoing emotion as fundamental human experiences. The imaginative and broad-ranging theories and research of Silvan Tomkins pointed to the important linkages between imagination, emotion, and consciousness (Tomkins, 1962, 1963, 1995). From the developmental standpoint, a large amount of research was stimulated in various forms by Jean Piaget (1962) and by the proposals for a life-span developmental cycle (Erikson, 1950). Many studies of early cognitive functions in children also called further attention to the great significance of cognition in human development.

Today we can describe human beings as motivated first of all to make sense of the complex world into which they are born through exploration, curiosity, and the formation of efficient mental structures for storage and retrieval of information. Such structures are termed *schemas, scripts,* or *prototypes* (J. L. Singer & Salovey, 1991). It seems very likely that the early ability to represent events as memory images plays a critical role in helping preverbal infants and toddlers move around in their environment and identify safe and unsafe situations within their limited perspective. Children may also experience the emotions of interest and joy when the scenes of new settings can be matched to already acquired imagery (D. G. Singer & Singer, 1990). A great leap forward in growth occurs as children begin to be able to comprehend and label adult communications and, soon after, to repeat them. This opens the way for the formation of schemas in which related scenes and their associated emotional tones can be encoded and stored for more rapid retrieval.

A major issue that has emerged from current cognitive research deals with the fact that even our perception of the external "real" world takes time, albeit milliseconds. We are never actually dealing directly, as in the old stimulus–response model, with a world "out there" (Antrobus, 1993; Libet, 1993). Even processing externally generated signals to produce what we would call a perception requires the passage of time, and the subsequent ability to remember this perception shortly afterward takes even more time. Memory can be viewed as a process that emerges from an initial scanning of sensory stimuli, organizing this material almost instantaneously into meaningful cognitive structures, and then within seconds reflecting further on this material even if it is no longer present. This further reflection will usually lead to linkage of the originally perceived material to prior content stored in the organism and an increase in the chances of later voluntary retrieval or to spontaneous recurrence of the percepts in the stream of thought. In the course of time, individuals may replay, reshape, or rehearse the original percepts, increasing the likelihood of later rapid retrieval or intrusive recurrence as recognitions or recollections. Marcia Johnson has dealt extensively in a series of research studies with the differential memory implications of material that has been perceived with or without more extended reflection (see Johnson & Multhaup, 1992). In Figure 3.1, one can observe the structure and the ways in which perception and memory are organized.

Examining this figure, we can see that at the base (P_1) of the *perceptual* cube, the process involves first of all locating and tracking an externally generated signal, extracting from it relevant features, and perhaps resolving it into something approximating a gestalt or organized structure. At a more complex level (P_2), the perceptual response goes beyond this to develop what Kreitler and Kreitler (1976) would have called "meaning structure" by examining the object relatively quickly, placing it into a broader environmental context, structuring it, and identifying it, perhaps even verbally labeling it at this point. The research on memory makes it clear that if one

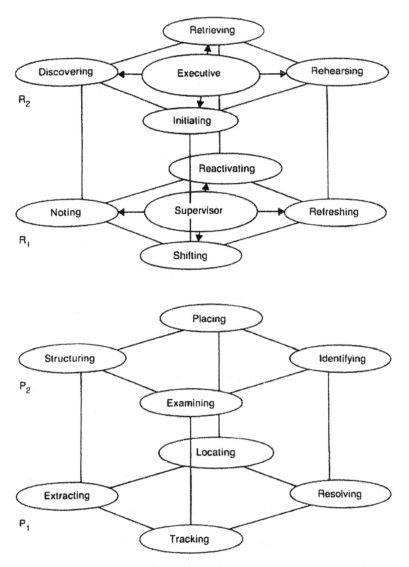

Figure 3.1. Short- and long-term memory encoding as a function of perceptual and reflective processing. R_1 and R_2 = reflection and extended reflection; P_1 and P_2 = perception and extended perception. From *The Handbook of Memory and Emotion* (p. 36), by S. A. Christianson (Ed.), 1992, Hillsdale, NJ: Erlbaum. Copyright 1992 by Erlbaum Associates. Reprinted with permission.

dealt only with the diagrammed activities at the base of the process, retrieval subsequently would be difficult. The full cube, including the P_2 processes, might involve the operation of relatively short-term memory. What next must happen for this percept to persist over an extended time, however, is for it to shift into the *reflective* mode, in which there may well be some sense of conscious control and intention through reactivating the percept,

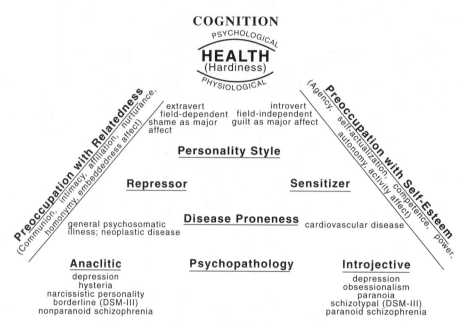

COGNITION

PSYCHOLOGICAL

HEALTH
(Hardiness)

PHYSIOLOGICAL

Preoccupation with Relatedness
(Communion, intimacy, affiliation, nurturance, homonomy, embeddedness, affect)

Preoccupation with Self-Esteem
(Agency, self-actualization, competence, autonomy, activity affect) power,

extravert	introvert
field-dependent	field-independent
shame as major affect	guilt as major affect

Personality Style

Repressor   **Sensitizer**

Disease Proneness

general psychosomatic illness; neoplastic disease   cardiovascular disease

Anaclitic   **Psychopathology**   **Introjective**
depression   depression
hysteria   obsessionalism
narcissistic personality   paranoia
borderline (DSM-III)   schizotypal (DSM-III)
nonparanoid schizophrenia   paranoid schizophrenia

Figure 3.2. A model of psychological and physiological health as a function of the balance of communion–affiliation and agency–autonomy. DSM-III = *Diagnostic and Statistical Manual of Mental Disorders* (3rd ed.). Adapted from *Repression and Dissociation* (p. 461), by J. L. Singer (Ed.), 1990, Chicago: University of Chicago Press. Copyright 1990 by the University of Chicago Press. Adapted with permission.

noting and refreshing one's view of it by repetition, and perhaps even mentally shifting placement of the objects (R_1). This then leads to the most extended level in the reflective area (R_2). This is closer to what we call *conscious imagery*, in which there is an initiation of a search, a further retrieval and rehearsal of the material, and even a sense of discovery. Chalmers (1996) suggested on the basis of her research that the element of conscious intention may be critical before an image can be described as being effectively vivid enough for subsequent adaptive usage.

Human beings, then, are first of all motivated to make sense of the complex world about them through perceptual and reflective processes and through the formation of schemas, scripts, and prototypes as well as through the continuing retrieval, rehearsal, and reshaping of memories. In addition, increasing evidence from developmental and personality research suggests that people are also motivated continuously to find, on the one hand, attachments and belongingness with others and to establish, on the other, a sense of independence, personal power, and autonomy. Figure 3.2 schematizes this triangular human motivational structure. The notion of the triangle is intended to represent the differences in emphasis that may emerge as individuals strive to balance what D. Bakan (1966) called "communion and agency" and Angyal (1965) termed "homonomy versus autonomy." Beneath the umbrella of wanting to establish meaning and organize experience, human beings are also continuously striving on the one hand to feel loved, admired, or respected; to feel close to another individual; or to identify themselves as members of a particular ethnic, religious, or national group. On the other hand, people seek also to sustain a sense of uniqueness and self-direction, of privacy in thought or of specialness in particular competencies or skills.

An analysis of psychopathological conditions as developed by Sidney Blatt (1990; Blatt & Schichman, 1983) has attempted to demonstrate that psychopathological conditions such as depression and psychotic patterns can be delineated along what they termed the *introjective* (autonomy) and *anaclitic* (attachment) dimensions. The triangular shape of this diagram allows one to estimate potential pathological or maladaptive implications of extreme positions on the dimensions. The sides of the triangle represent the relative emphases for an individual on concern about participation in a social context versus concern for autonomy and enhancement of self-esteem through one's unique competencies or for maintenance of privacy. The left side of the triangle characterizes efforts to seek intense affiliation or attachment, intimacy, and group membership—perhaps it even reflects what Schachtel (1959) termed the "embeddedness affect": the sense of loss of selfness through the communion or intimacy often symbolized in passionate sexuality, intense love, or religious or patriotic faith. If the triangle were bisected, on the right slope we would find the emphasis on uniqueness, personal power, and autonomy. McAdams, in a series of research studies, has continued to demonstrate the viability of this model of agency and communion as a way in which people define themselves through their behavior styles and interests over their life spans (Bauer & McAdams, 2004; McAdams, 1985, 1987, 1990, 1993).

Figure 3.2 suggests that individuals at the apex of the diagram who also show what might be called *psychological hardiness*, or relative freedom over the years from tendencies toward both physical and psychological pathology, would have the kinds of personalities with a strong balance between the need for affiliation (high communion) and autonomy (high agency). It is possible for some individuals to develop normal personalities and be effective and adaptive in various ways in this society while at the same time choosing to place a great emphasis on belongingness and affiliation. Others can find satisfying, meaningful lives by putting more emphasis on their autonomy and agency. It should be noted here that the high-communion figures tend somewhat more often to be female, but this I believe chiefly reflects the socialization patterns of our society and may not be a genetically given outcome. Indeed, we may be finding that many men will identify themselves with that high-communion tendency as society increasingly tolerates it.

In summary, human beings are motivated first of all to organize their experience and to encode and store it for future retrieval. They are also motivated to anticipate novel situations on the basis of prior schemas. As Tomkins (1962, 1963) and I (J. L. Singer, 1974) have suggested, different patterns of emotion may be aroused depending on the degree to which such anticipations coincide with the information presented. Within this overarching cognitive structure, humans are caught in a continuing lifelong dialectic between striving for affiliation and social communion on the one hand and the need for autonomy and a sense of privacy, independence, and personal power on the other. Ongoing conscious thoughts and the imagery or interior verbal monologues in which such thoughts are shared represent a special feature of the human need for autonomy. A balance between the two poles, if sustained over time, may account for what Maddi and Kobasa's (1991) research on *hardiness*, a form of health resilience, has long supported.

Individuals vary along a dimension of experience that is private. People seem to sustain a quasi-possessive belief in the secrecy of their thoughts. William James (1890/1950) referred to the human experiences of "my thoughts." Our memories; daydreams or night dreams; our spiritual, cultural, or sensual absorptions; and our projected futures all seem to us capable of remaining hidden from the scrutiny or awareness of others. If we are religious believers, we may assume that, to paraphrase the quote from Wordsworth cited earlier, "only God could penetrate this veil of inner experience." Our thoughts are known to others when we choose to share them. Like the secret agents in novels, we can be forced to reveal our hidden secrets only under certain extreme forms of compulsion—the ritual of the religious confessional, a voluntary contract with a psychoanalyst or a hypnotist, or often a mutual self-disclosure that strengthens the bond of an intimate relationship. The phenomena with which we will deal in the balance of this book stem therefore from the right-hand side of our diagram: the combination of our cognitive capacity, our awareness, and our adaptive use of the sphere of consciousness. In an era of mass communication and public confessionals, consciousness is, in a sense, a person's last region of independence. The ability to generate internal storytelling through combinations of verbal narrative and imagery can also be a great resource in the psychotherapeutic process when patients are willing to share this privacy with a trusted professional.

A LITERARY VIGNETTE: THE STREAM OF CONSCIOUSNESS IN PSYCHOLOGICAL PERSPECTIVE

I have chosen to present an example of the stream of consciousness that is drawn from James Joyce's *Ulysses* (1934) because it incorporates many of the features of perception, reflection, cognition, and the affiliation–autonomy complex. This fictional choice has the advantage of the poetry and beauty of writing by one of the greatest masters of English prose of the 20th century. One can, however, find comparable examples in psychologists' collections of the streams of thought of "real" people such as those available in Pope (1978) or Hurlburt (1990). These encompass many of the same issues but of course lack the poetic qualities of the following example.

The novel from which the following excerpt is drawn describes for the most part the inner thoughts of three characters during a specific day in the city of Dublin early in the 20th century. Our excerpt enters the mind of the young Irish would-be artist, Stephen Dedalus. This young man is presented as he gazes at the sea out of the window of his small apartment (located in an abandoned military tower). He launches into a series of images, memories, and interior monologues that deal with the recent death of his mother. He recalls his refusal, despite her deathbed pleas, to return to the Catholic faith he had rejected and to pray for her:

> Woodshadows floated silently by through the morning peace from the stairhead seaward where he gazed. Inshore and farther out the mirror of water whitened, spurned by lightshod hurrying feet. White breast of the dim sea. The twining stresses, two by two. A hand plucking the harpstrings merging their twining chords. Wavewhite wedded words shimmering on the dim tide.
>
> A cloud began to cover the sun slowly, shadowing the bay in deeper green. It lay behind him, a bowl of bitter waters. Fergus' song: I sang it alone in the house, holding down the long dark chords. Her door was open: she wanted to hear my music. Silent with awe and pity I went to her bedside. She was crying in her wretched bed. For those words, Stephen: love's bitter mystery.
>
> Where now?
>
> Her secrets; old feather fans, tasseled dancecards, powdered with musk, a gaud of amber beads in her locked drawer. . . .
>
> Memories beset his brooding brain. Her glass of water from the kitchen tap when she had approached the sacrament. A cored apple filled with brown sugar, roasting for her at the hob on a dark autumn evening. Her shapely fingernails reddened by the blood of squashed lice from the children's shirts.
>
> In a dream, silently, she had come to him, her wasted body within its loose graveclothes giving off an odour of wax and rosewood, her

breath bent over him with mute secret words, a faint odour of wetted ashes.

Her glazing eyes, staring out of death, to shake and bend my soul. On me alone. The ghostcandle to light her agony. Ghostly light on the tortured face. Her hoarse loud breath rattling in horror, while all prayed on their knees. Her eyes on me to strike me down. . . .

Ghoul! Chewer of corpses!

No, mother. Let me be and let me live. (Joyce, 1934, pp. 11–12)

We can now review this passage from the perspective of the modern psychological research on cognition and emotion. We begin first of all with what is essentially the young man's perceptual experience. The author, James Joyce, seems especially sensitive to the fact that many of our private thoughts emerge first from our reactions to specific external sights, sounds, smells, or tastes but then move from these more and more along a continuum of associations to earlier memories or even complete fantasies. This awareness is clearly evident, as Humphrey (1954) demonstrated in his remarkable analysis of the long interior monologue of Molly Bloom at the end of the novel. Stephen, at the outset, simply notices the "woodshadows" and the waves, using, as this literary young man might, metaphors that sound very much like those of the Greek poet Homer. This perceptual response, however, soon shifts through associative connections to a memory of the words and perhaps even the melody of a song that Stephen sang to his mother shortly before her death. From that point on, the associations become more remote from direct perceptual experience. Images of his mother weeping in her bed and begging him to resume his faith occur. These images then lead to recollections of his discovery of various private souvenirs of his mother's youth found in her bedroom. His early memories of her mothering behavior with her children follow. Finally, perhaps one might say from deepest consciousness, there recurs a memory of a dream he had in which his dead mother appeared to him in her burial clothes. Next he pictures the whole family kneeling and praying around her deathbed. The thought that he has been a betrayer of the dead now comes to mind along with a clear experience of guilt. Stephen finally screams out mentally, "Let me be and let me live." This last private cry seems to be an assertion of his rejection of the pressures for attachment and communion with the others. It manifests an insistence on his autonomy and his determination to develop his own creative capacities.

Having first indulged his introspective and artistic personal script (the shift from just looking to playing with words and images), Stephen Dedalus becomes quickly overwhelmed by images reflecting his conflict over the need for attachment and love of his mother and his family versus his struggle for independent assertiveness, all played out in thought. Then, he must strive to control and direct the very torrent of images he had allowed to appear initially.

If we take a look again at Stephen's consciousness as reflected in this vignette, we see how first he gazed idly at the sea, a purely perceptual reaction but one in which, beyond checking and noticing details, he was beginning to label the experience (see the P_1 and P_2 levels in Figure 3.1, shown earlier). He soon begins to fit the sea imagery into a broader context of personal memory and to reflect (see Figure 3.1, R_1 and R_2) not just on the cognitive motive but also on his need for closeness and attachment to his mother and family. This sense of warmth about belongingness, however, arouses yet another motive, his need to be independent, to assert his intellectual powers (such as his denial of Catholic ritual) but also his persistent need for self-realization as an artist. The struggle is carried out privately and mentally. Any passerby would simply notice that a young man is leaning from the window of his apartment in the Martello Tower and gazing seaward. Stephen's reverie is abruptly disrupted by his being called to come to breakfast by his roommate, "stately, plump Buck Mulligan."

THE UNIQUE PROPERTIES OF CONSCIOUS EXPERIENCE

Ongoing conscious experience was a central theme for writers in the 20th century from James Joyce through Saul Bellow. As the new medium of film developed over the century, imagery and fantasy were widely used even in the silent film days in pictures like Charlie Chaplin's *The Gold Rush*. With talking films and television one notices widespread use of voice-over effects to represent interior monologues as well as quick cuts to memory images or to fantasies of the characters as they go about their business. Ordinary viewers have clearly accepted these phenomena as natural reflections of their own experience; they often are delighted to find how similar the daydreams or self-talk of television or film characters are to their own private mentation. Only scientific psychology and behavioral science lagged behind in the study of consciousness. Part of this was occasioned by the fact that William James himself placed so great an emphasis on consciousness as central to human experience that he did not seem to allow for a significant motivational and intentional role for unconscious processes. Beginning around 1910, the behaviorists questioned the introspective approach to consciousness and preferred to work with animals or with directly observed learning behaviors in humans. They seemed largely uninterested in private mental processes.

The clinical reports and theorizing of Sigmund Freud, Carl Jung, and Pierre Janet in Europe emphasized the importance of unconscious motivations and attitudes and even genetically inherited symbolism. This "discovery" of unconscious processes shunted aside many of the great insights of James until almost the last quarter of the 20th century. I may, however, claim that my own research interest in daydreaming back in the 1950s and the significant contributions of Tomkins in his linkage of consciousness to emotionality (Tomkins, 1962, 1963, 1995) were exceptions to this trend.

The problem with the emphasis on unconscious processes introduced by the European clinicians I have mentioned was that although they called attention to phenomena that could be demonstrated in hypnosis (Luria, 1932), in symptom formation, humor, apparent slips of the tongue, and seemingly self-defeating defensive behaviors, these phenomena could not then be effectively integrated with developments that cognitive psychology studied scientifically. Erdelyi (1985) has shown that to some degree Freud anticipated various features of modern cognitive psychology. Nonetheless, only in the last 2 decades of the 20th century did a body of systematic research develop pointing to what Kihlstrom (1987) called "the cognitive unconscious." It is hard to integrate the elaborate types of unconscious fantasy of which Freud and Jung wrote with these more recent demonstrations of out-of-awareness processing. Children and adults can produce complex and elaborate language structures without conscious awareness of the grammatical forms they are using. It has also been shown systematically that words not consciously perceived (rarely more than single ones) or pictures not actually seen by study participants can influence their conscious reactions when new words or pictures are presented that are linked in some systematic fashion to the prior ones. The phenomenon of "priming" is widely accepted now as central to human learning. It is also clear that extensive practice both of motor skills and of the processing of phrases or schematic structures will gradually be automatized and subsequently emerge without conscious awareness as demanded in particular experiments or as needed in practical situations. Terms such as *implicit memory, implicit perception,* and *tacit knowledge* are extremely important for modern cognitive science's efforts to describe complex processing, encoding, and retrieval of new information. The burgeoning research area of identifying latent or unconscious prejudices through the computer-generated Implicit Attitudes Test is an even more recent example of how mainstream psychology has found experimental approaches to studying out-of-awareness phenomena (Cunningham, Preacher, & Banaji, 2001; Hassin, Uleman, & Bargh, 2005).

If processes outside of conscious awareness are "real"—even if they may not be as elaborately organized or "smart" as the psychoanalysts or analytic psychology followers of Jung might argue—then we can begin more clearly to see a place for consciousness in relation to the broad-ranging and yet limited capacities of unconscious thought. As mentioned earlier, Bernard Baars (1997) has made an important contribution in demonstrating the various ways in which consciousness can be studied scientifically by what he terms "contrastive phenomenology." This approach seeks examples by which one can pin down more precisely what specific roles consciousness may play in human thought by contrasting conscious experience with experiences that operate out of awareness. For example, he described how through PET scans researchers can notice the extensive metabolic activity of particular brain areas when a person is first learning new information, as in studies by Haier and colleagues (Haier, Siegel, MacLachlan, et al., 1992; Haier, Siegel, Tang, Abel, & Buchsbaum, 1992). This research shows how active large areas of the brain are when one is first learning a computer game like Tetris and then how much less evidence of high-level activity is shown once the game has been well learned. Baars proposed that in general, those sensory areas of the brain that are conscious are almost always likely to be showing more metabolic activity. Similarly, when one is paying attention to one object or activity in contrast to another, the neural activity may be greater. It seems likely that what might be called superliminal or above-conscious-threshold activity will lead to greater signs of brain activity than the processing of material out of awareness.

Experiments have been conducted in which one reads simple sentences such as "Mary had a little lamb" with the words interspersed with irrelevant material: for example, "Mary ball had ship a movie little ocean lamb." These experiments demonstrate the extent to which consciousness becomes important in sustaining a single line of thought. Similar results have been demonstrated many times in experiments of the type developed originally by Donald Broadbent of England (Broadbent, 1958), in which one is required to process information continuously through earphones in one's left ear while the right ear occasionally is receiving other kinds of material. If one "shadows" the left ear material by repeating it softly aloud as the words are presented, one will usually not encode or subsequently retrieve anything coming into the right ear. Exceptions occur—for example, when one's own name is transmitted to the right ear or when certain subtle schematically relevant words are presented to the nonshadowing right ear.

Another implication of the contrastive approach proposed by Baars (1997) relates to consciousness itself as a state of the organism. Many people may remember tragic situations such as that of Karen Quinlan, who suffered severe brain injury following a heart attack. Because of questions raised on religious and ethical grounds, she lived on for a number of years in a comatose state with no evidence of brain function. When she did eventually die it turned out that the really critical damage to her brain involved only the small areas of the intralaminar nuclei, which were located on either side of her thalamus, the well-known "relay station" buried in the cortex. It is clear that the combined functioning of the reticular formation and the intralaminar nuclei of the thalamus may be essential to sustain consciousness. Thus, even though the great frontal areas of the cortex may be essential for providing the contents of consciousness, they can be considerably damaged without interfering with the state of consciousness itself. Damage to the

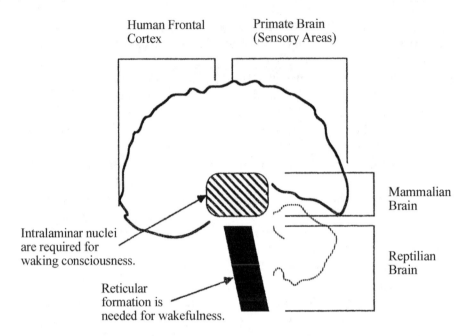

Human Frontal
Cortex

Primate Brain
(Sensory Areas)

Mammalian
Brain

Intralaminar nuclei
are required for
waking consciousness.

Reptilian
Brain

Reticular
formation is
needed for wakefulness.

Figure 3.3. A schematic model of consciousness in the brain. Consciousness creates access. Like major biological adaptations, consciousness serves multiple functions. The most important may be called the *access function*: to facilitate the flow of information between different elements of the mental theater. All of the psychological demonstrations in this book illustrate the role of consciousness in creating novel access. From *In the Theater of Consciousness: The Workspace of the Mind* (p. 32, Figure 1-2), by B. Baars, 1997, New York: Oxford University Press. Copyright 1997 by Oxford University Press, Inc. Used by permission of Oxford University Press, Inc.

relatively small areas of the intralaminar nuclei of the thalamus, independently or in conjunction with the reticular formation of the brain, is critical. Figure 3.3 presents a schematic representation of the situation and also incorporates Baars's belief that animals may well be conscious even though they cannot produce the complex kinds of thinking that characterize the more advanced areas of the frontal cortex.

Baars (1997), drawing on large and ever-increasing bodies of research, suggested that consciousness may indeed be viewed as a kind of theater or "private arena" in which we create contexts and narratives for playing out the stories of our lives and our expectations about possible futures. He called special attention to the fact that consciousness viewed as a stage may still occupy a narrow area, considering the vast amount of information processing that takes place in our continuously active brains. This spotlighted attention has extremely important functions for the human being. In Figure 3.4 it is possible to identify the relationship between the broad range of cognitive processes of which the human brain is capable and the special role that

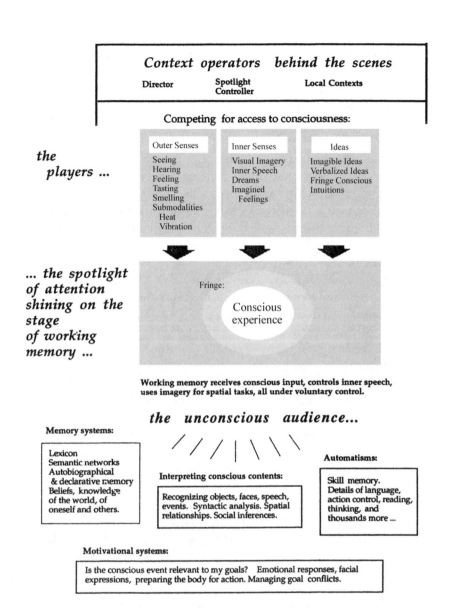

Figure 3.4. A theater metaphor for conscious experience. From *In the Theater of Consciousness: The Workspace of the Mind* (p. 42, Figure 2-1), by B. Baars, 1997, New York: Oxford University Press. Copyright 1997 by Oxford University Press, Inc. Used by permission of Oxford University Press, Inc.

consciousness may play. I would put somewhat greater emphasis on visual imagery, not only as a means of orientation in relation to various physical settings, which Baars emphasized, but also as a means of thinking about important people in our lives and about the interactions between those people and ourselves.

Baars (1997) listed the following critical adaptive functions of consciousness:

1. *Prioritizing goals:* Human beings need to entertain in consciousness, whether through interior monologue or imagery, the important goals or dangers that confront us. If we want ultimately to modify our behavior or to reorganize the values we have assigned to particular goals or dangers, we must think these through to some extent in the theater of consciousness. A therapist using such methods as calling for imagery, offering an interpretation, or reflecting back a patient's emotional responses is guiding the patient toward more effective use of consciousness with respect to important intentions or desires.

2. *Problem solving:* Consciousness is necessary for interpretation of stimuli and formation of meaningful connections. It serves as a gateway to drawing on working memory and to encouraging curiosity and exploratory activities for dealing with an anticipated perceptual situation or for planning a potential future situation.

3. *Decision making:* Consciousness plays an important role in coming to conclusions and in the executive control of one's own actions. It is important to note, however, that one must have time to react. Decisions such as whether to purchase a house or change jobs usually necessitate extensive conscious rumination. Certain overlearned behaviors can stand one in good stead in emergencies or in sports situations where instant reactions are necessary. Conscious practice of many of these moves may have helped in their becoming automatic later. When there are really urgent but weighty decisions to make, human beings must indeed take the time to dwell consciously on the issues.

4. *Prioritizing behaviors:* Consciousness helps in determining how much weight to give to organized sequences of behavior specific to a situation. Sometimes in emergencies one may produce flexible but often not entirely clear reactions because those may derive from overlearned but not necessarily relevant tendencies.

5. *Control:* One's thoughts, by clarifying the meaning of particular situations, may actually help in initiating and then, subsequently, controlling one's actions.

6. *Identifying error:* Consciousness plays a critical role in helping individuals identify mistakes, whether in written material or in social situations: Although it is possible that one can be

made uneasy by the occurrence of socially inappropriate behaviors or even one's own errors without awareness, it usually requires conscious thought to determine the reasons for such errors and to contemplate possible remedies.

7. *Confronting novelty:* Consciousness is critical for many kinds of learning experiences. This is especially important when one encounters novel situations for which there may not have yet been extensive practice.

8. *Establishing contexts:* Consciousness is critical for establishing meaningful contexts for events that occur. As I have written elsewhere, a conscious process such as imagery can provide a broader context in which to relate new information to past experiences and settings (J. L. Singer, 1974).

Baars (1997) summed up his review of consciousness by pointing to the critical role that consciousness plays in creating access to a variety of important cognitive processes, which have emotional implications as well. Figure 3.5 provides another clear instance of how critical conscious experience and working memory, or what Freud might have called "preconscious thought," play a role in linking the organism's responses to a great variety of mental contexts and well-learned but largely out-of-awareness resources. At any given time, conscious thought reflects only a small area of the vast panoply of human information processing. It also takes time for effective operation. Nevertheless, within that framework it is critical, and with the addition of the great language resources that we have as human beings it has provided us with special lexical and abstract skills that separate us from other animal species. When we turn in later chapters to specific interventions with clients that call on them to generate conscious images or short narratives, we can observe the workings of the theater of consciousness at almost all the levels proposed by Baars.

TWO MODES OF CONSCIOUS THOUGHT

There is an increasing coalescence among personality, cognitive, and developmental psychologists suggesting that human consciousness has evolved to reflect two modes of thought. Jerome Bruner (1986) labeled one as the *logical–scientific* or *paradigmatic* mode and the other as the *narrative* mode. The paradigmatic mode reflects what for some people may be considered the highest level of human thought, the capacity for organized sequential and abstract thinking as exemplified in rational mathematical and scientific processes, or careful rational thought about economics or business processes. Such thought is critical also for features of artistic production, as in a

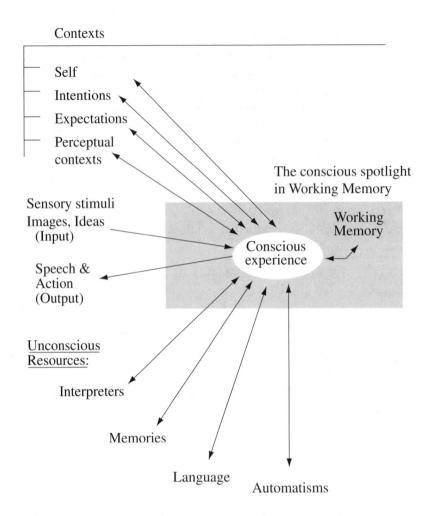

Figure 3.5. Access: the special role of consciousness. Consciousness creates access. Like major biological adaptations, consciousness serves multiple functions. The most important may be called the *access* function: to facilitate the flow of information between different elements of the mental theater. All of the psychological demonstrations in this book illustrate the role of consciousness in creating novel access. From *In the Theater of Consciousness: The Workspace of the Mind* (p. 163, Figure 8-2), by B. Baars, 1997, New York: Oxford University Press. Copyright 1997 by Oxford University Press, Inc. Used by permission of Oxford University Press, Inc.

composer's choice of instruments or an artist's choice of oils from his palette. The tools include the ability to use mathematics or formal logic or, nowadays, to rely systematically on computerized processes.

Narrative thought may well reflect a somewhat earlier evolutionary development, the forming of experiences into storylike sequences, which help sustain individuals and make communication simpler. These storylike forms of thinking give us a sense of past, present, and possible futures and open the way for the richness of interpersonal imagination.

It is a mistake to assume that the narrative mode is inherently less adaptive or that it is socially more primitive than the paradigmatic mode. They are basically complementary systems that work together to produce the highest level of thought. They may also operate effectively for different kinds of situations, as we shall see in the therapy descriptions presented later.

An example of the operation of the two systems in thinking was provided by Bruner (1986), describing a personal conversation he had with Niels Bohr, the Danish scientist generally considered along with Einstein as one of the towering figures of 20th-century physics. Bohr is widely known for his development of the concept of complementarity in quantum theory. He told Bruner that the idea came to him originally when he was confronted with the practical difficulty he had in reconciling his beliefs and feelings with respect to his adolescent son, who had just admitted stealing something from a local shop. On the one hand, he wanted to continue to love this boy and, on the other hand, he recognized how difficult this was in the face of his strong belief in justice. Bohr, meditating further and further about such things, began imagining figure–ground illusions in which you can only see one face at a time—for example, the classic one in which one view shows an old woman—then, when you reverse the figure, you see a young woman. This train of thought led him to realize the possibility of someone trying to think about the position or location of a particle and concurrently about its velocity, which in turn led him into a mathematical formulation of what has become a fundamental concept in modern atomic physics.

Bohr imagined his son, for whom he had great affection yet whom he also wanted to treat in a just fashion, upholding a principle of right conduct. This was a form of narrative thought. As he recognized the difficulty he had in finding a logical solution to his own conflicting feelings, he began to think of his situation in more general terms and, using his great logical thinking capacities, translated it into the paradigmatic mode through which, at least in the area of physics, he could formulate a general principle for addressing this issue, however difficult it might be in a social relationship. Alas, we do not know what he did about his son!

The notion of two modes of thought has been even further elaborated and subjected to extensive research by Seymour Epstein (1994, 1997) in the field of personality psychology. Epstein also proposed two major systems that can describe human thought. One of these is a rational system and the other is one that focuses primarily on the experiential mode. Epstein provided extensive arguments for why, from an evolutionary standpoint, the emergence of an experiential system is adaptive along with the rational system. The experiential system is characterized by narrative and emotion, whereas the rational system involves analytic logical thought; the use of abstract symbols, words, numbers, and sequences; and slower processing but also great flexibility because it is formulated in abstract terms such as algebraic symbols. Also, it is often characterized by a sense of control over one's thoughts, and it is almost always active at a completely conscious level. Although Epstein did not state this, there is reason to believe, as I suggested earlier on the basis of neurological studies, that the rational system is the aspect of human functioning most likely to be interfered with by extreme states of fatigue, drug abuse, or brain damage, especially in the prefrontal areas.

The experiential system is associated more with holistic than analytic thought approaches and also with strong emotionality, especially with efforts to experience positive emotion. It is characterized by connections primarily through association rather than through logic and by memories and their emotional correlates with past experience. In the experiential system, reality is particularly encoded in concrete imagery or expressed as well through analogy and metaphor or as part of a narrative process. Although the processing in the experiential system is rapid because the material presumably has been replayed mentally and therefore has moved toward greater autonomization, it is also harder to change this type of thinking because of the clarity and vividness of the imagery associated with the narratives formed. There is less subtle differentiation as part of this thought process, more tendency toward broad generalization, occasionally heavy reliance on well-established stereotypes, and a lack of precise integration. Epstein has written of the experiential system that it seems to the individual to be inherently valid and leads to statements such as "experiencing is believing" (S. Epstein, 1994, p. 711).

Bruner (1986) has proposed that the paradigmatic mode of thought seeks "truth"; the narrative mode of thought involves a striving for "verisimilitude," the appearance of truth or the conveying of a sense of believability because of the use of storylike or pictorial manifestations in one's thought. Bruner actually tried to provide evidence for the distinction by scoring literature, both fiction and nonfiction, along dimensions developed by specialists in narrative theory. A short story by James Joyce scores quite differently on complexity and the use of the subjunctive mood compared with an anthropologist's account of certain ritual practices in a particular community. Consider also the widespread appeal and influence of storytelling, from the Bible with its extensive use of parables and interesting stories as an approach to teaching morality through the interest we manifest to this day in fiction, whether in short stories or novels, on the stage, or in film or television.

The power of irrational fears can be seen in phobias about airplane flight, which occur even though individuals know that statistically they are safer flying than driving. Still, most people with such phobias acknowledge the great fear they experience in leaving the earth's surface. The power of pictorial representations so effectively used in advertising represents another example of the ways in which experiential thinking may have an impact on one's better judgment. The various forms of religion and religious practices also reflect the need of human beings to believe in storylike information. As many as 25% of adults in the United States have reported beliefs in ghosts, communication with the dead, telepathy, UFOs, and astrology (Vyse, 1997). With respect to religion, our widespread beliefs reflect the need to construct resurrection or transmigration stories, thus attempting to find ways of surmounting through such imaginings the logical reality that death is inevitable.

It should be stressed that one cannot assume that all experiential thinking is faulty. There are genuine consolations and social values in communal religious beliefs and practices. S. Epstein (1994) dealt at some length with the differences between his dual system and the classic Freudian psychoanalytic concepts of two forms of thought, primary and secondary processes. He attempted to show that Freud's notion of primary process as a major alternative to logical thought is too closely related to a reductionist notion of drives, and it manifests a development in thinking that from an evolutionary standpoint would be maladaptive (S. Epstein, 1999). The experiential system, by contrast, is a means through which more effective living may be possible along with the rational or paradigmatic mode.

It is important to stress that the distinction between the two forms of thought is not simply a proposal that is relatively unsusceptible to scientific scrutiny, as is the case with the psychoanalytic distinction between conscious and unconscious. Rather, this two-mode formulation is one that can be tested in a variety of experimental forms. S. Epstein (1997, 1999; S. Epstein & Brodsky, 1993) and Bruner (1986) went to some lengths to integrate their position with emerging study data, such as evidence of what have been called "nonrational heuristic" ways of thinking that prove to be efficient but prone to error in a variety of situations. Such data can be found in the extensive research of Kahneman, Slovik, and Tversky (1982); Kahneman and Tversky (1973); or Tversky and Kahneman (1983).

Some experiments have demonstrated the power of the experiential system even in the face of simple logical or rational knowledge. One of the objectives of the developmental work of Jean Piaget (1962) was understanding what stages children go through from their earliest years until the point when they can engage in relatively rational and logical thinking operations. For some reason, Piaget tended to minimize the degree to which the narrative or experiential facet of thought also developed systematically in the child. One could infer from his work that such thought was simply a form of primitive thinking.

In one study, D. G. Singer and Kornfeld (1973) demonstrated Piaget's (1962) well-known principle of conservation by showing 5-year-old children a short and long row each made up of 10 M&Ms, the long row having the M&Ms more widely spaced than the short row. The children could count them and ascertain that there were 10 M&Ms in each row. When the children were then given a choice of picking out only one row of M&Ms that they could then eat, they chose the longer looking row far more often, even though they rationally knew from counting that both rows included equal amounts of candy. This effect was less striking in 7-year-olds, who had reached the more advanced stage of thought, as predicted by Piaget. In effect, the 7-year-olds were able to say flatly that there were an equal number of M&Ms in each group. Nevertheless, they also tended to choose the longer row when it came to making an action decision. The same pattern prevailed for young adults, who though stating that the two rows were the same, when asked to choose, nevertheless showed a greater likelihood of choosing the longer looking row. The same finding occurred for the decision between taller and shorter glasses of a soft drink when it had been shown that the same amount of liquid had been poured into each of the glasses. The 5-year-olds still believed there was more in the taller glass. The 7-year-olds knew that they were equal, as did the college students, but when asked to express a preference for which to drink, even the young adults tended to prefer one that "looked like" it had more. This kind of bet-hedging thought is a striking example of experiential processing (D. G. Singer & Kornfeld, 1973).

Yet another study explored the *animism* phenomenon described by Piaget (1962) as characteristic of younger children's thought (the attribution of life to scientifically defined inanimate objects). It turned out that a significant number of adults also believed that rivers, clouds, or even pencils were living. Medical students whose training specifically focused on biological distinctions did not show any such attributions (D. G. Singer, Cohen, & Tower, 1978).

Kirkpatrick and Epstein (1992) offered a group of participants the chance to win some money by picking a red jelly bean out of one of two kinds of bowls. One was a "small bowl" that contained 10 beans, only 1 of which was red, and the other was a "large bowl" in which there were 100 jelly beans, of which only 10 were red. To test their degree of motivation, the subjects had to pay a dime for each trial. Having been informed of the ratios, they all clearly indicated they understood that the bowls provided equal chances for success (1 in 10), but nevertheless they frequently commented as they chose the larger bowl (making the "illogical" choice) that they felt foolish doing so.

A whole series of such experiments has demonstrated that the visual and phenomenal component of an experience may often, for otherwise mature and normal adults, override the logical–sequential system of thought, even when the individual can clearly indicate awareness of the rational odds in a situation. The entire gaming industry in the United States, from Las Vegas to Atlantic City to the extremely successful Native American reservation gaming operations in northeastern Connecticut, would not operate effectively if it were not for the frequent overriding of rational judgment by the more emotional–experiential system of the individual. S. Epstein's research has shown that although nonrational thinking can often lead to error in specific situations, there are a variety of ways in which the experiential approach may actually be more adaptive than the rational approach.

I have so far stressed the fact that for adults as well as children, seeing something in the environment or in one's mental imagery may too often lead to erroneous beliefs. In chapter 4 and in the later review of specific therapeutic uses of imagery, I attempt to show that the narrative or experiential mode of consciousness may have adaptive and practical uses. The human condition is such that as individuals or societies, we cannot seem to function purely on the basis of abstract, rational, and logical or verbal thought processes. The great power of art, culture, and spirituality in human life cannot be ignored. To explore whether one might conceive of a society and of satisfying personal lives built completely on thinking in Bruner's (1986) paradigmatic mode would take us too far afield, because it is the subject of extensive fictional as well as philosophical literature. I am focusing more narrowly on the fact that our mental reproductions of sensory experiences (imagery) and our storytelling thought sequences reflecting memories or anticipatory fantasies have important value in the work of therapists.

The Israeli cognitive psychologist Isaac Lewin (1986–1987) has proposed a three-dimensional structure for thinking about cognitive processes more generally. It seems to incorporate the two forms of thought stressed so far above. It points the way to viewing logical–verbal and imaginal processing in a context of reality–fantasy and looseness of control so that possibilities for both forms may show adaptive potential. In this model,

1. A distinction is made between an imagery system and a verbal or lexical system. These are two ways in which events are encoded for later retrieval. There are also two general forms by which individuals attempt to create ongoing internal models of experience. The verbal model is clearly closely associated with abstraction, but it is still an essential part of any narrative thinking.
2. A second dimension has to do with the degree of rational or logical thought at one extreme and, at the other, the extent to which there is acceptance of the irrational or considerations of processes involving multiple possibilities.

3. The third dimension deals with the degree to which the individual demonstrates voluntary control or directedness in the thought process.

I. Lewin (1986–1987) drew on a variety of theoretical and experimental studies in cognition. He noted in the individual an active effort at sustaining a goal-directed sequence of thoughts versus an openness to spontaneously occurring mentation that often reflects a high level of "task-unrelated" images and thoughts or forbidden or peremptory ideation. He argued for the importance of considering the degree to which each of these thought processes occurs (Horowitz, 1977, 1991; I. Lewin, 1986–1987; J. L. Singer & Bonanno, 1990).

Exhibit 3.1 portrays these dimensions of consciousness or cognitive processes. The imaginal representations and verbal-based structures columns are further subdivided into two columns each, one for imaginative cognitive processes and the other for those that are bound by reality and logic. The top panel of the exhibit designates the processes as involving free-floating thought, and the bottom panel designates them as involving directed and controlled thought. This framework contains almost every type of conscious experience, including formal controlled learning in an imaginal area or in a verbal area as well as consideration of the extent to which conscious experience is controlled by a specific intent of the person or seems to be free-floating.

The emphasis in this book is on the kinds of imagery that can occur in psychotherapy, but we must not neglect certain types of imaginative verbal material, such as interior monologues, remembered conversations, or mentally rehearsed family arguments. We will also deal with daydreaming in its free-floating form as well as with the more directed or controlled daydreams guided by a therapist. An examination of imagery in psychotherapy must also review reports by patients of their night dreams, especially as these relate to the continuity between day and night dream material. Spontaneous memory images or the mental recurrence of dramatic or traumatic experiences often form part of the therapeutic encounter. One must also take account approaches that encourage the patient in a more deliberate and directed fashion to produce a variety of what might even be termed *thought experiments*. These more controlled uses of imagery, which may be found in the bottom panel of Exhibit 3.1, serve as a means of examining alternative possibilities of behavior in both past and future situations.

Although the approach in this book stresses the more imaginative dimension of human experience, it would be folly to deny the importance of the logical or paradigmatic form of thought. Therapists must rely on clients' abilities at various times to organize their thinking along verbal lines and in relation to reality and logically bound structures. Guided imagery

EXHIBIT 3.1
Examples of Some Cognitive Processes in Three-Dimensional Space

Imaginal representations		Verbal-based structures	
Imaginative	Reality and logically bound	Imaginative	Reality and logically bound
Free floating			
Majority of dream experiences	Spontaneous memory images: "a vacation"	Associative thinking	Some verses of a known poem occur to the mind spontaneously
Hallucinations	Recurrence of dramatic or traumatic experiences	Daydreaming of a verbal nature: relaxing, meditating, ruminating	Obsessive thoughts and ideas
Daydreaming			
Directed and controlled			
Nonrepresentational visual art	Learning and problem solving by preverbal children and animals (Tolman's "cognitive maps")	Writing of science fiction	Problem solving in an abstract and well-organized way
Effort to imagine a legendary monster	Intentional eidetic experience	Invention of a new mathematical concept or area	Learning "facts" in school (history, geography, etc.)
Musical or poetic imagery within tonal or metric design	An effort to "see" a friend's face and to "hear" her voice when she is not around	Imagining arguments that did not take place (e.g., a Platonic dialogue, scenes for a drama)	Leaning a foreign language
	Subject's task in a "mental practice" experiment or specific memories evoked in therapy or in research		An effort to give a verbally accurate report of a dream

Note. Examples of cognitive processes within the three-dimensional classification model: verbal versus imaginal, directed and controlled versus free floating, and imaginative versus reality and logically bound. Adapted from "A Three Dimensional Model for the Classification of Cognitive Products," by I. Lewin, 1986–1987, *Imagination, Cognition and Personality, 6,* pp. 50–51. Copyright 1986 by the Baywood Publishing Company. Adapted with permission.

approaches are often used, particularly by the European mental imagery schools, in which the entire therapy seems to be carried out in the form of ongoing symbolic "imagery trips" without any emphasis on integration or discussion, but it is hard to understand how such approaches could truly be effective unless one takes a quasi-mystical view of people's latent symbolism capacity. The relative success of cognitive therapies attests to the importance of patients' verbal–rational thought.

Consciousness and imagery are special features of the general cognitive processing system of the individual. Although this narrative or experiential system is adaptive and valuable, it must also be seen as collaborative with rational or rational–verbal–sequential systems of thought if many types of psychotherapy are to be applicable to daily living. The frequently demonstrated effectiveness of cognitive–behavioral therapies and, to a somewhat lesser extent, rational–emotive therapy points to the importance of guiding patients to use more paradigmatic thought processes. As we shall see in the next chapter, reaching that stage of communication along logical–sequential lines may first depend on effective production of imagery and narrative thought capacities. The sharing of relatively specific imagery between patient and therapist may increase the likelihood that the content of their "theories of mind" will overlap, a result that is likely to create an increase in empathy.

4

IMAGERY AS A PRECURSOR AND CENTRAL COMPONENT OF NARRATIVE THOUGHT

> If we must suffer, it is better to create the world in which we suffer, and this is what heroes do spontaneously, artists do consciously, and all men do in their degree.
>
> —Ellmann (1990, p. 1)

Naked and alone we humans are cast at birth on Earth's shores. We must endure our increasingly lengthy lives bearing the burden of an evolutionary gift or curse—we are wired to experience memories of past misadventures as well as of joyous encounters. We also become aware of a range of future possibilities, including the grim reality of impending death. Our consciousness presents us with the continuing challenge of organizing past experience into retrievable schematic structures that afford us a sense of meaning, preparing us to confront new information with some degree of control.

THE ROLE OF IMAGERY AND EXPERIENTIAL THOUGHT IN THE HUMAN CONDITION

Our emotional system, as the research of Mandler (1984), Tomkins (1962, 1963, 1995), and Izard (1977) has shown, is closely tied to our cognitive expectations and our ability to assimilate new situations into previously encoded schemas and scripts. Moderate amounts of new or unexpected information may pique our curiosity and arouse emotions of interest or excitement. The extremely unexpected or novel may first frighten or shock us. If we can quickly match such material with prior schemas, we may experience joy, or, as in the case of jokes or aesthetic originality, such matches may evoke laughter and positive emotionality. Persisting high levels of unexpected information that cannot be assimilated into prior cognitive structures may first evoke anger and then sadness and distress (Mandler, 1984; J. L. Singer, 1974, 1984; Tomkins, 1962).

We share with other animals a sense of alertness to dangers and to opportunities for escape, food, or sex, but in the far more complex world humans have created, we depend on our conscious reflection or our well-encoded unconscious store of schemas and scripts for effective adaptation (Hassin, Uleman, & Bargh, 2005; Kihlstrom, 1987). The metaphor of consciousness as a stream can be supplemented by a more active metaphor of our memories, plans, fantasies, and daydreams serving as invisible antennae that use past experiences and anticipated futures to ready us for the unexpected.

Although our relatively overlearned and mentally organized schemas, scripts, and prototypes may operate much of the time outside of conscious awareness, they are reflected in consciousness by the quasi-sensory representations or analogues of our images. We mentally picture past events and faces of those important to us and remember scenes from books, movies, or television that may be relevant to our current or anticipated milieu. This stream of conscious associations is quasi-sensory, because it includes remembered conversations and voices of significant persons in our lives as well as revivals of tastes, touches, and smells. The aesthetic power of great literary figures like Shakespeare, Dickens, Joyce, and Proust lies in their ability to use language that suggests very concrete images of sights, sounds, touches, tastes, or smells. These images evoke in us the shock of recognition of our own ongoing conscious sensory experiences that for lack of richness of available vocabulary cannot easily be communicated to others.

Consider Shakespeare's Hamlet, confronted by the Danish courtiers who urge him to reveal the whereabouts of the body of Polonius, whom he has killed. Notice the vivid use of various sensory images in just these few lines:

Rosencrantz: What have you done, my lord, with the dead body?

Hamlet: Compounded it with dust, whereto 'tis kin. . . . .

Rosencrantz: Take you me for a sponge, my lord?

Hamlet: Ay, sir, that soaks up the King's countenance, his rewards, his authorities. But such officers do the King best service in the end. He keeps them, like an ape an apple, in the corner of his jaw; first mouthed, to be last swallowed. When he needs what you have gleaned, it is but squeezing you, and, sponge, you shall be dry again. . . . .

King: Now, Hamlet, where's Polonius?

Hamlet:	At supper.
King:	At supper! Where?
Hamlet:	Not where he eats but where he is eaten. A certain convocation of politic worms are e'en at him. Your worm is your only emperor for diet; we fat all creatures else to fat us, and we fat ourselves for maggots. Your fat King and your lean beggar is but variable service—two dishes but to one table. . . .
Hamlet:	A man may fish with the worm that hath eat of a King, and eat of the fish that hath fed of that worm. . . .
King:	Where is Polonius?
Hamlet:	In heaven. Send thither to see. If your messenger find him not there, seek him in the other place yourself. But, indeed, if you find him not within this month, you shall nose him as you go up the stairs into the lobby. (*Hamlet,* Act IV, Scenes ii and iii)

When you read this passage from the play you inevitably find yourself mentally picturing, perhaps even mentally touching, tasting, or smelling, the various examples offered by Hamlet that pertain to death, to the ultimate equality of high-ranked persons and humble ones, the sleaziness of the "yes-men" courtiers, and the ugliness of hypocrisy. If we pay attention to Shakespeare's imagery, we find ourselves more fully engaged with Hamlet as a person, with his cynicism and existential despair. The play becomes more than a standard story of revenge. It is rather a probing exploration of important life concerns that human beings all share and that pass through our consciousness as our senses respond to the outside world of smells, touches, and tastes while our memories or fantasies alert us to our own awareness of our social status, our guilt or shame, and our fears of impending death.

The concrete images we are aware of if we pay careful attention to our ongoing consciousness are not necessarily random epiphenomena that reflect the continuous activity of our brains' neural networks. They can also serve an adaptive evolutionary purpose so that, to resume my antennae metaphor, they function as feelers to help us use past memories and future anticipations in orienting ourselves to each new environment in which we find ourselves.

In the last chapter, I mentioned the generalizations about human thought proposed by Bruner (1986) and by S. Epstein (1997, 1999). They include the concept of a narrative or experiential system that involves associations of events, images of possibilities, and concurrent emotions and is juxtaposed against the human capacity for logical–sequential analytic thought, which might have developed later in human evolution.

Whereas our logical or rational thought system is characterized by effortful, conscious evaluations, abstractions, subtle distinctions, and conscious justifications, our experiential system seems effortless and is expressed in specific images, metaphors or analogies, and narratives. It is often characterized by strong emotion and by a sense of inherent validity. It has an "experiencing is believing" quality (S. Epstein, 1999, p. 56).

Although it might be argued that our capacity for what has been called propositional or abstract logical thought is one that puts us at a higher level than all other biological species, it is questionable that such an ability alone is sufficient for effective human adaptation. The recent extensive research by Robert Sternberg and his group at Yale has pointed to three basic forms of thinking ability that must combine to produce what they call "successful intelligence," which is required for effective accomplishment in school, work, or even social relations (Sternberg, 1997, 1999a, 1999b; Sternberg & Grigorenko, 2002). These capacities include (a) the *analytic*, which reflects the established measures of IQ and which is comparable to S. Epstein's (1999) rational thought; (b) the *practical*, which involves an ability to envision and act on goal-related social and physical activities, much like what might be called "street smarts"; and (c) the *creative*, which involves an ability to reformulate and reshape established schemas and scripts into novel structures. Sternberg (1997, 1999a, 1999b; Sternberg & Grigorenko, 2002) has shown that skills (innate or fostered) in each of these modes are differentially distributed in the population and across cultures and that individuals who excel in one or more of the three show special accomplishments. Optimal combinations may be necessary for broad-ranging success in business, science, politics, or the arts (see chap. 8).

Our capacity for generating imagistic thought, for vividly replaying memories, or for thinking of social or even material possibilities, even if bizarre at times, exemplifies Sternberg's (1997, 1999a, 1999b; Sternberg & Grigorenko, 2002) practical and creative capacities. For the purposes of this book, I propose that effective psychotherapy ultimately demands that we help our patients to free up in themselves or to develop further all three capacities. Approaches like Ellis's (1989) rational psychotherapy, Beck's (1976) cognitive psychotherapy, or Kelly's (1955) personal construct method perhaps focus more on fostering the paradigmatic thinking of clients, whereas interpersonal and narrative therapies draw more on imagery and creative thought processes (McLeod, 1997; Mitchell, 1988). We will address this application of the triadic theory of successful intelligence to various forms of psychotherapy in our later consideration of specific treatment approaches.

Humans' imagery system as reflected in relatively concrete or specific autobiographical memories or future-oriented daydreams and mental rehearsals of possible interactions makes up a great deal of our ongoing conscious stream of thought (S. Epstein, 1999; J. A. Singer & Salovey, 1993; J. L.

Singer, 1974). The next section examines how images become ordered into storylike sequences that help us to make more sense, sometimes to good effect, sometimes in self-defeating ways, of our thoughts of the past and of possible futures.

The human capacity to generate mental reproductions of sensory experiences has been the subject of extensive research from the earliest days of scientific psychology. After the lacuna of about 50 years (1910–1960) pointed out by Holt (1964), interest in imagery reawakened, and efforts to devise research methods to establish the "reality" of such analogue mental activity were carried on experimentally by Segal (1971), Shepard (1978, 1984), Kosslyn (1976), H. S. Rosenberg (1987), Finke (1989), Bower (1990), and Farah (1985), as well as by myself (Antrobus, Singer, & Greenberg, 1966) along with Antrobus (1999). The research on the relation of imagery to verbal reports of conscious experience has been extensively reviewed by Richardson (1969, 1984, 2000). The psychophysiology and psychological or psychopathological correlates of imagery have been examined by Sheikh and by Klinger and Kunzendorf, among others (Klinger, 1978, 1990a, 1990b; Kunzendorf, 1991; Kunzendorf & Sheikh, 1990; Sheikh, 1983; Sheikh & Korn, 1994).

An impressive series of studies directed by David Rubin (2005) has shown the importance of personal visual imagery in heightening the recall, recollection, and "believability" of reports produced in tests of autobiographical memory. His psychological and direct brain-imaging research shows that personally witnessed events and other directly experienced situations combine a more diverse set of behavioral and brain systems than do "secondhand" or semantically summarized impersonal memories. It is clear that the phenomenon of mental imagery can be demonstrated as a measurable human activity and that it is reasonably possible to rely on self-reports of its occurrence for many practical purposes, from memory studies to athletic preparation or health psychology research. As S. Epstein's (1999) work suggests, the experiential mode of thought involves imagery and narrative. Whereas imagery can be functional in reproducing recent sensory experiences or in athletic preparation, in our daily conscious experience its use most often is likely to be in the sequences of images that form autobiographical narratives. In discussing applications of imagery to psychotherapy, we must necessarily turn our attention to the relatively new field of life narratives.

NARRATIVE AND THE LIFE STORY IN ONGOING CONSCIOUSNESS

What keeps individuals in psychoanalytic therapy for years, reporting on their memories, fantasies, daily encounters, and night dreams even in the face of the sparse evidence of symptom reduction or personality change (Bornstein, 2001)? I propose that a major component of the process is the opportunity for patients to verbalize to a sympathetic listener their own continuing efforts to create meaningful life stories from the often confusing, seemingly random interactions, traumas, self-doubts, compulsions, and even surprising successes that characterize human life. Much of our ongoing consciousness involves the effort to give meaning or to make sense of our experiences by telling and retelling stories. In almost every culture, adults or older siblings tell family histories; religious legends; and faith-related or superstitious accounts of dangers, salvations, spirit worlds, and invisible societies of elves, fairies, angels, saints, and animal gods. In the past century, vast numbers of individuals all over the world who were once fated by their poverty to be unlettered in human history have attained literacy and also gained access to the story-telling electronic media of radio, film, television, and, most recently, computers. We live now in a world almost saturated with storytelling (D. G. Singer & Singer, 2001, 2005). It seems only natural that we should be seeking to form our personal experiences into meaningful stories, trying again and again to shape and reshape remembered or antici-pated events into scripts we ourselves "write" and can edit to give ourselves some clearer sense of specialness, of identity (McAdams, 1985, 1993; McLeod, 1997; Sarbin, 1986; J. A. Singer, 1997; J. A. Singer & Salovey, 1993; Tomkins, 1995).

Of special importance in the increasing recognition that the narrative mode of thought is critical for defining consciousness has been the develop-ment of reliable and quantifiable procedures for analyzing life story material (McAdams, 1989, 1993). Later chapters make some suggestions about how therapists can use scoring methods to help them and their patients in assessing imagery sequences and narrative thought and also how researchers can use such scoring procedures to assess psychotherapy processes and out-comes. Useful starts in this direction were pioneered by Luborsky and Crits-Christoph (1990) and by M. Horowitz (1991).

CHILDREN'S PLAY AND THE ORIGINS OF NARRATIVE

At what stage of life does narrative thought begin? We can only estimate from experimental studies when babies and toddlers may be capable of private imagery. It is not until the early preschool years that children are sufficiently verbal to show storytelling or life-narrative tendencies. These emerge in their make-believe or pretending game play (D. G. Singer & Singer, 1990).

Although most children show some involvement in pretending and in symbolic play by around 3 years of age, sometimes with soft toys or dolls, sometimes with blocks, or even with imaginary playmates (M. Taylor, 1999), there is considerable variation in the frequency and complexity of such play. Considerable research has examined the factors in the child's family life or in the settings or the availability of toys and companions that foster such play. Adult encouragement by regular bedtime storytelling or direct initiation of symbolic play, or even exposure to TV programming such as *Mister Rogers' Neighborhood,* has been shown in research to enhance the likelihood of such play. A body of research studies demonstrates how training encourages this type of play in preschoolers or young school-aged children (D. G. Singer & Singer, 1990; D. G. Singer, Singer, Plaskon, & Schweder, 2003; J. L. Singer & Lythcott, 2002). It is important to understand that even though symbolic play is a reflection of the basic human mode of experiential or narrative thought, the processes involved, with their richness, variety, and manipulability, may vary across children and may lead to individual differences in acquisition of imagery skills, vocabulary range, and ability to use such play for impulse control or delay and for the control of aggression (D. G. Singer & Singer, 1990; J. L. Singer, 1973). We can hypothesize that a child confronted with so many large-sized and confusing people and objects like trucks, buildings, and animals gains by make-believe play a sense of mastery in cutting them down to manageable, manipulable sizes and forming them into stories that fit well into his or her own limited range of schemas and scripts. Through such play, the child can gradually assimilate the extreme novelty of the grown-up world or the magical world of fairy tales, superstitions, and religion based tales (like the story of Jonah and the whale) and form new schemas (Piaget, 1962; D. Singer & Singer, 1990).

Children at first speak most of their thoughts out loud, but in the school years, with disciplinary requirements and with the acquisition of reading, they learn to internalize the narrative play into ongoing private thought. With instruction in grammar, mathematics, and science, human beings gradually acquire the ability to use formal, rational thought—the logical–sequential or rational mode of S. Epstein (1999), the paradigmatic mode of Bruner (1986). There are undoubtedly genetic or other constitutionally based variations on how often and how effectively we can apply this later acquired ability, the "analytic or IQ test–measured mode," as Sternberg's (1999b) research described it. Thinking most often follows the earlier learned narrative path, which has limitations but also adaptive value, especially in relation to interpersonal situations and other problems calling for practical or creative forms of intelligence. Even a field perceived to be the epitome of formal thought, the law, may depend more than most people realize on Epstein's experiential mode of thought. In his great lectures and later book on common law, Oliver Wendell Holmes, later one of the most respected of all Supreme Court justices, opened his presentation with the statement, "The life of the law has not been logic; it has been experience" (quoted in Menand, 2001, p. 341).

Before we move on to examining more specifically how the narrative features of thought (made up so often of sequences of imagery) relate to personality and to psychotherapy, let us look at some examples of the early manifestations of such thought in children's spontaneous play and then in psychotherapy with children. Here is an example of some 4-year-olds at play in the yard of a New York City nursery school, a verbatim transcription made by Rosalind Gould in 1964. Notice how the two boys, Jim and Chris, work into their play their efforts to make sense of gender, overheard conversations by adults about marriage, fairy tales they've been read or told about that refer to "princesses," cartoons or scenes from television, and even that then-new singing group they may have watched on TV called the Beatles. Keep in mind that their play involves their mental representations of these adult issues and does not include actual toys or physical implements. They indeed are creating a miniaturized world that they can control.

Chris:	I hate women!
Teacher:	Why do you say that, Chris?
Chris:	Because when ya' marry them ya' hafta get your blood tested.
Teacher:	What else do you think about women, Chris?
Chris:	I think they're kookie! I'm gonna marry a princess because they're better—they're prettier.
Jim:	Yeah, because they have jewels and gold and they have crowns.
Olivia:	[*Comes over to the boys*] What are you doing?
Jim and Chris:	We're digging and looking for princesses.
Olivia:	Well I have a bride dress at home.
Chris:	Aw, who cares about that.
Jim:	Yeah. Ya' need a princess suit. [*To teacher*] Don't tell her we're gonna marry a princess.
Chris:	Princesses hate to wear their princess suits all the time or else they'll be stripped of their beauty.
Olivia:	[*To teacher*] What means "stripped of their beauty"?
Chris:	Aw, go away! We hafta keep digging.

Teacher:	Digging for what?
Chris:	Digging for a princess of course.
Jim:	Yeah, ya' don't find them in New York. We're digging our way to find one.
Chris:	Well, ya' just don't marry one like the regular way. Ya' hafta save one first. Princesses fall in love with princes. Did ya' ever eat a princess?
Jim:	NO! [*They dig for a while silently*] I dream about army things.
Chris:	Well, I dream that I'm a lieutenant with a lovely princess.
Olivia:	Boys! Boys! I just found a real live earring from a princess. [*She hands them a piece of crumpled paper*]
Jim and Chris:	Get out of here! [*They chase her away*]
Chris:	[*Running around the hole he has dug*] Romance! [*Running full circle again*] Princesses! [*Running full circle a third time*] Jewels! Let's get digging for those princesses!
Jim:	No, we don't really want them. We hafta wait till we're grown up for that.
Chris:	Yeah, till we're twenty-one!
Jim:	Yeah.
Chris:	And then we can buy a real drill and shovel and a pick.
Jim:	And a whole car and one of those things that go rrr-rrr-rrr.
Teacher:	You mean a pneumatic drill!
Jim:	Yeah.
Chris:	But I wanna dig for princesses.
Jim:	No!
Chris:	Oh, shucks. [*To another boy*] Josh, do you wanna marry a princess?
Josh:	Sure I do.
Olivia:	Do you know where you could get a real princess? In Ireland or England or something.
Chris:	Yeah, then we could find one and . . . we could see the Beatles while we're there!
Jim:	I love the Beatles. Yeah! Yeah! Yeah!

Chris: [*Running back from the group of girls in another part of the yard*] I just went up to the princess' house and guess what—they scared me away. (Gould, 1972, pp. 22–24)

This lively example of imaginative play shows how these children tried integrating adult behaviors into their own limited schemas and scripts, their own beginning identification of possible selves, and even their early formulation of a self-as-child versus self-as-adult identity. We as adults may not go "digging for princesses" in our ongoing thoughts, but we may often enough catch ourselves creating narratives of audacious seductions, great Olympic athletic accomplishments, masterful achievements at work, or what we will do after we win the lottery!

The open verbalizations of the 4-year-old's fantasy play gradually are internalized over the next few years. Mark Twain, in his novel *Tom Sawyer* (Twain, 1876), described a somewhat older boy in the Missouri of the 1830s who runs along pretending to be a steamboat captain, carrying out his fantasy partially mentally but also blurting out orders to the crew or imitating the whistles, the chug-chugs of the engine, or the other noises as the ship maneuvers on the Mississippi River. Undoubtedly, Twain was drawing on his own recollections of his boyhood play.

A recent reminiscence by a Turkish-born writer, Orhan Pamuk (2005), described how in middle childhood in the apartment of his beloved grand-mother he would play a similar game. The sitting room became the captain's station for a large ship, suggested to him by the horn sounds of boats passing through the nearby Bosphorus. "As I steered my imaginary ship through the storm, my crew and passengers [panicking] . . . , I took a captain's pride in knowing that our ship, our family, our fate, was in my hands" (Pamuk, 2005, p. 36).

This internalization process has become a central theme in theory and research on the development of attachment. Research such as that of Meins et al. (2003) and of Fonagy and his groups (e.g., Fonagy, Gergely, Jurist, & Target, 2002) as well as some of my own work with Dorothy Singer among others (Borelli & David, 2003–2004; D. G. Singer & Singer, 1990; Slade, 2002) has pointed to the importance of early secure attachment to at least one loving parent who shows sensitivity to pretend play and exhibits "mind-mindedness," a recognition of the quality of a child's mental experience. Such support fosters the internalization or "mentalization" of imaginative play in middle childhood.

The vignette from Gould's observation of presumably healthy children in spontaneous play is not all that different from the imagery sequences and narratives produced by troubled children in play therapy (D. G. Singer, 1993). A case in point is that of a boy of 6, Robert, who came to the attention of his pediatrician when he became terrified after being asked to urinate as part of a routine physical examination. It turned out that the boy had suffered from a toilet phobia for more than a year, a dysfunction that now limited him to urinating only in one special toilet at home, usually with one parent present and with the toilet opening covered by light tissue. With the beginning of his attendance at elementary school impending, the family recognized it was urgent that he be helped within the next few months. A course of psychotherapy followed with a combination of relaxation, systematic desensitization, play therapy, and art therapy (D. G. Singer, 1998).

Robert's phobia was traced to his first observing the filter system and drain of the family's new swimming pool, which aroused a conditioned fear of being swept through it. This fear soon generalized to his toilet, and in his effort to make sense of this seemingly incomprehensible terror he began to imagine snakes and reptiles emerging from the toilet drain to attack him. He revealed these fantasies to the therapist only after a short course of play therapy in which he used toy trucks and other vehicles to create simple, nonthreatening narratives. During this play sequence he came to trust this strange adult. With the reassurance of safety with the therapist, he began to create narratives in which he molded clay reptiles or drew pictures of them and then drew spears and slingshots to attack them or cages in which to confine them. He progressed to using toy toilets and dolls and gradually began to report that "this can't happen because there really are not snakes in there" (D. G. Singer, p. 86). He could then tolerate systematic desensitization of the phobic images, and eventually, with in vivo desensitization he could actually visit the school toilets for practice before the term began. After further practice there, he began to use toilets at home and on visits to relatives. He tore up his snake drawings and began to produce benign pictures and stories of sailing. He was ready to begin the school term on his own and presented the therapist with drawings of flowers and a carefully printed "thank you." A long-term follow-up revealed no recurrence of the toilet fear and a normal pattern of urination (D. G. Singer, 1998).

This brief case summary exemplifies both the hazards and adaptive possibilities of the experiential or narrative thought mode. Robert, confronted with a "massive" new image of the swimming pool and warned of its dangers, may well have developed a conditioned fear response along the special brain pathway described in the research by LeDoux (1996). When this conditioned fear response generalized to the flushing system of toilets, Robert sought some cognitive explanation for the fear in his limited range of schemas and scripts and drew on the images of crocodiles, snakes, or biting fish he may have seen in television cartoons or movies or even been teased about by older children and unwitting adults. He began to generate a narrative of toilet dangers that soon nearly completely incapacitated him in regard to toilet habits, especially when it was partially reinforced by his parents' indulgence and failure to seek help early for his problem. At the same time, Robert's imaginative capacities and ability to create playful narratives in other areas sustained him, and once reassured and relaxed by the therapist, he began to use his creative abilities along with some analytic intelligence to consider alternative possibilities. Overcoming the conditioned fear was most difficult, and the systematic desensitization (which drew on his imagery skills) and in vivo exposure of the therapy were necessary along with cognitive restructuring.

MAXIMIZING THE ADAPTIVE FUNCTIONS OF IMAGERY AND NARRATIVE

All human beings, except perhaps those severely brain-damaged individuals who are intellectually retarded or autistic, are likely to manifest Epstein's experiential thinking. Research on young children has suggested that certain learning opportunities play a role in helping children develop more effective use of their inherent imagery and narrative thinking capacities. Parents and other adults who form secure attachments in children through loving, consistent, and verbally communicative relationships as well as through encouraging the children in their make-believe play and role play (e.g., board games) or construction play (blocks, Legos, crafts) enhance children's abilities to regulate their imagery and narrative thinking tendencies and their capability for differentiated and integrated mental representation (Blatt, Auerbach, & Levy, 1997; D. Singer & Singer, 1990). Individual-difference studies have yielded evidence that children who engage regularly in pretend or symbolic play, either alone or, especially, with others, show more ability in vocabulary, imagery, awareness of reality–fantasy distinctions, delaying or waiting, control of impulsivity or physical aggression, cooperation, leadership, and creativity (Russ, 2004; Russ, Robins, & Christiano, 1999; D. G. Singer & Singer, 1990).

As Bruner (1986) has suggested, the narrative mode of thought is associated with verisimilitude, that is, seeking to develop an imitation of what may be real, whereas the paradigmatic mode of thought is more associated with determining the exact truth. Life involves many circumstances in which factual truths are critical. These include, among others, financial management, warfare, computer skills, science, and engineering. Logical or analytic intelligence is needed for the demands of these activities. This mode of intelligence, though linked to genetics, can also be enhanced by environmental influences such as parenting and good teaching in school and work settings (Sternberg & Grigorenko, 2000). We can scarcely minimize the adaptive importance for human life of our paradigmatic logical or abstract thought. But the great variety of social settings in which people find themselves prove to be sufficiently ambiguous that the truth seeking of abstraction and logic may not suffice. Humans need effective means of constructing mental simulations of possibilities. But life generally and the great variety of social settings in which we find ourselves are more ambiguous. We need effective means of simulating possibilities in intimate relations, in the creative features of the arts, humanities, and even aspects of science as well as in many daily forms of social intercourse. Our imagery and narrative abilities, if we can control them and test them against various realities, are very useful. As we move in the following chapters to psychotherapy practice, I will try to show how imagery and storytelling can be used effectively by the therapist and patient. An important feature of a great variety of therapeutic approaches may well involve training patients to identify, enhance, and regulate their imaginative skills.

5

IMAGERY AND NARRATIVE IN VARIOUS FORMS OF MODERN PSYCHOTHERAPY

The *New Yorker* magazine once featured a cartoon depicting a typical parade down the city's Fifth Avenue, much like those for St. Patrick's Day, Polish American Day, or Columbus Day. In this parade, groups bearing banners like "Freudians United," "Jungians Assembled," and "Gestalt Therapy Forever" formed a procession for what was obviously Psychotherapy Day. This depiction may not be so far-fetched; researchers have identified more than 200 forms of psychotherapy that were practiced in the 20th century (Kazdin, 2000) and may still be in use around the world. If we were talking of faith- or intuition-derived forms of religious worship (even within the major religious groups like Hinduism, Christianity, Judaism, Islam, and Buddhism), such large variations would not be surprising. Psychotherapy, however, is on the whole accepted as a practice derived from psychological and medical science. The scientific endeavor of experimentation, theory testing, and data collection is inherently unifying. The satellites launched from Russia, China, and the United States as well as the surgery and disease-immunization procedures practiced across national boundaries reflect the same principles derived from common research-tested applications of mathematics, physics, physiology, and neuroscience. At the forefront of scientific knowledge, even though physicists may disagree about certain still-untested concepts—such as string theory as an approach to unifying the quantum physics of atomic particles with the grand sweep of cosmic nebulae—there is agreement that such divergences are ultimately resolvable through systematic experiments and data collection as well as mathematical formulations.

Although psychological science has not yet attained the precision of measurement and prediction of other physical or biological sciences, it has the tools and procedures (if not the funding or, for political, sociological, or sometimes ethical reasons, the opportunities) to move closer to establishing common scientific principles for assessing and modifying personality difficulties. It would be presumptuous to attempt to set up guidelines for unifying all psychotherapies or psychopathologies, but I hope to point to some avenues for approaching that goal by focusing on the integrative possibilities of imagery and narrative processes in a range of psychotherapies.

A HISTORICAL PERSPECTIVE

Figure 5.1 lays out an ambitious and fairly comprehensive overview of the emergence of modern psychotherapies from their origins in the 1880s, when the young physician Sigmund Freud, exposed to the clinical uses of hypnosis during a traveling fellowship in France, returned to Vienna to enter a joint practice with Joseph Breuer treating neurotic patients. Freud's clinical experience with hypnosis led to his invention of psychoanalysis as a form of treatment of psychopathologies at the start of the 20th century. A complete examination of this chart and the influences within and across columns is more appropriate for a full historical study. I will, however, guide the reader quickly through the maze of methods and names, focusing primarily on my proposal that the right side of the diagram represents psychotherapies relying most strongly on the narrative or experiential and imaginative features of human thought whereas the left side of the diagram reflects approaches that put greater emphasis on the rational and cognitive aspects of human thought. The right side, especially in the more intrapsychic, emotion-focused, "wilder" Jungian, Reichian, Gestalt therapy, guided imagery, and humanistic approaches, may loosely reflect Nietzsche's (Kaufmann, 1968) famous Dionysian worldview in contrast with the more Apollonian orientation of psychotherapies on the diagram's left, like those of Kelly (1955) and Beck (e.g., Beck, 1976), the early "rational therapy" of Ellis (see, e.g., Ellis, 1989), and the cognitive–behavioral approaches in general. Another directional trend in this diagram can be identified as a shift from a highly individual or intrapsychic emphasis reflected in classical (pre–object relations) psychoanalysis and its Jungian offshoots toward a more social or interpersonal orientation (e.g., Sullivan, on the right side of the diagram; see Sullivan, 1953). The chart ideally would need to take on a topological

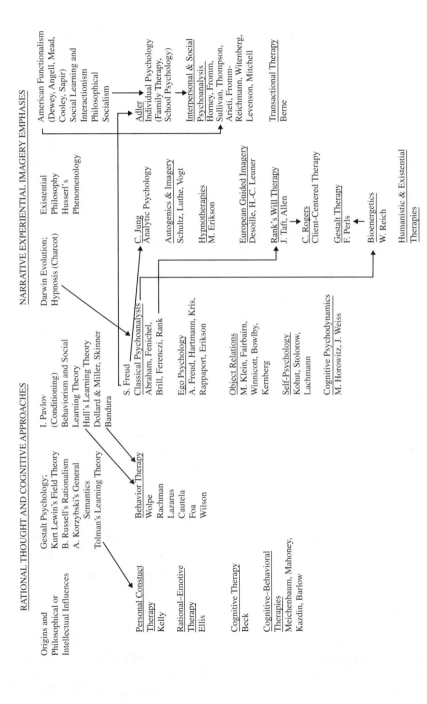

Figure 5.1. The emergence of modern psychotherapies. The top row represents origins and philosophical or intellectual influences on the various schools of thought displayed at the bottom of the figure.

mathematical form, so that it could be circular, and the neo-Freudian and particularly the American functionalist sociology- and psychology-influenced school of Harry Stack Sullivan could link up with the social learning theory origins of the cognitive–behavioral therapies.

Let me walk the reader more carefully through Figure 5.1. I have put Freud and what might be called classical or orthodox psychoanalysis at the center because I believe that although psychoanalysis and its modifications and variations are no longer as widely accepted and esteemed as they were for the first 80 years of the 20th century, a strong case can be made for the proposition that all the forms of modern psychotherapy have in some fashion been influenced by the writings of the Viennese neurologist. If one puts arrows into the chart (as I do when lecturing), one can show that Freud stimulated Dollard and Miller's social learning therapy or Bandura's social learning model as well as Beck's cognitive therapy. Carl Rogers's client-centered psychotherapy, first presented in 1942 as a contrast to psychoanalysis, was itself traceable to the influence on Rogers of the teachings of Jessie Taft and Frederick Allen at the Pennsylvania School of Social Work and the Philadelphia Child Guidance Clinic, respectively. Both of them strongly reflected the ideas of Otto Rank, one of Freud's earliest and closest associates.

Classical psychoanalysis, most thoroughly represented in Fenichel's *The Psychoanalytic Theory of Neurosis* (Fenichel, 1945), although it still has its adherents, was gradually modified into the ego psychology approach, which emphasized defense mechanisms, and to a closer tie to general psychology by the introduction of autonomous ego functions in the work of Anna Freud, Hartmann, Ernst Kris, Rudolph Loewenstein, and David Rapaport in the 1940s and 1950s. The British school, stimulated originally by Melanie Klein, soon moved into a less id-dominated and more interpersonal direction under the intellectual leadership of W. R. D. Fairbairn, John Bowlby, and Donald W. Winnicott, among others. This object-relations group independently moved the whole system closer to the interpersonal neo-Freudians, who were themselves initially stimulated by Adler, Szandor Ferenczi, Horney, and, especially in the United States, by Harry Stack Sullivan and Clara Thompson. In general, these groups have moved away from the metapsychology and largely untestable features of Freudian theory toward "observable" and researchable concepts such as "attachment" or, as in the work of Joseph Weiss and Mardi Horowitz, toward integrating testable links between psychoanalytic constructs like fantasies and cognitive psychology's "schemas" and "scripts."

The "mainstream" psychoanalytic column is positioned at the center to represent my proposal that, at least in Freud's persisting conception, the goal of psychoanalysis was "where Id was, there shall Ego be" (Freud, 1933/1964, p. 80), a position that in essence argues for the ultimate importance of rational–logical thought. This emphasis is less critical to most of the treatment approaches on the right side of the diagram, especially those of Jung, the European imagery schools, the humanistic approaches, Reich's bioenergetics, or Perls's Gestalt therapy. Even Rogers's client-centered therapy puts priority on emotional experience rather than logical–sequential thought.

To the right of the center column, we find an emphasis on the narrative, imagery-based, and experiential features of the human condition. Although Freud himself gave up hypnosis as a treatment in the 1890s, he continued to emphasize imagery associations and the hypnosis-derived use of the couch (J. L. Singer, 1974). He also persisted in emphasizing the powerful influences of unconscious drives and fantasies because he believed these to be the special features of his contributions to psychology. Aspects of his early treatment and theorizing, such as *catharsis,* the curative power of a vivid reliving of early memories, continued to be used by later clinicians and are key features of various primal scream, regression, and rebirthing approaches, and Freud's conceptual references to displacement of sexual energy were taken literally by Wilhelm Reich and his followers, who used massage and orgone boxes to redirect the libido of their patients. Vestiges of hypnosis, along with Reich's notions of free sexuality, were intermingled by Frederick Perls with somewhat watered-down notions drawn from the scientific work of the Gestalt psychologists and the neurological research of Kurt Goldstein into what is today called Gestalt therapy, an approach that puts great emphasis on the experiential and storytelling side of the human condition. A continuation of hypnosis or quasi-hypnotic interactions combined with storytelling as a means of redirecting a patient's thoughts and behavior characterizes the school of Milton Erickson, a hypnotist who also often resorted to Christlike parables as a feature of therapeutic interactions. Freud might well have been appalled by these extensions of his approach in what he would consider irrational directions.

The therapies that bear some relation to the great European influence of the Swiss psychiatrist Carl Jung are grouped just below his name. In the first decade of the 20th century, as psychoanalysis emerged not only as a form of psychotherapy but as a major intellectual movement, Jung was Freud's chosen heir apparent. The complexity of these men's personal and intellectual relationship has been well documented by now and need not be detailed here. Jung, like Freud, was a scientifically trained physician, and some of his work on word-association methods and on personality traits has had a lasting influence in psychology through the measurement of emotion for lie-detection procedures and in the many psychometric studies of traits like introversion and extraversion. Jung greatly expanded the notion of the role of unconscious processes in human motivation. His emphasis on the spiritual, mystical, and creative elements of the unconscious led to his intellectual parting with Freud, who persisted in limiting unconscious motivation to a Darwinian "human-as-animal" sexuality. Jung eschewed Freud's reduction of human motivation to bodily functions and put much more stress on humans as mythmakers and storytellers, on their use of cross-cultural archetypes or symbols. He developed a therapeutic technique called *active imagination*, in which patients sought through vivid imagery to reenact their dreams and fantasies.

During this same period in Germany, several physicians, notably J. H. Schultz and Oskar Vogt and, later, H. Luthe (Schultz & Luthe, 1969) developed an approach that used vivid imagery for relaxation and for counteracting a huge variety of physical symptoms. Their extensive reliance on imagery as part of autogenic treatment has been documented in numerous case reports, mostly in German medical journals, and may have reflected some Jungian influence. The full history of how autogenics fits into the spectrum of the European mental imagery movement remains to be fully researched. Somewhat independently, in France through the work of Desoille, Roger Fretigny, and Andre Virel, among others; in Italy in the work of Roberto Assagioli; and in Germany in the fairly extensive research work of Leuner (1978), there emerged what may be called the *guided imagery* or *waking dream* approach to psychotherapy. This therapeutic intervention consists mainly of patients producing imagery sequences that become, in effect, dreamlike narratives. There is a minimum of interpretation or discussion. The therapist's role is that of a "guide," helping the patient to keep the flow of images moving. These therapeutic approaches represent extremes of reliance on narrative thought or the experiential system with a strong imagery component.

Further down the "Jungian" column we encounter a somewhat more "Americanized" group of therapies, albeit with origins that are also traceable to the influence of one of Freud's earliest and closest adherents, Otto Rank. Rank was particularly concerned with beginnings (the birth experience), limits, separations, and anticipated endings and their emotional components. He was less caught up in the complexities of the unconscious or in the vicissitudes of instincts such as sexuality and aggression. His approach zeroed in on emotional relationships and on how a child's or adult's responses in psychotherapy mirrored important life experiences of beginnings, attachments, and anticipated separations. His work influenced Jessie Taft, a psychologist at the Pennsylvania School of Social Work in Philadelphia, whose social worker cohorts began to use variants of the Rank approach in their counseling of clients. Carl Rogers was initially drawn to Freudian psychoanalysis in his work as one of the first American clinical child psychologists. When he was exposed to the social work approach of the Pennsylvania school he began to rethink the therapeutic process, and in the 1940s he outlined what he first called *nondirective* and, later, *client-centered* counseling and psychotherapy. His emphasis was on enhancing the patient's emotional experience and, through an attitude of "positive regard" and reflection of feelings, on furthering his patients' abilities to reshape their life narratives, clarify their own feelings, and come to terms with a more constructive awareness of self.

Rogers also introduced systematic research on the processes and outcomes of psychotherapy, moving beyond the anecdotal methods that prevailed in the psychoanalytic world. By the 1960s, Rogers was the most respected and famous clinical psychologist in America. As he moved more and more toward focusing on the purely experiential features of psychotherapy, he opened the way for the emergence of the humanistic psychotherapies. These approaches, products of the social milieu of the 1960s and 1970s, incorporated some of Rogers's work, Gestalt therapy, the guided imagery methods from Europe, and aspects of existential philosophy. Whereas a complex thinker and intellectual like Jung might have been uncomfortable with the derisive attitudes toward "intellectualization" or "mind-fucking" expressed by Frederick Perls and other humanistic psychotherapists, the common element in the therapies in this column is their major reliance on the more emotional, imagistic, and purely experiential rather than rational side of human thought.

Further to the right in our chart of psychotherapies, we see a shift from the intrapsychic focus toward a greater interpersonal, social orientation in the theory and treatment techniques. I believe that much of this shift is traceable to the influence of another of Freud's heirs apparent, the physician Alfred Adler. Although Adler, once he had broken with Freud, began to call his approach *individual psychology*, he was increasingly oriented toward socialism politically and toward a view of humans as continuously striving to reconcile their drives for power with a recognition of social interest, the value of service to society, or constructive relationships with others (Ansbacher & Ansbacher, 1970). Adler broke with classical psychoanalysis as he came to emphasize actual family relationships, sibling rivalries, human competition and strivings for power, and the role of personal fictions or self-enhancing myths as the areas for therapist interventions. Much of what is today termed *narrative psychotherapy* was anticipated in his approach. In the early 1920s, when Adler's socialist connections to the early post–World War I Austrian government put him into a position of national influence, he introduced the first programs of school psychology and family psychotherapy, reflecting his interactionist orientation.

Adler's early contacts with another younger Freudian psychoanalyst, Karen Horney, brought interpersonal psychoanalysis to prominence in the United States in the late 1930s and 1940s. Horney was increasingly convinced that Freud's intrapsychic, biological drive emphasis overlooked the critical role of actual family interactions in the origins of neurosis. She became more and more convinced that family structure itself and the anxieties aroused in children by family difficulties often reflected broader social dysfunctions and the neurotic features of entire societies. Her widely popular American books, along with those by another former Freudian, Erich Fromm, captured the imagination of many American psychiatrists, psychologists, and social workers as well as the general public (Fromm, 1941, 1955; Horney, 1939, 1945). Horney and Fromm joined with the American psychiatrists Clara Thompson and Harry Stack Sullivan and others to break away from the New York Psychoanalytic Society and the American Psychoanalytic Society, which represented classical psychoanalysis, in order to form a new psychoanalytic institute focusing more on interpersonal psychoanalysis.

Sullivan has become the intellectual progenitor of interpersonal approaches in psychotherapy and, more generally, in psychological research (Kiesler, 1996). Influenced by the early-20th-century American school of functional psychology reflected in the work of John Dewey and George Mead, among others, Sullivan laid out a systematic revision of Freud's system into an interpersonal and operationalized form, a form that opened the way for extensive systematic research, as Kiesler (1996) has demonstrated. The interpersonal psychotherapists remain on the right half of the diagram because they mainly emphasize narrative and experiential processes and use imagery and dream interpretation in treatment. Yet, as I suggested above, their relationship to the interactionist, pre-behaviorism functionalists led to the social learning approaches that characterize the treatment methods on the left of our diagram.

The left side of our chart brings forth one immediate implication. The many psychotherapeutic variants on the right stem from direct practice rather than from psychological, scientific-method research backgrounds, whereas the rational, thought-based cognitive or behavioral therapies are more closely tied to preclinical behavioral science investigative domains. This difference in origin does not automatically make the cognitive–behavioral approaches more effective as therapies; that must be empirically demonstrated. It may well be that because of their earlier beginnings and great variety, the more narrative and experientially focused therapies have already helped many more people with many more types of psychological or psychosomatic difficulties in Europe and America. With the exception of Rogers's client-centered therapy, however, few of the more experiential or "psychodynamic" therapies have been subjected to careful process and outcome research in contrast to those on the diagram's left, which have been almost continuously under research scrutiny (Kazdin, 1998, 2000).

We can trace the cognitive–behavioral therapies to two general psychological lines of research, and the more purely cognitive therapies seem likely to reflect some philosophical influences as well. In the first half of the 20th century, two major psychological research approaches emerged: Gestalt psychology, developed in Germany, and behaviorism, deriving from a combination of the Russian physiologist Pavlov's conditioning experiments and American functional psychology. The behaviorally oriented research on animal learning of Edward Thorndike and John Watson spread widely in the United States and became a key feature of the many new psychology departments being formed, especially in the Midwest. Gestalt psychology, with its emphasis on human perceptual studies and, to a lesser extent, on learning and motivation, became more prominent with immigration to this country during the 1930s of many German and other European scientists, including Wolfgang Köhler, Kurt Kafka, Max Wertheimer, and Kurt Lewin. By the 1930s and 1940s, two clear schools of learning theory could be identified. One was led by Yale's Clark Hull, deriving chiefly from behaviorism but with a subtle influence from psychoanalytic drive theory. The other school of learning theory (also conducting behavioral research largely with rats) was led by Edward Chase Tolman at the University of California in Berkeley. Tolman, at first a strong behaviorist, was more and more intrigued by the more holistic, cognitive orientation of the Gestalt group and especially by Kurt Lewin, whom he considered (along with Freud) one of psychology's true geniuses. I have not emphasized B. F. Skinner, who came to prominence a little later, not because his objective behaviorism was not influential in the area (quite the contrary), but because although his conditioning approaches are much used with children, the autistic, and the retarded and in many kinds of case management, they play only a small role in psychotherapy.

Though Hull was primarily interested in developing an exquisite and precise learning theory involving conditioning and drive reduction with rats, two of his close associates at Yale, John Dollard and Neal Miller, had begun to explore how behavioral concepts could be integrated with psychoanalytic concepts. Both men went to Vienna to meet Freud in the 1930s and also to be psychoanalyzed by some colleagues of his. Miller later conducted his classic studies of conflict in rats, which yielded similar results to the experimental and theoretical analyses on conflict in humans carried out by Kurt Lewin and his students in Germany and later in the United States. Dollard and Miller collaborated on studies of social learning and imitation and then on their famous book on psychotherapy (Dollard & Miller, 1950) in which Hullian learning was integrated to some degree with psychoanalytic conceptions. This influential book almost certainly was a progenitor of the modern behavior therapies, introduced to America through the South African psychiatrist Joseph Wolpe and other close associates such as Rachman and Lazarus. For our purposes in this volume, the behavior therapies approached treatment as a learning process by combining systematic forms of relaxation or (in the case of aversive conditioning) arousal, with repetitive conditioning techniques relying heavily on patients' production of imagined scenes of frightening settings or unwanted actions as the targets for change. In contrast with Dollard and Miller's acceptance of unconscious motivations or fantasies, the first group of behavior therapists dealt primarily with clients' conscious rational motivation for change and improvement, encouraging and expecting them to practice the repetitive exercises of the conditioning techniques. No significant effort was made to uncover complex underlying sources for phobias or compulsive behaviors. Instead, the rational thinking of adults was relied on to take advantage of the opportunities for reshaping their behavior through conditioning practice. Only the imagery component of these treatments reflected the experiential mode of thought, and, wherever possible, direct in vivo practice was preferred to imagery.

The behavior therapies, by focusing on very specific, narrowly defined symptoms such as fears of heights, animals, and public speaking, made possible systematic outcome research. This scientific link was attractive to many psychologists trained in the precise methods of learning theory. Evidence of the relative effectiveness of these therapies accumulated in the 1970s and 1980s. At the same time, it was becoming clear from the narrow range of psychological symptoms that could be treated with conditioning therapies and the limited numbers of more complicated personality types that actually proved to be suitable for these approaches that greater attention needed to be paid to other facets of the more rational components of human thought. Independently of behaviorism, a separate movement toward rationally oriented psychotherapy, cognitive psychotherapy, had been emerging in the late 1950s and 1960s.

Because of his acknowledged debt to Gestalt psychology and to the field theory of Kurt Lewin, Tolman's approach to learning theory introduced, even in the rats he studied, the psychological role of expectancies, plans, and cognitive maps, in contrast to Hull's stimulus–response focus on drives and conditioning. As we know now, the cognitive orientation gradually emerged on the basis of empirical findings as the dominant approach, not only in animal studies but also in investigations of human perception, memory, and learning. In the atmosphere of this intellectual groundswell, approaches to clinical practice also began to reflect this more holistic, conscious, and somewhat logical–sequential orientation. Philosophical trends may also have had a subtle impact on the emergence of cognitive therapies. One may think of the nearly century-long effect of the extreme rationalism of the long-lived Bertrand Russell and his former pupil, Wittgenstein, at Cambridge. Wittgenstein and other British philosophers like Gilbert Ryle, John Austin, and Alfred Ayer placed great emphasis on the importance of clarity in language as a guide to greater precision in all aspects of thought and behavior.

A popularized and quasi-therapeutic elaboration of the role of precision in language and in logical thought was introduced early in the 20th century by a Polish engineer, Alfred Korzybski. It attained wide interest and, under the title of general semantics, played a subtle role in influencing the early cognitive psychotherapies of George Kelly, Albert Ellis, and Aaron Beck.

Probably the first major player in this movement was the American George Kelly (1955), who devised a full-scale personality theory, a set of operationalized concepts and measurement procedures, and a formal psychotherapy that continues to be practiced to this day, especially in England. Kelly took the approach that a human being can be regarded as a scientist, someone who constantly formulates hypotheses about the social world around him and who, on the basis of "tests" of these hypotheses through interpretations of the outcomes of social interactions, develops hierarchies of personal constructs. The narrowness or breadth, rigidity or flexibility, and comprehensiveness of one's personal constructs are keys to adaptive behavior or personal adjustment. Psychotherapy involves helping a client reshape and differentiate perceptions of relationships to significant others by the identification and measurement (quantitative and qualitative) of his or her role repertory system or personal construct hierarchy and the gradual modification of self-defeating role-playing. Although rehearsing new roles or reexamining the rigidity of one's construct system through imagery are features of this therapy, the emphasis throughout is on rational discourse and respect for the client's ultimate logical capacities.

Albert Ellis, perhaps influenced especially by Bertrand Russell's philosophy, independently developed rational psychotherapy. He sought to confront the many prejudices and self-defeating systems of beliefs we all develop through limited social learning and exposures to specific family distortions or influences of religious and cultural superstitions. Ellis was particularly concerned with prudish sexual attitudes and with the naive, irrational expectations people brought to intimate relations. His therapeutic approach involved extensive use of humor and active mockery to help clients recognize their own narrowness and irrationality. He came to recognize increasingly the importance of emotionality in the therapeutic interaction and renamed his popular cognitive therapy *rational–emotive psychotherapy*.

Aaron Beck, a psychiatrist originally trained in psychoanalysis, became increasingly disenchanted with the cultish, tradition-bound, and untestable nature of classical Freudian therapy. He believes, like Ellis and Kelly, that humans can be reached through their capacities for rational thought, and he devised a thoroughgoing system for helping people to recognize their self-defeating beliefs and patterns of quasi-superstitious behavior. The thoroughness, organization, and testability of Beck's cognitive therapy has led to its emergence as the most influential of current psychotherapies. Beck and a group of psychologist–researchers like Bandura, Lazarus, Meichenbaum, Kazdin, Foa, and Barlow, among others, also have accepted the contributions of the behavior therapy approach with its emphasis on repetitive practice. Practitioners on the left side of our diagram now most often use cognitive–

behavioral approaches rather than the purely cognitive treatment mode of the type originated by George Kelly in the 1950s.

SPECIFIC APPLICATIONS OF IMAGERY IN PSYCHOTHERAPIES

Although the balance of this volume will address specific applications of imagery in particular forms of the two major types of psychotherapy in current use, it may be helpful to the reader to anticipate these examples with a survey tied to the structure of Figure 5.1. It should be apparent that much of the work carried out in classical psychoanalysis, in its more direct offshoots and in the neo-Freudian and interpersonal approaches, is heavily dependent on imagery and memory narratives. The reliance on reports of one's dreams or daydreams that characterized psychoanalysis in its classical form has continued on into the object relations, self psychology, and integrative approaches of Mardi Horowitz and Joseph Weiss. In all of these approaches, the client engages to some degree in free association throughout a therapy session. The listening therapist is likely to perk up and reinforce those phases of the ongoing talk when the specific imagery of early memories, recent dreams, or vivid fantasies about oneself or the therapist are reported.

The increasing emphasis on shorter term psychodynamic therapies has led to many therapists intervening more frequently to focus the patient's attention on particular problem areas or on memories of problematic relationships in early life. Though dream reports remain the ostensible "royal road to the unconscious," as Freud put it, shorter term treatments are, of necessity, less likely to become involved with the patient's detailed associations to dreams, which can eat up a whole psychotherapy hour. Only dreams or waking fantasies that offer clues to problems of transference to the therapist or other very significant figures in the client's life are likely to become the focus of a session.

It is my experience from reading case reports, listening to case presentations, and reading the psychoanalytic journals that the psychoanalytic interventions of an Adlerian or interpersonal orientation found on the extreme right of Figure 5.1 are characterized even more than the classical Freudian by a focus on the interactions of patient and therapist and by directing patients' attention to imagery and fantasy that especially bears on those processes. Adler originally fostered the notion of the recall of family "fictions," of narratives about sibling as well as parental relations, but with, perhaps, less emphasis on dream reports. Transactional therapy, with its emphasis on identifying and modifying one's roles, relies heavily on active role-playing and also seems less oriented to dream imagery reports and associations to their content.

The vertical line of therapies descended from or in various ways influenced by Jung have the greatest concern with the evocation of fantasy material linked to a presumed rich unconscious life. Yet even Jung became impatient with the more passive kinds of free association to dream reports. With his method of active imagination, he encouraged patients to, in effect, reenter the dream experience and relive dream images as if they were currently under way. This approach undoubtedly led to a flowering of what became a widely practiced approach in France, Italy, and Germany: the *guided waking dream method*. The patient, after a quasi-hypnotic period of relaxation, is encouraged to imagine him- or herself lying in a meadow or strolling through a forest and then to generate a series of images, which are reported to the therapist. In the more structured method used by Hans-Carl Leuner and his followers, each session begins with a different setting: a meadow, a forest, climbing hills or mountains, exploring a cave, looking through a family picture album, and so forth. Interpretation is minimal in these approaches because it is believed that the sequence of imagery opens areas hitherto suppressed or unrecognized and that this enlightenment of the unconscious is often inherently curative (Leuner, 1978; J. L. Singer, 1974; J. L. Singer & Pope, 1978).

The approaches on the left side of our diagram have much less emphasis on the "free-floating" uses of imagery, fantasy, or memory, and they have almost no resort to dream reports. However, although the behavior therapies are very much action oriented, they do rely extensively on fairly specific imagery. Systematic desensitization calls for the establishment of a hierarchy of imagined settings associated with increasing levels of fearfulness after using the same kinds of relaxation exercises found in the European guided imagery treatments. Variants of this reexperiencing of phobic scenes under relaxed conditions may also call for generating mental scenes of peacefulness or pleasure to reduce one's fearfulness (Lazarus, 1971, 1981; J. L. Singer, 1974). Images of noxious scenes or events may be used to counteract the occurrence of unwanted urges or compulsions (Cautela, 1967, 1970a, 1970b; J. L. Singer, 1974). Modeling of individuals who engage in effective actions—for example, public speaking or self-assertion—is also a regular feature of the behavior approaches (Lazarus, 1981).

The more cognitive approaches also have relied heavily on focused uses of imagery. These uses began when George Kelly (1955) introduced his personal construct therapy, in which the rather formally structured role repertory method called on clients to imagine key family or other significant figures and then to imagine how these figures were linked together to generate sets of personal constructs or organized belief systems about friendship, helpfulness, neglect, or hostility. The gradual integration of cognitive therapy methods and pure behaviorist approaches with the increased theory and evidence from cognitive psychology evident in the work of Aaron Beck,

Donald Meichenbaum, Alan Kazdin, Michael Mahoney, and David Barlow, among others, has increasingly incorporated uses of our imaginative capacities in relatively controlled forms as part of therapeutic interventions. The major differences between these approaches and those on the right side of Figure 5.1 lie in the greater emphasis on free-floating imagery in the more psychodynamic treatments and also in the greater importance placed on early memories and life narratives in the psychoanalytically derived groups. As I show in the balance of this volume, however, it may be possible to find ways of integrating the various approaches in the interests of fuller and more effective interventions.

In summary, our survey of psychotherapies dating from 1900, almost all traceable in some way to Freud's introduction of a psychological approach to treating neuroses, suggests a number of commonalities as well as differences. If we accept the notion that human thought and communication vary in terms of relative reliance on a narrative, episodic, and experiential–imagistic mode, on the one hand, and a logical, orderly, sequential, and verbally precise style, on the other, then a majority of the forms of psychotherapy in current use place greatest emphasis on the rational style. At least in North America, the more cognitively oriented psychotherapies may be most widely promoted because they are now emphasized in university training programs on the basis of their better record of scientific researchability and empirical assessment. The so-called empirically validated or assessed therapies are, however, too narrowly defined in terms of symptom range or diagnostic categories to encompass the wide variety of complaints and concerns of people who seek treatment at clinics or from private practitioners, as Westen and Morrison (2001) have shown. I therefore argue that despite their surface differences in self-representation, advertising, or group affiliations, most therapists are increasingly integrating methods and techniques that draw on both the paradigmatic or logical features of human thought and the narrative–experiential modes. In the following chapters, I show how use of the human capacity for narrative and imagistic thinking can be integrated into variants of the two major groups of psychotherapies: the cognitive–behavioral and the psychodynamic–interpersonal.

6

THE PSYCHOTHERAPEUTIC
SITUATION

My intent in this volume is to guide the clinician in the use of imagery processes for constructive purposes. Effective thought clearly calls for an integration of cognitive and narrative–experiential processes. An often-neglected feature of cognitive ability, the use of sensory-linked mental reproductive skills or images, is our focus here.

Having set the background from a historical standpoint, let us now look more closely at the specifics of the psychotherapeutic situation faced by adults seeking individual help from clinicians for a variety of personal problems, from formally diagnosable conditions to the range of interpersonal difficulties to which our human condition is prey. Exhibit 6.1 presents the various facets of the psychotherapeutic situation. My intent in this chapter is not to review the entire structure of a dyadic psychotherapy but to call attention to the ways in which the imagery abilities or limitations of the patient and, perhaps to a lesser extent, of the therapist, come into play in their interaction.

All psychotherapy must be understood as occurring within socioculturally determined structures that may range from government to private settings of clinics or practices, from medical to school or religiously affiliated institutions or storefront clinics, and with large variations in the socioeconomic environments of the participants. The nature of the family structures prevalent in the society may also be important determinants of what both

EXHIBIT 6.1
The Psychotherapeutic Transaction

The patient	Therapeutic technique and interaction	The therapist
■ Demographics (e.g., age, sex, socioeconomic status)	■ General techniques • Verbal communication • Nonverbal communication • Recounting of life history and self-disclosure by patient (forms bond) • Working alliance around patient's problems	■ Demographics (e.g., age, sex, socioeconomic status) ■ Degrees of abstract, practical, and creative intelligence ■ Personal experience
■ Symptoms • Physical • Interpersonal or emotional difficulties and disruptions (e.g., affect disturbance, dread, depression, anger, impulsivity)	■ Specific techniques • Free association and total honesty • Imagery experience (learning, enjoying, and controlling it) • Attribution, labeling, and cognitive restructuring	■ Professional education and experience ■ Cognitive and affective styles ■ Communication skill and precision of expression
■ Basis of referral (e.g., medical, self, legal) ■ Education, culture, prior accomplishments and skills	• Questioning assumptions • Small-scale rehearsal of ineffective behaviors and identification of false expectations, missed communications • Practice of new behaviors	■ Accurate empathy and imagination ■ Self-knowledge ■ Activity, wit, and humor
■ Expectations and hopes: A cognitive map more or less differentiated about • Self • Sex role, gender-related beliefs • Course of therapy and relation to therapist • Childhood holdovers • Nature of interpersonal relationships • Magical or realistic anticipations	• Modeling (covert and direct) • New reference groups • Body experiences, relaxation, biofeedback, autonomic system awareness	■ Value orientation ■ Consultation with others ■ Ethical knowledge, sensitivity, and commitment
■ "Ego strength": successful experiences (social, vocational), general competence and skills, semi-objectivity, delaying capacity, freedom from addictions ■ Cognitive style and imagery ability ■ Physical health and health-related attitudes and behavior ■ General morale	■ Specific behavior techniques • Word or thought stopping • Systematic desensitization • Flooding • Aversive conditioning • Covert modeling • Imagery control and elaboration • Empty chair dialogues or psychodramatic role-playing	

patient and therapist bring to their encounter. No serious study of psycho-therapy can ignore such influences.

The left-hand column describes what the patient brings to a therapeutic encounter, including the symptoms, from some physical difficulties to the emotional and interpersonal stressors, that provide the impetus for seeking psychological help. The nature of a referral source may be a strong determinant of motivation or may lead to sets of positive expectations or even to resistance to treatment if the referee is perceived as threatening or misguided. In the famous case of Dora written up by Freud, the adolescent girl's apparent awareness that the pressure from her father to seek help for her symptoms was really a manipulation to foster his own adulterous intentions doomed the treatment from the start (Freud, 1905/1962).

For our purposes, the most relevant category of what the patient brings to treatment is that of hopes and expectations. Here we find the complex images and the daydreams about what therapy can offer; what a therapist can do; what beliefs one holds about one's actual, ideal, or dreaded self (J. L. Singer, 1999); what memory demons from childhood recur persistently; and what myths or illusions about the nature of personal relationships were fostered by family, religion, one's peer culture, or the popular media. Hope, defined through agencies, pathways, and goals that are features of what the patient brings, may also play a critical role as a therapeutic intervention, as the research reviewed by Snyder, Ilardi, Michael, and Cheavens (2000) has shown. The patient's hopes, expectations, and beliefs about the process and outcome of psychotherapy may be expressed verbally in summary terms or abstractions, such as "I hope to get well"; "I think the therapist is a wise, well-trained person"; and "I suppose if I do what the therapist says, I'll start feeling better." Many elaborate and fairly detailed imagery sequences may underlie these verbalizations, such as representations of specific interactions between patient and therapist and then between patient and significant others such as lovers, spouses, children, parents, bosses, or friends.

Early research was carried out by Herman Witkin and Helen Block Lewis (Witkin, Lewis, & Weil, 1968) on cognitive styles such as field dependence or field independence. Patients who are field independent are likely to talk on for longer periods without therapist prompting or questioning, and they may also be more at ease in generating vivid images or remembering dreams. Field-dependent patients seem to do better with a more active, "interventionist" psychotherapist. More recent studies by Sidney Blatt and his collaborators, who reanalyzed studies of psychiatric inpatients at the Menninger Foundation, also found important signs of cognitive style differences along somewhat similar lines, with indications that depending on the type of psychotherapy offered, such styles in patients, either of dependency or of autonomy, led to more effective outcomes (Blatt, Straynor, Auerbach, & Behrends, 1996).

I am proposing that the competent therapist, whether in initial assessment or early in ongoing treatment, must be looking for information from the patient that covers—in as concrete a form as possible—the categories outlined here of what the client brings to the treatment process. My stress on specificity derives from accumulated clinical understanding that general statements and abstractions lack the emotional immediacy and clarity of communication that are necessary features of effective psychotherapy in any of its forms. If patients can generate and then describe vividly imagined events, whether relatively veridical episodic memories or fantasies and anticipations, the therapeutic process takes on a reality and excitement that can foster effective learning and can motivate personality change.

What does the therapist bring to the psychotherapeutic situation? The right-hand column of the diagram outlines a range of background characteristics, intellectual skills, and educational and experiential exposures relevant to the therapeutic process as well as skills in verbal expression and the ability to empathize with the emotions and also to imagine the experiences of the client. Again, for the purposes of this volume, I stress the imaginative capacities of the professional who must try to represent mentally what the patient has described about growing up in a small town like What Cheer, Iowa, or a foreign city like Bergen, Norway, and sustain a vivid sense of the patient's "significant others," Aunt Ida, or brother Louis. We will later treat in some detail how the therapist's imagery can be useful in a variety of constructive ways for aiding the client and also for providing some degree of personal gratification in the difficult work of treatment.

The central column of the chart deals with a variety of possible interactions between the two protagonists in the therapeutic drama. I am limiting my discussion of psychotherapy to the verbal interaction of two adults. There are treatment approaches that include physical activities ranging from massage to yoga positioning; special kinds of exercise like the Feldenkreis or Alexander approaches; or, more recently, mindfulness meditation. The nature of the interaction is primarily verbal. As in any conversation, nonverbal cues like the direction of gaze; facial expressions of emotion like smiling, frowning, or surprise; and body movements such as yawning, stretching, or scratching are obviously all relevant facets of the communication process.

In the patient's recounting of a life history, a summary of facts is important, but so is the role of imagery. When the patient's narration takes on too abstract a form, critical memories, fantasies, or those often self-defeating beliefs from earlier years may not emerge. Here the therapist can encourage the patient to strive to retrieve specific event memories whenever possible. Encouraging a patient to picture home life scenes like family meals, family excursions, and critical episodes at play with peers or in school may yield richer data. In contrast to matter-of-fact verbal summaries, one may get detailed accounts of specific settings and encounters with significant persons, all tinged with emotional expression. Often such specific images evoke the self-defining memories that research has shown to be of considerable importance in conveying current affect-laden attitudes (J. A. Singer & Salovey, 1993; J. A. Singer, Singer, & Zittel, 2000).

As the patient unfolds his or her "story"—this disclosure of events, some perhaps never before shared with another person—a bond begins to form between the two individuals in the room. The patient experiences a revival of images of sometimes relatively rarely retrieved events along with strong emotions of joy, sadness, or dread. The listening therapist tries to imagine the settings and interactions from the patient's account, striving as much as possible to avoid mixing in personal recollections but using his or her imagery and the patient's vocabulary to attempt to perceive situations from the patient's perspective. This sharing of imagery is an important component of what becomes the *therapeutic alliance*, the situation in treatment most consistently associated with a good outcome.

Psychotherapeutic treatment involves sets of specific techniques, some of which overlap the many "schools" but many of which are defining features of particular types of psychological intervention. The use of free association, the interpretation of dreams, and the analysis of transference are targeted processes that differentiate classical Freudian analysis and its offshoots such as Sullivanian interpersonal psychoanalysis from cognitive–behavioral therapy and Rogers's client-centered counseling. Many clinicians are put off by the use of the term *technique* because it implies a mechanical or perhaps inauthentic stance for a psychotherapist. A stilted application of procedures by an uncaring professional may not work well in the interpersonal situation of psychotherapy in contrast with surgery, where the physician's personality or sincerity have little importance compared with the technical knowledge and manual skill needed during an actual procedure. If, however, we psychotherapists eschew a technology of intervention, are our clients paying just for interviews with caring, nice people? Why do we seek and offer "training," attend graduate professional schools, pay for workshops, and take licensing examinations? To the extent that psychotherapy presumably derives from scientific knowledge and research, it necessarily depends on techniques and procedures that reflect its informational base. Competence in psychotherapy often involves a seamless, emotionally sensitive application of techniques, but if the procedures used are not reasonably tested and researched, why should we expect to be paid? What would delineate us from good friends or even from charlatans or misguided believers in magic?

The methods listed under "Specific techniques" in the middle column of Exhibit 6.1 all are used in some form of psychotherapy, and many depend on the patient's ability to use imagery. Free association, so central to the various forms of psychoanalysis, grew out of Freud's shift from hypnosis to simply encouraging patients to "see" one image after another and then to report these sequences to the physician (J. L. Singer, 1974). By 1900, when Freud described the psychoanalytic method in his book *The Interpretation of Dreams* (Freud, 1900/1962c), he had moved to encouraging the patient to engage in a more general free association that included much more verbalization. This shift from an imagery emphasis, according to some researchers, may actually have weakened the therapeutic power of the free association method (Horowitz, 1978; Reyher, 1978; J. L. Singer, 1974).

Although many features of psychotherapy call for verbalization, clarity of communication, questioning of assumptions, or identification of misguided attributions, almost all treatment approaches do rely on patients' awareness of the reality and potential of their imagery capacities. Therapists may not explicitly label this activity *training*, but the likelihood is that many individuals in treatment, whatever their specific diagnoses or interpersonal problems, benefit from recognizing how and when to use imagery, how to enjoy it, and sometimes how to control it.

Imagery is used in various treatments when patients engage (with the therapist's overt or tacit encouragement) in mentally replaying some ineffective behaviors and also in mentally rehearsing new ways of relating to people. Of course direct enactment of such new styles of behavior is critical for a positive outcome, but imagined efforts can be very useful in readying patients to make the effort. Similarly, modeling, in a covert form, is increasingly being used. Research by Geller, Cooley, and Hartley (1981–1982) has shown that people who report a successful outcome of psychodynamic psychotherapy are likely to sustain images of the therapist not as a godlike or parental figure but as someone who encourages the patient in reexamining assumptions or identifying defenses or otherwise using some of the techniques that were part of the treatment.

Important signs of progress for many patients include their recognitions that they need new reference groups, new sets of friends or social and civic connections, and perhaps even opportunities to be of service to others. The eventual efforts to effect such life changes outside of therapy are crucial and can often be regarded as positive outcome measures when evaluating therapeutic gains. Within the therapy session, the awareness of one's need to make moves away from dysfunctional families or peer groups may come in images of alternative lifestyles sometimes suggested by reading or the popular media. Patients may then mentally play out pictured scenarios of steps that they need to take, people they might contact, and settings they should explore.

A vivid and sadly humorous example from my own practice can be briefly described. The patient grew up in a family that was largely alienated from the broader society in respect to social activities, religion, and civic responsibilities and was focused almost entirely on "money-grubbing" and even some quasi-illegal ventures. As an adult, he was doing well financially as a stock trader but had recently divorced from his wife and had limited visitation with his two young children. His only leisure activity was gambling, betting on all kinds of sports events without much success. He even wagered on exhibition baseball games during spring training, when outcomes are almost certainly unpredictable.

Confronting the narrowness, joylessness, lack of service to others, and what one might even call the existential meaninglessness of his life, this man began to envision possible alternatives. What groups could he join? How could he be helpful to others within his current lifestyle? His children were in early elementary school, so he started to picture himself attending school functions. That seemed a practical first step for him. More and more excited by the possibility he began to shout loudly, "That's it! That's it! I'm going to join the PTA!" His therapy hour ended with his repeated loud cries about the PTA. My next patient came into the office with a puzzled expression, remarking, "Am I crazy or did I hear someone yelling 'I want to join the PTA!'?"

The middle column of Exhibit 6.1 concludes with a listing of specific techniques used in behavior or cognitive–behavioral therapies. These methods grew out of the objective learning theories and were touted to some degree as contrasting with the "fuzzy," intrapsychic, and overly theoretical or speculative psychodynamic psychotherapies. These techniques still depend to a considerable degree, however, on the patient's ability to generate vivid imagery so that private inner experiences cannot be ignored, even though one also relies on overt actions, practicing, and in vivo experiences as part of the therapy (J. L. Singer, 1974; J. L. Singer & Pope, 1978). For example, the earliest and perhaps the most widely used and researched behavior therapy technique, systematic desensitization, introduced by Joseph Wolpe (Wolpe, 1958), depends on the patient's imagining a hierarchy of the frightening situations that make up his or her phobia—for example, riding to the 1st floor of a building in an elevator with one's spouse, riding to that 1st floor alone, and, eventually, riding to the 10th floor in an elevator alone. One then repeats each step in therapy under relaxed conditions or, in a modification, using imagery of a peaceful scene to juxtapose against the frightening one (Lazarus, 1971; J. L. Singer, 1974). Ultimately, when one can move in therapy through the hierarchy from least to most frightening imagined scenes, one may be more willing to attempt the real life confrontation of an elevator ride. Although no one claims that imagery practice alone can do the job, the patient's ability to generate vivid and controllable imagery may be a critical ingredient for the effectiveness of systematic desensitization (Wilkins, 1971). In subsequent chapters, I discuss practical uses of imagery in relation to the procedures and objectives of the various techniques of behavior and cognitive–behavioral therapies.

In summary, this chapter has guided the reader through most of the features of modern psychotherapy, with a special focus on the many ways that both the patients' and even their therapists' capacities for generating imagery or engaging in related forms of experiential thought are relevant. One can envision certain forms of psychotherapy that do not seem to call for elaborate internal representations. The effective behavioral management techniques using positive reinforcements after a child with a conduct disorder or an autistic patient performs appropriate actions are examples. Yet in the 551 treatments, techniques, or psychotherapies for children and adolescents listed by my Yale University colleague Alan Kazdin (2000), a significant number call for the patients to generate some type of imagery, narrative, or experiential response. In older adolescents and adults, we cannot ignore the power of the human imagination as part of a personality change or self-healing process.

7

USING IMAGERY
IN PSYCHOANALYTICALLY
ORIENTED THERAPIES

One of my conscious intentions in writing this book was to look for common features across psychotherapies and to relate such features as much as possible to basic research in psychology and the behavioral sciences. Although the right side of the Figure 5.1 in (see chap. 5) suggests that there are many psychotherapies traceable to Freud's classical psychoanalysis, which dates to 1900, most of these can be integrated around a relatively delimited sequence of procedures. There are many different psychoanalysis institutes in the Americas and in Europe, each presumably representing some variation in adherence to classical or orthodox Freudianism, each focusing somewhat more or less on the psychosexual drives or stages or on the concepts of self-delineation, object relations, and interpersonal interaction. They vary somewhat in whether the patient's use of free association is a primary requirement, on the use of the couch (so familiar to us from the movies or from *New Yorker* cartoons), in the frequency of sessions per week, and in the rules about therapist training. The politics and sociology of the psychoanalytic "movement," though an interesting topic for scholarship, is not our concern here; rather, I have outlined those technical steps that characterize almost all psychotherapies that describe themselves as psychoanalytically oriented or psychodynamic.

EXHIBIT 7.1
Common Approaches or Defining Processes in
Psychodynamic Psychotherapies

---

1. Narrative life review
2. Free association
3. Identification of resistance and defense mechanisms
4. Review or reconstruction of early memories with emotional experience
5. Examination and interpretation of dreams or waking fantasies
6. Identification and interpretation of persisting "pathological" belief systems or self-defeating fantasies
7. Identification and analyses of transference to the therapist or to significant others
8. "Working through" or corrective examination of recurrent self-defeating beliefs, fantasies, or defensiveness
9. Encouragement in trying new patterns of response in therapy and in social life
10. Enhancing gradual separation from therapist

Psychotherapists, when polled, are increasingly likely to label themselves as "eclectic." Clinicians trained in cognitive–behavioral therapy, when actually practicing, are often likely to pay some attention to their patients' resistance or transference-like reactions (Safran, 1990). One of the founders of behavior therapy, Arnold Lazarus, a highly regarded practitioner, now incorporates many features of psychodynamic therapy into his work, as his writings attest (Lazarus, 1981).

Exhibit 7.1 displays what I propose are the common features of the psychoanalytically derived psychotherapies. It is not my intent to review the whole process of psychodynamic psychotherapy but rather to identify those features of it that involve imagery and examine in some detail their effective use by the clinician.

TELLING ONE'S STORY AND FREE ASSOCIATION

All psychodynamic psychotherapies are oriented around the narrative and experiential thinking modes of clients. Symptom relief and personality change depend ultimately (as Freud certainly believed) on the realistic, logical capacities of the clients and their ability to gain insight into their irrational drives, persisting childhood fantasies, or misinterpretations. Thus, the goal of therapy ("where Id was, there shall Ego be" as Freud [1933/1964, p. 80] wrote) depends ultimately on the paradigmatic or logical capacity of the individual, what Freud called "the secondary thought process." At the start of treatment, however, and through much of it, the patient is encouraged to provide spontaneously occurring thoughts and memories and descriptions of daydreams or night dreams, of fears or worries—indeed, to strive for complete honesty in capturing ongoing thought, however bizarre it may seem on reflection.

The patient's imagery is especially important in this initial phase of the treatment encounter. It is too easy to fall into a conversation replete with summary statements and abstractions: "I guess I had a normal childhood"; "Things went pretty well for me until we moved and I started doing poorly at school"; "One of the things you learn as you grow up is that you can't really count on your parents when you run into problems with your friends." Statements of this type may be useful only if the patient can then move to detailed, concrete instances, examples of events that in their recounting carry the impact of being temporarily reexperienced with a vividness seemingly approximating the perceptions and emotions that accompanied their initial occurrence (J. L. Singer, 1974).

All psychotherapies that are psychodynamically oriented, then, begin with the patient telling a story or a group of stories. In a thoughtful analysis of the nature of narrative and its use as a psychotherapeutic process, McLeod (1997) has suggested, on the basis of a review of the literature, that storytelling functions as a communication that "carries information about *action, purpose, identity, feeling, intentionality and the world in which the storyteller lives*" (p. 53). Recent efforts to identify the key structural elements that emerge from research on psychodynamic therapies show that they can be organized around themes that bear out McLeod's summary. Strupp and Binder (1984) characterized these themes as acts of self, expectations about others' reactions, others' reactions to the narrator, and one's own interpretations about oneself. Luborsky and Crits-Christoph's (1990) core conflictual relationship theme approach—a quantitative method much used in research on the course of psychotherapy and the transference phenomenon—begins with a wish, expressed by the patient; the response of another person; and then the patient's reaction to that response. The extensive research of Mardi Horowitz, some of it in collaboration with myself on the role relationship model configuration, attempted to integrate this examination of patients' stories into a broader cognitive psychological framework (Horowitz, 1997; Horowitz, Eells, Singer, & Salovey, 1995; Eells et al., 1995). Figure 7.1 represents an example of how one can organize a set of statements and expressed beliefs from the narratives of a patient videotaped in the first five sessions into a configurational structure that may guide subsequent therapeutic interactions or at least aid in formulating treatment strategy and tactics.

This figure is related to the extensive social cognition research on individuals' self-representations by Tory Higgins and his collaborators (Higgins, 1987; see chap. 9). We can diagram how a patient's descriptions of specific social encounters along with images of their possible outcomes and their effects on his or her emotional states or self-representations can be

COMPROMISES

OUGHT SELF
Problematic Compromise RRM

ACTUAL SELF
Quasi-Adaptive Compromise RRM

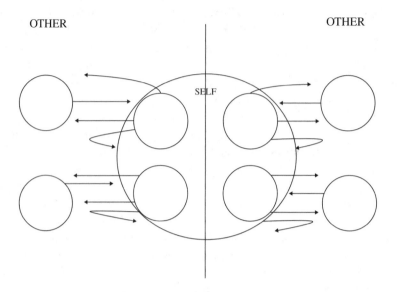

OTHER

OTHER

SELF

DREADED SELF RRM

IDEAL DESIRED RRM

WISH–FEAR DILEMMA

Figure 7.1. Horowitz's role relationship configuration model. RRM = role-relationship model. From "The Role-Relationship Models Method: A Comparison of Independently Derived Case Formulations," by T. D. Eells, M. J. Horowitz, J. L. Singer, P. Salovey, D. Daigle, and C. Turvey, 1995, *Psychotherapy Research, 5,* p. 156. Copyright 1995 by Taylor & Francis (http://www.tandf.co.uk). Adapted with permission.

deduced from narrative accounts at various points in psychotherapy. Research sponsored by the MacArthur Foundation's Program on Conscious and Unconscious Mental Processes (Horowitz, Eells, Singer, & Salovey, 1995) showed that independent raters of the videotapes could agree in outlining the patterns of patients' consciously expressed beliefs as well as their implicit psychological schemas and scripts to construct their role-relationship models. I discuss the specific relevance of this approach to the application of the theory of self-guides and self-discrepancies later. Here, I wish to call attention to the way patients may assert conscious beliefs in abstract form, such as "You can't really trust someone you love when it comes down to it," and then proceed to draw broad generalizations about interpersonal relationships. They may support their deductions by narrating vividly imaged events from memory or describe anticipated social interactions with comments about how such incidents impact their emotions and beliefs about themselves. It is important for the therapist to help the client move beyond the summary statements to the concrete episodes because these may offer clues as to how the patient may be magnifying or misinterpreting presumed memories or fantasies about situations and establishing idiosyncratic, inaccurate, self-defeating self-images or guiding rules of social conduct.

Some practitioners influenced originally by the interpersonal approach of Harry Stack Sullivan or the lifespan crises of Erik Erikson have sought to help their patients by providing some structure to those who may be floundering in an effort to provide an early life narrative. For example, one can suggest that a patient bring to mind early memories around the following themes.

1. *Food and eating.* A patient, picturing early scenes she recalled at the dinner table, described her mother's continuing revulsion at her father's eating habits—smacking his lips, snorting, dribbling food. This young woman quickly realized how she has since incorporated that scene into her own reactions. When dining with a young man on a first date she often impulsively takes a dislike to someone who may slurp his soup or dribble some spaghetti.

2. *Cleanliness, toilet behavior, body control.* A young art dealer described with a mixture of embarrassment and growing anger how his aristocratic, immaculately groomed mother would follow him into the toilet at home, even as late as his middle childhood, to be sure that he had a full bowel movement. A meticulous man, finicky about cleanliness, he realized after recounting this memory that he still was overly focused on people's backsides.

3. *Early sensuality, sexuality, and affectionate behavior.* A young woman remembered how her older brother, whom she greatly admired, began to abuse her sexually once she began to grow past puberty. Her efforts to talk about this to her parents were brusquely dismissed. She saved herself from serious distress by putting great emphasis on athletics and finding in her coach a person who became a benign surrogate parent.

4. *Schooling and work attitudes.* A young man remembered a sequence of incidents when he was just a boy in which his parents told him again and again about the school and career successes of some older cousins, warning him of the dangers of school failure. He was shown the picture of another cousin who did poorly at school and was drafted into the military, badly wounded in action, crippled, and continually dependent

on other family members. This patient realized that his own crisis of anxiety and depression was associated with his inability to sustain the initial pressure of graduate school. He was concealing the fact that he wasn't attending classes from his wife and his parents (see chap. 9).

5. *Religious beliefs, values, and social orientation.* The patient I described in chapter 6, a moderately successful stockbroker in therapy because of impulsive marital infidelity and other rash behavior that made him extremely anxious, recalled a series of incidents from his early years in which his father and uncles made scornful comments about patriotism, religion, and "goody-goody" relatives. They gambled and engaged in various near-criminal behaviors and had no cultural interests.

The critical feature in these narrations seems again and again to be the identification of specific events, usually well imagined and involving some concrete detail. Recollections of childhood incidents are unlikely to be fully veridical restorations of long-past events, but there is good evidence that greater specificity rather than abstract summary has important mental health and adaptive implications (Blagov & Singer, 2004; McAdams, 1993; J. A. Singer, 1997; J. A. Singer & Salovey 1993).

Although psychodynamic therapists still acknowledge the importance of free associations, encouraging the patient to verbalize his or her naturally occurring stream of thought throughout a full therapeutic hour, it is unlikely that they will rely solely on this method. The pressures to shorten treatment and our greater awareness today of problem areas for focusing attention limit extensive use of Freud's classic procedure. In cases in which patients simply repeat symptom complaints, seem blocked, or make "small talk," therapists do call for efforts at verbalizing ongoing thought. Here too, when such verbalizations take on too abstract a form, specific encouragement of the reporting of imagery sequences often can prove extremely effective. Freud's early efforts in the beginning of psychoanalysis called for him to actually press a patient's forehead and ask for one picture after another.

Joseph Reyher, almost a half century ago, adapted imagery association approaches to a technique he called *emergent uncovering psychotherapy*. He encouraged patients to allow sequences of scenes or events to develop as they relaxed in a chair or on a couch and then to narrate them. Reyher and his associates conducted a series of research studies that demonstrated that this approach quickly produced more conflict-relevant material and less defensiveness and evoked more emotionality (see Reyher, 1978).

Other psychodynamically oriented therapists such as Joseph Shorr, Anees Sheikh, Eric Greenleaf, and Mardi Horowitz have also made use of variations on the approach of using imagery sequences in preference to purely verbal free associations, which often involve abstract, overintellectualized commentaries. The various guided imagery techniques that developed in Europe under the influence of Carl Jung, Oskar Vogt, Robert Desoille, and Hans-Carl Leuner, among others, also reflect the presumed clinical value of encouraging imagery or waking dream methods in place of nonspecific free associations (J. L. Singer, 1974; J. L. Singer & Pope, 1978). The example I presented of my patient Mrs. Vogel in chapter 2 reflects an instance of the use of such a method when free association seems to be ineffective.

IDENTIFICATION OF RESISTANCE AND DEFENSE MECHANISMS

Imagery may assist in identifying resistances, avoidant tendencies, and the defense mechanisms, all critical activities for psychodynamic or interpersonal psychotherapies. The blockages in free association or the repetition of clichés, homilies, and abstract summaries of complex thought patterns or interpersonal transactions may reflect avoidant tendencies.

A highly educated but socially inexperienced female patient announced in a somewhat affirmative manner at the start of a session that she had just had her first sexual experience and had "lost her virginity." "It was wonderful!" she exclaimed. When asked for more detail, she rather abstractly described an encounter with a stranger at a party who then led her to his apartment. Asked about her emotional response she said, "It was fine. You know how men are." After some evasion she finally described the situation, in which the man literally pounced on her, stripped off her clothes, inserted his penis, immediately reached a climax, quickly helped her on with her clothes, and led her to the door. Again asked about her reaction, she said, "I felt good that I could really excite a man. Isn't that what's supposed to happen?" Without further inquiry and her more vivid description of the events, one might have accepted her initial summary and missed the self-deprecating and self-defeating belief system she bore, an assumption that her affection, passion, and arousal were irrelevant to a sexual encounter because "you know how men are."

Encouraging patients to provide specific details of recent or even more remote events may help to identify more clearly their own hesitations, avoidant tendencies, misleading beliefs, or long-standing family mythologies. Defensive efforts such as intellectualization or reaction formation may become transparent when vivid imaginings of events are requested. A scholarly college student who has made several visits to a striptease theater to collect "sociological data" on audience responses may soon recognize his own natural prurient interest when vividly describing the experience. A young female teacher expressed her shock at the "sinfulness" of a teacher she read about in a newspaper account who had seduced a teenage boy and bore his child. As this woman recounted the events and tried to picture mentally how a "mature professional" could engage in such unethical behavior, she suddenly became aware of the mental image of a boy in one of her own classes. He seemed especially appealing to her because of his combination of good looks and enthusiasm for learning. Although she was not likely to act on this attraction, she became aware of how often she seemed to resort to extreme reactions of scorn for "sinners," often thus avoiding confrontations with important and often healthy desires of her own.

TRANSFERENCE IN DREAMS AND FANTASIES

The examinations or analyses of transference phenomena are generally acknowledged as defining features of psychodynamic psychotherapies. The identification of the process of transference was probably one of Freud's greatest discoveries, and it has evoked a vast number of clinical articles. Freud observed that during psychoanalysis the patient may revive memories of key early childhood figures, usually parents, and then confuse the appearance, behavior, or comments of the therapist with those of these earlier persons, thus leading to apparent distortions, resistances, or even, if such figures were highly valued, to greater efforts at therapeutic work, the so-called *positive transference*. Transference was often signalized by sudden excessive affections, the sort of sexual advances that forced Freud's older and very "proper" colleague, Joseph Breuer, to give up psychotherapeutic treatment. Freud attributed transferences to the specific conditions of the psychoanalytic process. He proposed that identifying and analyzing the "transference neurosis" provided a unique opportunity to observe and work on the major memory revival distortions that underlay neuroses right in the office.

Freud soon came to realize that transference distortions were a common feature of everyday life as well as of neurotic or psychotic behavior, and by broadening his view he opened the way for great advances in clinical psychology and in personality and social cognitive theory (J. A. Singer & Singer, 1992, 1994; J. L. Singer, 1985; J. L. Singer & Salovey, 1991). Despite numerous anecdotal instances reported in the voluminous literature on the phenomenon, there is as yet no systematic evidence that the development and subsequent analysis of a full-blown transference neurosis is a truly defining feature of psychoanalysis (J. L. Singer, 1985). The research of Susan Andersen and her colleagues has demonstrated that the transference-like carryover of attitudes toward the significant figures in one's life is an experimentally demonstrable feature of normal social cognition (see Glassman & Andersen, 1999). Reports and transcripts of psychotherapy and the research of Luborsky and Crits-Christoph (1990) make it clear that a great deal of effort in dynamic psychotherapy involves identifying specific transferences from earlier figures to new persons in one's life, not only to the therapist but even more so to spouses or key friends (J. A. Singer & Singer, 1992, 1994; J. L. Singer & Salovey, 1991).

Luborsky and Crits-Christoph's (1990) research with dozens of patients was built around the scoring of transcripts for relationship episodes using a formulation built around the patient's account of wishes or desires in the episode with the other person, the other's apparent reaction, and the patient's subsequent response. One could accumulate such instances by direct inquiry for narrations or by their spontaneous occurrence in the patient's free associations. Using judges and statistical procedures, one can identify a limited number of core conflictual relationship themes and ascertain whether they fit to some degree with the original model proposed by Freud. In their study, Luborsky and Crits-Christoph, and their collaborators (for a summary of this work, see Luborsky & Crits-Christoph, 1990) showed that most core conflictual relationship themes involved wishes and conflicts in relation to others and to the patient's own reactions. They could often be linked to earlier parental relationships, were partly out of awareness, might eventually relate somewhat to the therapist (albeit less negatively), and might also be evident not just in therapy session associations but also in dreams, daydreams, or accounts of external social encounters. The formulation of Horowitz and his collaborators described and diagrammed earlier in this chapter overlaps with the Luborsky group's approach, differing chiefly in the notion that the schemas of the patient may involve expectations, reflections of recurrent current concerns, and broader belief systems, thus going beyond the notion of "wish" as a critical feature in a relationship episode.

The important issues for our purposes in this volume bear on how the psychotherapist can elicit vivid and emotional and hence meaningful episode descriptions that will allow the patient to identify the importance, personal relevance, and potential for change in his or her transference responses. I propose that the transference episodes relating to the therapist have the in vivo, intensely real quality that behavior therapy research has shown to be especially important in producing symptom relief or behavior change (Kazdin, 2000). At the same time, there is no research evidence that it is these therapist-transference analyses that are critical for change. Most patients are really more concerned about their relationships outside of the safe haven of the office, and it is the transference responses to significant others when vividly exposed and examined in therapy that are often of importance. Indeed, the consistent success of the cognitive–behavioral treatments demonstrates that examining such extramural relationships can be quite effective. Let us consider some examples of how the patient's and even the therapist's imagery can help to identify and to clarify or modify the patient's often self-defeating transference reactions.

Transference Within the Psychotherapy Session

A neuroscience research specialist had sought psychotherapy because of recurring bouts of anxiety, insecurity about her work, and loneliness. Undoubtedly very bright and technically skilled as well as well spoken, she seemed in her first few sessions unable to do more than recite her symptoms, recount the day's events, or report on details of her education and her current research activities. I asked her if she could use imagery to recapture early memories about her family, following the protocol described earlier for obtaining childhood scenes relating to food, cleanliness, affection, and values. She became even more evasive and increasingly angry. I quietly explained the clinical reasons why I wanted her to try this exercise, but she grew even more openly angry. Next, asked at least to try to produce a spontaneous image, she sat quietly for a moment, and then, with tears coming from her eyes, she described her fantasy. It was a vivid memory dating to age 4 or 5. When guests visited her home, her father would stand her on the table and tell her to recite with dramatic gestures works he had trained her to memorize, poems by Longfellow, Emerson, and Edgar Guest and speeches from *Peter Pan* and *Alice in Wonderland*.

> I hated this stuff but my father was firm in keeping these displays until I was in elementary school. I've grown up always pushed to be a show-off. I resented it but I also loved him—he was more interested in me than my mother, who just loved her ladies' card games. So I couldn't really object openly to him. Then I get into therapy all these years later and you're asking me to perform. You even look like he did.

This transference reaction emerging in the imagery of her performances opened the way for further exploration of other carryovers of her ambivalent reactions to male authority "demands for showiness," most recently the insistence of her laboratory supervisor that she read a paper on their research at a scientific conference. Thus, the transference pattern of her often self-defeating passive–aggressive reactions could be examined within the treatment room and in a number of external settings.

Transference Emerging Through Dream Content

Although the phenomenon of dreaming and the often apparent creativity of the content of our dreams continues to be a fascinating subject for research in personality (Domhoff, 1996; E. Hartmann, 1998), there seems currently less indication that psychotherapeutic progress hinges on extensive and intensive exploration of what Freud called "the royal road to the unconscious." There are occasions, however, when waking or sleeping fantasies can provide useful clues to patient wishes or to transference reactions.

A female patient was struggling to overcome her antipathy to her parents now that she was married and had children. Among the sources of her ambivalence to her mother and father was the recollection that during her late puberty and early adolescence, her older brother had persistently molested her sexually, mainly by groping her body and masturbating against her. She sought a number of times to complain to her parents, but they seemed to change the subject or defend the young man, whom she felt was their favorite. She finally gave up her efforts but became detached from her parents, keeping secrets from them and avoiding confidences and warmth. Fortunately, she found a supportive mentor, a teacher and athletic coach, who encouraged her and sustained her unselfishly through her adolescent years. Now she hoped that she might reconcile with her parents so that her children could experience them as grandparents.

During the weeks she was struggling to overcome her anger, she came in one day reporting a vivid dream. In the dream, she was in my office, easily recognizable from the furniture and a reproduction I had of a jungle painting by Rousseau. Her mother was seated across the room, and the young woman wanted to start telling her of her years of humiliation and resentment and "clear the air." She was blocked, as she had been in childhood and still was as an adult. Then she noticed that a goat, a bearded, presumably male animal, was seated in the room. Somehow she felt emboldened and found herself for the first time really able to quietly but forcefully describe her early experiences and her current feelings to her mother.

At first we were both puzzled by the dream image, especially the goat, although she felt exhilarated at how outspoken she had been in the dream. It occurred to me that setting the conversation in my office was surely a hope that our therapy sessions could help her break through her years of withdrawn bitterness. I said nothing of the thought (baffled at first by my apparent presence as a goat!) but asked her for some associated images. She herself quickly remarked that she hoped somehow the work she had done in therapy could help her relate more maturely to her parents. Then, she found herself picturing mentally her drive to my office, which was located in a wooded suburb. She began to smile and told me that just around the corner from my home she always passed a wire fence surrounding a small field. A goat belonging to one of our neighbors was often seated in rather "dignified" fashion by the gate. She then pictured the well-liked and trusted mentor of her adolescent years, a rather formal but concerned man who actually had a small beard—a goatee. The comfort she experienced in coming to her therapy sessions and her memories of her past mentor had been transferred to me. If only I were there she could really talk to her mother. Identifying the situation through her dream and then through her waking memory imagery opened the way for her then to explore how she might indeed confront her parents, perhaps even emboldened by imagining me and perhaps the older man along with her in the room. With some further discussion and a kind of imagery rehearsal in the next session, she found herself able soon to visit her parents, and with some hesitation and stumbling, she gradually laid out the full story to them.

Transference in a Waking Fantasy

Another example of transference, this time emerging in a sequence of waking thoughts, exemplifies how a patient's imagery built around the therapist may open a series of memories and beliefs that prove useful for promoting personal awareness and change. For many years before I moved to Yale University, I saw patients in an office located on New York's Fifth Avenue, across the street from the Metropolitan Museum of Art. A patient I had been treating for some time came into the office smiling. "I finally saw your wife," he said. "She got into the elevator just as I got out to come here. She looked just as I had been imagining her for several months. She was tall, very slim, and seemed very sophisticated, dressed in basic black, wearing white pearls and white gloves."

To the best of my knowledge, my wife was many miles away in the suburbs. Nor did she typically dress in that style or own a set of pearls. I had no idea who the woman this young man had encountered could be—perhaps the patient of another psychoanalyst on the same floor. Without correcting my patient I simply asked him how he had formed his impression of my wife's appearance and what other images came to his mind about her or me and our family. On the basis of the neighborhood, my own style of dress in suits and ties, and the paintings in my office and waiting room (actually reproductions), he had developed the notion that I came from a socially prominent family and was a prototypical Fifth Avenue or Park Avenue sophisticate, perhaps even on the board of the museum. He believed that I lived the lifestyle to which he aspired and that he could learn from me.

Asked for further memories or images that came to mind, he pointed out that his parents were poor immigrants. They were intelligent and kindly people who had worked all their lives at factory jobs. Then a vivid series of images occurred to him. A younger brother of his father had obtained more education, become very successful in business, and married a woman from a patrician background. The couple traveled in circles of the same kind often depicted in the newspapers as attendees at society charitable balls. The patient had scarcely any contact with his uncle and aunt but heard accounts of their activities from his parents and found himself over the years fantasizing about how he might attain their social status. Referred to me for psychotherapy, he quickly drew conclusions from the neighborhood and transferred some of his long-standing ambitions onto me.

This sequence of images and the inferences he drew about himself, his belief systems, his parents, and his life possibilities and self-esteem led him to reexamine his own goals and self-representation. Some of the anxieties in his school and work situations that had occasioned his referral for psychotherapy now became comprehensible. He began to work toward identifying a more realistic and appropriate recognition of his own skills and potentialities, free of his childhood fantasies about a quasi-mythical lifestyle, and an understanding of his parents and their value.

Identifying Transferences Outside Therapy

The majority of clients' transference reactions are almost certainly those occurring in their relationships with significant others outside the treatment office. The demonstrable treatment successes of short-term interpersonal psychotherapies and cognitive–behavioral therapies point up the likelihood that focusing on such extramural relationship distortions may be sufficient for effective psychoanalytic intervention (J. A. Singer & Singer, 1992, 1994; J. L. Singer, 1985). Much of what one does in psychodynamic psychotherapy, therefore, still hinges on identifying self-defeating transferences, or what Sullivan called the "parataxic distortions" that occur in our daily lives with the key figures around us.

Here is an example of an imagery approach that helped a patient to recognize a transference in his work situation that was a major contributing factor to his continuing anxiety and depression. This middle-aged businessman was an executive in a busy company who had recently begun to suffer recurrent fears of failure and anxieties about job loss. In our first few sessions, his communications were terse and full of generalities and clichés. He seemed at a loss to explain why he was so anxious and saddened other than from a strong sense that the company would fail and he would lose the only job he had held in his adult work career. He seemed unable to bring up earlier memories and showed many of the features of a "repressor personality" style (Bonanno & Singer, 1990; Weinberger, 1990). His therapy sessions consisted of his recounting of the day's events and business crises. I became aware that I was becoming restless, indeed almost bored and irritated by his communication style. I cautiously pointed out to him that we needed to try a different approach and suggested we consider a form of guided imagery of the type developed in Europe by Desoille (see J. L. Singer, 1974) and by Leuner (Leuner, 1978; J. L. Singer, 1974). At first hesitant, he agreed to try relaxing, shutting his eyes and producing a sequence of images of walking through a field.

To the surprise of both of us, the images that he recounted proved to be vivid and full of events. A recurrent theme was his encounters with menacing older men, often like wizards or enchanters, who threatened him so that he had to flee. I remarked on the persistence of this theme and asked him if any memories came to mind. He struck his head and began to describe a series of childhood incidents of severe physical abuse by a demanding and also often inebriated father who eventually deserted the family. Having heard enough about his daily work encounters I asked him to describe in more detail some of his business crises. What now emerged with some trepidation were a series of incidents in which his boss, a powerful and officious man, was making technical errors that could jeopardize the business. My patient felt that he knew correct alternatives to these business decisions but was certain he would be fired if he sought to contradict the chief executive. After further discussing his images about what might happen and mentally rehearsing different strategies for presenting his case, he realized how much of his trepidation related to transferring his memories of long-standing exposure to his abusive father onto his boss, with no real basis for his assumptions about the latter's probable reaction.

After a few more sessions of mental rehearsal and reexamination of his memories of his father and of his CEO's mannerisms, the patient made a kind of existential decision that whatever the outcome, it was important for him to confront his boss and lay out his work proposals. To his great surprise his boss, albeit first taken aback by the firmness of an assistant he considered a "yes-man," listened respectfully to his suggestions. The patient's proposals were adopted with some modifications, and the company situation improved. The relationship with his CEO soon became one of more equality and goodwill.

"WORKING THROUGH" AND THE LATER STAGES OF PSYCHODYNAMIC THERAPY

The course of psychotherapy after the identification of defenses, transferences, and recurrent early memories is of great importance. It calls for helping the patient to repeatedly identify self-defeating belief systems about self and others and to identify recurring defensive maneuvers that may now be vestigial, however effective they seemed in earlier years. Patients also need to be helped to try new ways of relating so as to free themselves of often crippling transferential reactions, as we saw in the businessman of our last example. To the extent that the effective therapeutic alliance between client and therapist has depended in part on a positive transference, often an overestimation of the wisdom and daily living skills of the therapist, this distorting dependence must be cleared up. The professional in this dyad is no wizard like Gandalf in *The Lord of the Rings* but a humble if responsible helper who cannot resolve the inevitable, ongoing, real-world problems of the patient. What the therapist can do is encourage the patient to develop continuing mental strategies and tactics for examining conflicts and stresses and for taking note of holdover defenses or transferences and thus incorporate into daily behavior the best features of the therapeutic process. The research by Jesse Geller and associates (Geller, Cooley, & Hartley, 1981–1982) on the later memories and imagery about therapy of patients who have experienced either unsuccessful or successful outcomes from psychoanalytically oriented treatment is very enlightening. Patients who did not make really significant gains in treatment reported more recurrent transference-like images of their therapists, either images of a very negative cast or Gandolphlike overestimates. The patients who reported clear improvements after treatment did not dwell on personalized images of the therapist. Instead, they noticed that when they confronted conflicts or relationship dilemmas they found themselves envisioning their former therapists suggesting questions or processes to them. The therapist lived on primarily as an "enabler," not as some lofty or otherwise grandiose figure.

Imagery methods are of continuing importance in the later phases of psychotherapy. They involve further attempts to identify defenses, earlier life episodes that may have fostered misleading belief systems, or transferences that are self-defeating. One must also encourage patients to try new ways of relating—to make new moves in hitherto habitually frightening, anger-arousing, or seemingly conflict-laden situations. Such new moves may call for rehearsals in the treatment room and at home. Experienced therapists often find themselves engaging in subtle kinds of life-training activities that are not much written about in the psychoanalytic literature. In well-conducted later phases of treatment, we find in actual practice considerable overlap between psychodynamic and cognitive–behavioral therapies. Some excellent examples of integrations of cognitive and psychodynamic approaches and their applications in the terminal phases of psychotherapy are available in Messer and Warren's (1995) account of short-term treatment and in a fine article by Safran (1990). In the next chapters, I examine what basic research can suggest about the uses of imagery in the major alternative forms of treatment, the cognitive and behavior modification approaches.

8

IMAGERY APPLICATIONS IN COGNITIVE–BEHAVIORAL THERAPIES

Cognitive–behavioral psychotherapy has emerged since the early 1970s as the major alternative to the psychodynamic–interpersonal approaches for the psychological treatment of emotional distress and relationship difficulties. It now closely rivals the earlier Freud-derived methods in frequency of use by U.S. or Canadian clinicians, and its influence in Europe is spreading. Most impressively, cognitive combined with behavioral therapies have been the most extensively researched approaches with respect both to outcome evaluations and studies of process. The movement in the late 1990s toward developing careful intervention manuals and using these to develop empirically assessed psychotherapy treatments for a large array of diagnosed psychiatric conditions has been largely dominated by the cognitive–behavioral therapy (CBT) approaches. As Figure 5.1 indicates, behavior modification and cognitive therapies had different historical origins, but since the late 1970s most behaviorally or cognitively oriented therapists and researchers had come to recognize the value of integrating the action exercises of the former method with the information-processing examinations of the latter procedures. Along with this blending of techniques, which emerged from the research of Beck and his group (Beck, Rush, Shaw, & Emery, 1979), Kazdin (1978), Lazarus (1971, 1981), Mahoney (1974), and Meichenbaum (1977), among others, we find in actual practice increased use of imagery methods across a broad spectrum of these CBT systems. It is a curious irony that treatment methods that sought initially to distance themselves from the speculative mentalisms of psychoanalysis have increasingly moved to using procedures that draw on our human capacity to generate mental reproductions of past or possible future events (Crits-Christoph & Singer, 1980; J. L. Singer, 1974).

THE EMERGENCE OF COGNITIVE PSYCHOTHERAPIES

The personal construct approach to psychotherapy that appeared in George Kelly's profound two-volume work (Kelly, 1955) deserves pride of place as the forerunner of current cognitive therapies. Ellis's (1989) rational (later rational–emotive) therapy, though developed roughly at the same time, did not have the same systematic and rigorous methodological quality as Kelly's approach. Ellis had greater promotional skills and has long outlived Kelly (who died in 1966 at age 61), so the rational–emotive orientation has taken on the authority of a "school" and has a greater continuing influence, at least in the United States. From the standpoint of the relation of personal construct theory to imagery methods, we find the key in Kelly's assertion that all behavior can be construed as anticipatory in nature (Kelly, 1955, Vol. 2, p. 744). In effect, then, Kelly's view of human action assumes that we operate through expectations and mental plans that almost always involve some fleeting imagery using past event memories to set up possible futures. With his method of beginning psychotherapy by calling on a patient to develop a role construct repertory list identifying (and, of necessity, imagining) "your mother or the person who played the part of your mother in your life," "a teacher you liked," and "your closest girl(boy)friend before you started going with your wife(husband)," (Kelly 1955, Vol. 1, p. 227), Kelly seemed to be invoking mental representations. Without reviewing the complexities of Kelly's derivation of a series of personal constructs or organized belief systems from his initial involvement of the patient in identifying the key persons and, later, the key situations in his or her life space, we can see that this cognitive method depends as heavily on the patient's images or fantasies about key life figures as does the gathering of early childhood memories so characteristic of the psychodynamic method reviewed in the last chapter.

In Aaron T. Beck's (1967) cognitive therapy, which continues to be the most influential and most researched cognitive approach, we find a grouping of the cognitive distortions to which humans are prey. Identifying these distortions or faulty cognitive processing mechanisms and helping the patient to modify or overcome them becomes a critical focus of therapy. They include all-or-nothing thinking, overgeneralization, selective negative focus, arbitrary inference, negative prediction, and personalization (Beck,

1967). In describing each of these, Beck depends heavily not only on patients' verbal summaries (e.g., "I'm a loser!") but also on patients' memories of specific past events or images of anticipated future ones. Clearly, as Beck has told me personally, effective cognitive therapy depends greatly on moving beyond purely verbal exchanges to encouraging patients and therapists to resort to their auditory or visual imagery capacities.

Behavior modification approaches emerged in the late 1960s and through the 1970s and were designed to avoid the mentalism of the then predominant psychoanalysis-derived therapies. The methods of behavior management derived from Skinner's systematic reinforcement and contingent reward procedures worked reasonably well, and their development has continued, especially for severely retarded, relatively nonverbal children or adults or as features of parent management methods for children with conduct disorders (Kazdin, 2001, 2005). In the treatment of phobias, obsessive–compulsive behavior, assertiveness, inadequacy, or personality difficulties, it became increasingly clear from research (Wilkins, 1971) and clinical experience (Lazarus, 1981; J. L. Singer, 1974) that the use of imagery as part of behavior therapy is critical. A first step toward introducing more emphasis on thought processes into behavioral treatment came with the integration of the analysis of belief distortions that were featured in cognitive therapy with the active practice procedures of behavioral treatments like systematic desensitization or covert modeling. The pendulum has swung so far toward mentalism that we find influential behavior therapy researchers now incorporating a once scorned system like mindfulness meditation into their treatment protocols (Marlatt & Kristeller, 1999; Z. V. Segal, Williams, & Teasdale, 2002).

WHY IMAGERY MATTERS IN COGNITIVE–BEHAVIORAL TREATMENT

In his cognitive theory of behavior change, Donald Meichenbaum (1978) proposed three main psychological processes to explain how imagery-based therapies can contribute to change. A client develops a sense of control from monitoring and rehearsing various images. This sense of control over images and inner thought in turn helps the client gain control over emotions and subsequent interpersonal behavior.

The second process involves the client changing the meaning of his or her maladaptive behavior. Imagery therapies convey a new perspective to the client and a new conceptualization of the problem. This changed meaning will be reflected in altered internal dialogue that is evident before, during, and after instances of the problem behavior.

The third process in imagery treatments is the mental rehearsal of behavioral alternatives that contribute to the development of coping skills. This process has been described by other authors as "the work of worrying" (Janis, 1958), "mental practice" (Richardson, 1969), and "covert modeling" (Kazdin, 1973). Meichenbaum claimed that as a result of engaging in this mental problem solving, the recurrence of the client's own symptoms will become a reminder to use the coping skills he or she has learned rather than engaging in further maladaptive behaviors.

Although Meichenbaum's (1978) proposal is tentative, it appears promising as a framework for understanding the role of imagery in therapy. Certain specific predictions can be made from the model. For example, extended rehearsal of coping behaviors in imagery should be an effective technique. In fact, research by Meichenbaum (1978), Sarason (1975), and Kazdin (1973) indicates the special value of imagining oneself or a model person engaging in a variety of constructive efforts. These findings tend to support this aspect of Meichenbaum's theory. It seems that envisioning concrete steps toward modifying beliefs or toward increasing one's sense of control are more effective than imagining or verbalizing a successful outcome without the necessary intervening steps. I believe that many therapists from diverse backgrounds may engage their clients in such activities, and this may explain why studies often show that different therapies yield comparably good outcomes.

Another model concerning the role of imagery in therapy was proposed by Lang (1977) and has been applied to the treatment of fear behavior. Lang claimed that images can be analyzed in terms of their stimulus propositions and their response propositions. Stimulus propositions are essentially descriptive of a scene—for example, a black snake moving on the ground. Response propositions involve assertions about the individual's behavior in response to a stimulus. These can involve verbal responses ("I scream"), behavioral responses ("I run away"), and visceral responses ("my heart is pounding"). Lang stated that it is the imagined response propositions that play a central role in the fear process. Treatment should accordingly involve modification of the client's imagined response propositions (i.e., the maladaptive way the person usually responds). Lang suggested that this analysis could be applied to other emotional states and problems in addition to fear. Envisioning a very positive outcome is sometimes labeled as a "mastery" emphasis. Lang proposed that this kind of imagery may yield a good result.

The clinical implications of this theory have been investigated in studies by Grayson and Borkovec (1978) and Crits-Christoph and Singer (1980, 1983). The study by Grayson and Borkovec (1978) used a 1-session imagery treatment of speech-phobic college students. The results indicated that subjects who, after an initial stimulus scene, imagined themselves behaving in a relaxed and competent manner had lower subjective ratings of fear in response to the phobic images than subjects who either imagined being anxious and incompetent or imagined themselves avoiding the phobic situations. Though supportive of Lang's (1977) theory, these results have limited generalizability because of the brevity of treatment and the nature of the sample used. The study by Crits-Christoph and Singer was less supportive of Lang's model. In that study, phobic patients were treated by either a positive imagery method or by a mastery imagery method over 12 sessions. The positive imagery method consisted of the pairing of relaxing, positive scenes with fearful phobic scenes, and the mastery imagery method consisted of changing subjects' imagined response propositions along the lines suggested by Lang. Results indicated that both treatments were equally successful compared with a no-treatment group in reducing the severity of the specific levels of distress and other unwanted thoughts and behaviors. In sum, no strong evidence exists to show that the method proposed by Lang is the crucial way to produce behavior change through imagery. It seems likely, however, that the systematic analysis of imagery into its components as provided by Lang may prove to be a useful tool for asking meaningful questions about imagery as a psychotherapeutic device.

The experience of self-efficacy is also worth considering as it relates to imagery treatments (Salovey & Singer, 1991). Bandura (1977) proposed from a learning perspective that various psychotherapeutic methods produce a change by altering an individual's expectations of self-efficacy. J. L. Singer and Pope (1978) have specifically related this concept to the imagery-based treatments. In brief, it is argued that people's projections into the future involve expectations about the outcomes of certain actions they might perform. Images and self-verbalizations of whether they expect to successfully produce certain outcomes are especially important in determining if they will initiate certain behaviors and how long they will persist in certain efforts (J. L. Singer & Pope, 1978). These expectations are based on personal experiences and observations of how well others (e.g., parents and siblings) have done in similar situations. The research reviewed by Bandura (1982, 1986) documents that changes in self-efficacy are related to improvement in the treatment of fear behavior.

Imagery treatments in particular can serve to improve expectations of self-efficacy. In many cases, individuals have developed fears or expectations of failure without actually having directly experienced the target situations. Some imagery methods (e.g., systematic desensitization, covert modeling) often help reduce the negative affect associated with the imagined situations and provide the person with an additional sense that they do have the coping skills to confront such situations. It also seems likely that the repeated practice of success-oriented fantasies in an imagery-based treatment would be a particularly direct way of strengthening self-efficacy expectations. In fact, a study by Kazdin (1979) found that covert modeling treatments do improve the self-efficacy expectations of unassertive clients. Changes in the levels of self-efficacy were also significantly correlated with improvement on behavioral and self-report measures of assertiveness. Thus, the concept of self-efficacy cuts across many types of therapeutic interventions and may be especially relevant in explaining the effects of diverse imagery treatments.

A simple personal example may suggest the power of images of self-efficacy in influencing effective action. My wife and I had the good fortune some years ago to be invited to spend a month at the Villa Sorbelloni, a Rockefeller Foundation retreat for a few scientists, humanities scholars, and creative artists. This beautiful estate is located at the top of a steep cliff overlooking Lakes Como and Lecco and the village of Bellagio in northern Italy. If we had some time free from our separate writing projects and wanted to visit the village or lakefront, we would have to walk down hundreds of steps. No longer young or agile at the time, when we first imagined the daily downhill walk and then the uphill return climb, we were filled with dread. Then we remembered the recent research findings of Bandura, which showed that breaking a larger task into more manageable subgoals was especially conducive to an accumulating sense of personal efficacy and performance. Each of us set up achievement goals, starting with only 10 steps at a time and then perhaps increasing the goal to 20 or 25 steps. Just the imagery alone emboldened us to try, and then as we walked we found this method quickly strengthened our sense of accomplishment so that the task, though never easy, could be regularly accomplished.

SYSTEMATIC DESENSITIZATION

Wolpe's (1958) technique of systematic desensitization was the first of the imagery-based behavioral therapies. The popularity of this approach is probably due to its simplicity. The main components of the procedure involve only the imagining of a graded sequence of anxiety-arousing scenes while deeply relaxed. The widespread and repeated success of the method is evident not only from anecdotal reports but from many controlled outcome studies. In fact, a review of controlled outcome studies by Smith and Glass (1977) concluded that desensitization-type behavior therapies produced greater average therapeutic effects than any other type of psychotherapy. The usefulness of systematic desensitization for the treatment of phobic behavior is especially well documented.

In spite of this extensive evidence supporting the effectiveness of the procedure, questions still remain as to the important ingredient in systematic desensitization. The use of an ordered anxiety hierarchy and progressive muscle relaxation have been found not to be essential for success. Kazdin and

Wilcoxon (1976) have argued that nonspecific factors such as expectation of improvement should not be ruled out as the reasons for the changes shown with the use of desensitization. Wilkins (1971), on the other hand, has found that the research literature seems to indicate that the significant ingredient of systematic desensitization and similar treatments is the use of imagery by the client. At the least, the evidence seems to indicate that the underlying theory of reciprocal inhibition proposed by Wolpe and the relationship of this approach to learning theory are highly questionable (Breger & McGaugh, 1965). Much more likely, treatment seems to work by changing the private anticipations, self-communications, and images that the client holds with respect to the critical situations for which treatment has been sought (J. L. Singer & Pope, 1978).

POSITIVE IMAGERY

The positive imagery approach appears to have a wide variety of applications (J. L. Singer, 1974). This procedure, also called *emotive imagery*, involves the use of highly pleasurable, relaxing images to counteract anxiety. Imaging these positive scenes (typically nature scenes) can reduce anxiety in real-life confrontations or through their pairing with anxiety-arousing images. The latter approach has been reported by J. L. Singer (1974) and Lazarus (1981) to help with the systematic desensitization treatment of phobias. A study by Crits-Christoph and Singer (1983) documented the usefulness of this type of imagery not only in reducing the amount of phobic anxiety but also in reducing general levels of distress and unwanted thoughts. Other uses of positive imagery include reducing childbirth anxiety (Horan, 1973), relieving the symptoms of peptic ulcer patients (Chappell & Stevenson, 1936), reducing laboratory-produced pain (Greene & Reyher, 1972), and helping to alleviate feelings of depression in severely depressed patients (Schultz, 1978).

An instance from my own practice may exemplify the role of positive imagery in systematic desensitization. A young woman I had treated with a more psychodynamic–interpersonal approach for several years had terminated with our mutual agreement that she was now doing very well in her life and was also symptom free. She subsequently was happily married and bore two children. One day she called me to report that she had developed a rather specific phobia, a fear of driving with her children over a major New York City bridge, a route necessary for her to visit her parents. Although we had explored her family relationship quite extensively and she was moderately reconciled with her somewhat cold and distant parents, a panic overtook her on the occasion of driving her children across the bridge to visit her parents. After reviewing the dynamics of the situation, which she had quickly grasped on her own, she indicated that the vivid trauma of her panic on the bridge persisted and was beginning to generalize to other driving situations such as taking the children to the pediatrician. Contemplating the situation in advance seemed especially troublesome. I realized that it was important to help this woman deal quickly with the phobia lest it spread to a crippling agoraphobia, handicapping her in caring for her children, because her husband, a surgical resident, could not help her very much at this stage of his career.

This intuitive and sensitive woman was surprised by my suggestion that we consider systematic desensitization, because she thought of me as a psychoanalyst, but she readily agreed to try. She told me that she felt I had helped her reframe her life so extensively after the breakdown that occasioned her initial treatment that she trusted my judgment now. I described the steps of the standard technique to her, adding my own suggestion that we expand the relaxation phase beyond the Jacobsen exercises to include her imagining scenes that seemed to her to be associated with past experiences or imagined settings of peacefulness and carefree restfulness. As most people do, she vividly imagined nature scenes that she found especially peaceful. Two imagery sequences seemed especially effective, an oceanfront summer scene and a scene of walking or cross-country skiing through a woodland as snow was lightly falling. She found these images worked well for home practice without the more ritualized progressive relaxation that we used in the office. With only 12 office sessions and the home practice she completely reduced her anxious contemplation of the hierarchy of scenes about driving and was freely engaging in normal visits with her children. I had occasion to see her or talk with her by telephone over several years afterward, and there had been no recurrence of these phobic symptoms.

The psychophysiological effects of imaging positive scenes have been documented by Schwartz, Fair, Salt, Mandel, and Klerman (1976), who found that positive images, compared with sad or angry images, produce a unique pattern of facial muscle responses, and by Crits-Christoph and Singer (1983), who found that sharp drops in forehead muscle tension occur when clients shift from fearful to positive scenes. These results indicate that the clinical use of positive scenes involves more than simply teaching clients how to keep their mind off the problem of concern, and that the physiological concomitants of the affect aroused by the images play an important role. The special quality of the relaxation that can be achieved by such images may have a carryover effect on the anxiety-arousing images or situations. Crits-Christoph and Singer found that physiological response to phobic images was reduced after the repeated pairing of these images with positive scenes. The role of positive imagery is consistent with the relationship of imagery and affect discussed by J. L. Singer (1974, 1984) and originally postulated by Tomkins (1962, 1963).

COVERT CONDITIONING

Several different procedures fall under the category of covert condition-ing, most of them developed by Cautela (1967). These techniques were derived from extensions of operant learning principles and include covert sensitization, covert reinforcement, covert negative reinforcement, covert extinction, covert response cost, and covert modeling (Cautela, 1967, 1970a, 1970b, 1971, 1976; Kazdin, 1979).

Covert sensitization, or *covert aversive conditioning*, involves the pairing of extremely unpleasant images with scenes in which one engages in undesirable behavior. For example, a problem drinker might imagine he is about to take a drink of alcohol and then imagine that he vomits as he puts the drink in his mouth. This procedure has been applied relatively successfully to the treatment of sexual deviations (Barlow, Leitenberg, & Agras, 1969), alcoholism (Ashem & Donner, 1968), compulsive behavior (Cautela, 1966), and smoking (Cautela, 1970c). (I give an example of my use of this approach in moderate smoking control later in this chapter, when I discuss imagery in cognitive therapy.)

I was treating a young mathematician for anxiety, social fears, inhibi-tions, and career concerns using a psychodynamic approach. We were near-ing a termination, because his life situation had improved considerably and he was engaged to be married. He suddenly revealed to me that he had for some years been caught up in a particular sequence of compulsive voyeurism about which he felt great shame. He wanted to overcome this practice before marriage. His voyeurism was very specific and, fortunately, not conducted in public circumstances where arrest was likely. Typically, he would be sitting in his study in a large apartment house complex, working on some mathematical research. An image of sexual interest would come to mind and he would walk to his window, where he kept a powerful set of field glasses. He would then scan the dozens of apartment windows across the courtyard while his sexual excitement increased. There was usually a good chance that he would spot a window in which he could see a woman who might be provocatively dressed or actually undressed, in which case he began actively to masturbate, usually to climax.

The compulsive "peeping Tom" behavior of the young man was easily traceable to issues that had been confronted extensively in the earlier phases of therapy. An only child whose mother was unwittingly sexually provocative and often overprotective, he developed something close to a classical Oedi-pus complex, drawn to his mother and intimidated by a forceful and demanding father, a prominent public figure. He had several memories from childhood of seeing his mother undressed and of bursting in on his parents in their adjacent hotel room as they were embracing while partially un-clothed. In the course of treatment, he had made considerable progress in recognizing that his assumptions about his parents often reflected his own earlier immaturity and that, for example, his father was actually a deeply loving person beneath a gruff exterior.

Yet for all the patient's insight and reshaping of his relationships, he was seemingly trapped in his voyeurism by the inherent positive reinforcement of the masturbation he had practiced in this form for many years. He willingly accepted my suggestion of trying a covert aversive conditioning approach. I encouraged him to generate a particularly noxious set of images, pictures of people with repellant skin diseases—scabs and sores, yellow pustules, venereal infections. After some practice we would go through the specific sequences that led to his actual voyeurism: his imagery and craving thoughts while at his desk, moving to the window, grasping the binoculars, and scanning the neighborhood apartment windows. For each step, he practiced juxtaposing a truly unpleasant skin disease image immediately after the "unwanted desire" image. Within a month of twice-weekly therapy plus home practice, the graph of the frequency of his voyeur episodes showed a sharp drop, and the practice had disappeared in 2 months. He married, and some years later could report to me that he had not experienced any recurrence, even though his career as a mathematician often called for long periods of working alone.

Covert reinforcement procedures involve the use of positive, pleasant images as a reinforcement to increase certain behaviors. A client who has deficits in social skills, for example, might imagine himself going to a party and engaging in various social behaviors. Each time the client exhibits a desirable behavior in the imagery, the therapist instructs the client to imagine the pleasant scene to reinforce the behavior. Escape from an aversive situation can also be used as the reinforcer, in which case the technique of covert negative reinforcement is being used.

The method of *covert extinction* relies on imagining that the reinforcing stimulus that maintains the maladaptive behavior does not occur. With drug abusers, this would involve imagining that the drug high does not come after injection. In using covert response cost, the client is instructed to imagine the response to be reduced followed by the imaginary loss of a reinforcer—for example, "imagine you are about to take a drink; now imagine that your brand-new car has just been demolished." Most of the research on the above techniques consists of case reports, and consequently their relative usefulness compared with other techniques remains untested.

The final method of covert conditioning, *covert modeling,* has generated the greatest amount of interest. This procedure is derived from the modeling or vicarious learning literature, especially the work of Bandura (1986). However, rather than actually observing a model, a client imagines a model performing the behavior that the client wishes to develop. A series of progressively more demanding situations might be used in treatment.

Several case reports and analogue fear treatment studies have indicated the potential of this technique for some purposes. More convincing evidence of the clinical usefulness of covert modeling comes from a series of studies by Kazdin (1974, 1975, 1976, 1979). These studies have shown that covert modeling can be effective for treatment of unassertive behavior in a clinical population. Covert modeling was found to be superior to imagining scenes without the modeling component and to no-treatment control groups. Various parameters of the covert modeling imagery scenes have also been manipulated. Treatment appears to be enhanced by increasing the similarity between the imagined model and the client (Kazdin, 1974), by the use of several different models across sessions instead of the same model (Kazdin, 1976), by imagining positive consequences following the model's behavior (Kazdin, 1975), and by allowing clients to elaborate on their modeling images rather than limiting the context of the images (Kazdin, 1979).

IMPLOSIVE IMAGERY OR FLOODING

The technique of *implosive imagery*, or *flooding*, was introduced by Stampfl and Levis (1967). This procedure consists of an intensive, prolonged approach to a phobic situation using imagery. The patient is supposed to experience stress and anxiety without the relief usually provided by avoiding or escaping the situation. The assumption of the method is that anxiety will gradually diminish, much as in an extinction procedure. Thus, this approach also has its foundation in learning theory. An analogous procedure is in vivo flooding, in which the exposure is a real confrontation to the public stimulus. Clinical and research studies have shown this procedure to be effective.

COPING WITH STRESS AND PAIN

Imagery is one component of Meichenbaum's (1974) "stress inoculation" technique. This procedure uses self-instruction and imagination of alternative successful coping behavior to help a person get through stressful situations and develop an effective coping strategy. Turk's (1980) research on the use of images and other cognitive techniques as mechanisms for tolerating laboratory-produced pain has contributed to our knowledge of how imagery may be effective in combating stress. The emphasis is placed on the ability to use imagery to distract oneself and to generate very strong experiences that might be capable of psychophysiological counteraction.

A variety of other imagery procedures have been used in CBT. Most of these have not been widely researched or used clinically.

ASSESSING IMAGERY AND FANTASY CAPACITIES

If one chooses to use an imagery-based technique in therapy, the problem of measuring clients' imagery becomes crucial. Unfortunately, the assessment of imagery for clinical purposes, except in the indirect form of projective techniques, is undeveloped. Tower and Singer (1981), in a review of the literature on the measurement of imagery for clinical purposes, found few measures that could identify and predict imagery capabilities. In spite of the inherent problems in this area, therapists and clinical researchers should realize the importance of imagery assessment for obtaining maximal results in imagery-based treatment.

Tower and Singer (1981) have described how the measurement of imagery has several diagnostic uses. First, imagery can be used to help discover the nature of a client's problem, as with the traditional uses of projective tests. Second, assessment can provide information on the imaginal resources a client has available for doing the work of the treatment. Almost all of the procedures discussed in this chapter rely heavily on the client's imagery skills: his or her capacity for generating vivid images and controlling the images produced. Indeed, a study by Dyckman and Cowan (1978) documented that imagery vividness scores obtained during treatment correlated highly with the outcome of systematic desensitization therapy with persons who had a phobia of snakes. Third, it may be of interest to the therapist to assess a person's general style of processing information or responding. For example, some people, in their cognitive styles, are primarily verbalizers, whereas others tend to be visualizers (Richardson, 2000).

What types of instruments are currently available for measuring imagery capabilities? A variety of self-report measures attempt to assess imagery under the assumption that a person's subjective judgments concerning his or her own experience are of primary interest. These include the Betts Questionnaire Upon Mental Imagery (Betts, 1909), Gordon's Test of Visual Imagery Control (Richardson, 1969, 2000), the Vividness of Visual Imagery Questionnaire (Marks, 1973), the Imagery Survey Schedule (Tondo & Cautela, 1974), the Imagery Research Questionnaire (Lane, 1977), the Survey of Mental Imagery (Switras, 1978), the Individual Differences Questionnaire (Paivio, 1971), the Verbalizer–Visualizer Questionnaire (Richardson, 2000), the Creative Imagination Scale (Wilson & Barber, 1978), and the Imaginal Processes Inventory (Huba, Aneshensel, & Singer, 1981; J. L. Singer & Antrobus, 1972).

Physiological measures that have been used include breathing regularity (Golla & Antonovitch, 1929), facial muscle patterns (Schwartz et al., 1976), laterality of eye movements (P. Bakan, 1969; Rodin & Singer, 1976; B. A. Rosenberg, 1980), and brain waves (Schwartz, 1975; Short, 1953; and many others). The work of Schwartz and his colleagues has extended beyond simple indices of physiological responses to examining patterns of physiological processes associated with imagery and emotions. As functional magnetic resonance imagery techniques improve in flexibility, we can anticipate that they will be increasingly available to study ongoing imagery (Baars, 1997).

For many clinicians, these assessment procedures may seem too time-consuming or costly for use with their clients. Physiological measurement, however, need not be restricted to laboratory experiments with sophisticated equipment. Many processes, such as clients' lateral eye movements and facial muscle tension, can be observed by eye. Heart rate can be monitored by taking a person's pulse. Other types of measures, such as simple ratings of vividness and affective responses to images, can also be obtained easily in a clinical situation. It is my view that therapists should recognize their responsibility for obtaining such information regarding the imagery process. These data can then be used to adjust the treatment as necessary for each client to obtain maximum results.

ENHANCING IMAGERY

The imagery measurement techniques just described typically highlight a wide range of individual differences in imagery abilities. Many people report little or no capacity for generating vivid images. What should be done with such people in therapy? In the extreme case, clients who show poor imagery skills can be treated with alternative methods. Attempts can also be made to enhance the imagery of some clients. Relaxation techniques are one way to potentially make images more vivid. Mathews (1971) concluded that this is the probable function of relaxation training in systematic desensitization. By screening out external information and limiting task demands, one can, through relaxation, enhance the occurrence of imagery and increase the likelihood that a more intense affective response will be generated (J. L. Singer, 1974).

Lang (1979) described a training program he developed within the context of his propositional analysis of imagery. Therapists read prepared scripts to subjects who are then asked to image the scene suggested by the script and report the details of what they actually imagined. The therapist reinforces all statements by the subject indicating that the subject imagined what the therapist wanted. Data presented by Lang indicate that training in imagining response propositions in particular tends to produce greater psychophysiological effects to fear imagery. Such training results in more concordance between self-report and physiological indices of fear during phobic imagery.

Instructing clients to practice imagery at home and to attend to their spontaneous fantasies and daydreams can also enhance their imagery skills.

Crits-Christoph and Singer (1983) found that during imagery treatments for phobias, ratings of vividness of imagery increased with repeated practice of each new hierarchy scene. Therapists should be aware of these practice effects and also realize that clients often need considerable time to bring into focus a vivid image. (See chap. 10 for further examples of methods.)

THE ROLE OF IMAGERY IN COGNITIVE THERAPY

Alan Kazdin's impressive history of behavior modification succinctly brings out the origins of cognitive psychotherapies in contrast to the more purely behavioral approaches (Kazdin, 1978). As he wrote,

> Most cognition-based techniques stress the individual's perception and interpretation of external events rather than the direct influence of the surroundings themselves. [Such treatments] evolved out of dissatisfaction with stimulus–response explanations of behavior and in response to research that has demonstrated the role of thought processes in controlling behavior. (Kazdin, 1978, pp. 307–308)

He also pointed out that many of the symptoms that lead people to seek therapy are themselves reflections of thought processes such as obsessive ruminations, self-criticality, and problems in self-control.

Kelly's personal construct approach had been criticized, perhaps unfairly, for overstressing thought and not providing the client with "moves" for changing overt behavior. Such a criticism may have also been applicable to Ellis's rational–emotive therapy or Beck's cognitive therapy. Consequently, the cognitive approaches soon sought to integrate the more behavioral techniques such as homework assignments and behavior practice into their procedures. In Beck's earlier descriptions of his treatment approach, one finds practice focused primarily on writing down and reshaping thought, as described in the treatment of an anxious woman (Beck, 1976, pp. 257–262). By 1985, cognitive therapy emphasized much more active corrective experiences as part of the recognition that psychotherapy is, in effect, a form of education and that effective learning requires the use of a variety of active didactic procedures, a position I had also proposed (Beck & Emery, 1985, p. 186; J. L. Singer, 1974).

Let us review briefly some of Beck and Emery's (1985) approaches to modifying imagery. These authors pointed out that cognitive therapy often makes use of "induced imagery" in its procedures and that because maladaptive overt behavior is often also associated with particular recurrent images, the identification and modification of such images may be a critical step in treatment. In the next pages, I follow Beck and Emery's (1985, pp. 212–231) categories in discussing the modification of imagery in cognitive therapy but use examples drawn from my own or my supervisees' experiences.

IDENTIFYING MALADAPTIVE BELIEFS OR COGNITIONS

A 25-year-old man of "old American" Anglo-Saxon background noticed a book about the operas of the German composer Richard Wagner on my office desk. He told me afterward that he felt that he and I were "soulmates" and described his elaborate images about Germany in the period leading up to World War I—Emperor Wilhelm in his spiked iron helmet; the mustachioed field marshals Hindenburg, von Moltke, and Ludendorff; the scenes in Wagner's music drama of the superhero Siegfried wielding the sword he had forged to slay the great dragon Fafner. His subsequent associations helped him to recognize how he had built up an elaborate identification with Teutonic power in the pre-Hitler and the Nazi Party era. As a gifted young mathematician and early computer scientist, he had often been teased as a "nerd" and weakling by schoolmates and, seemingly, was shunned by girls for his shyness. His transferential identification with me as a soulmate was accurate only insofar as we both shared an admiration for the purely musical contributions of Wagner. However, we were far apart in our attitudes about Wagner as a person and also with respect to the young man's attachment to imperial Germany. The vividness of his imagery about German power helped us both to see the extent to which he was undervaluing some of the qualities of his own cultural background and his personal strengths as a scientist and a responsible man.

MODIFYING IMAGES AND SUBSEQUENT BELIEF SYSTEMS

In the case of the client discussed above, it was eventually possible to encourage him to generate alternative imagery about himself. He developed an imagery sequence in which he could picture developing his research skills further but also taking a more active role in local and national politics. He began to picture ways in which his personal qualities and strengths could be more effectively used in a form of political party activism that also offered social opportunities. I did not necessarily agree with his political stances, but I had to respect his seriousness and the responsibility reflected in his imagery and in his subsequent behavior.

TURNING OFF AN UNWANTED FANTASY

Beck and Emery (1985, p. 215) described how hand clapping, practiced first during therapy sessions and then used at home by a patient or even by his wife at his instigation, could terminate an unwanted fantasy of dying. In my own practice, a patient was a moderate smoker (seen for other reasons) who was interested in reducing her frequency or ending the practice completely. Tracking her craving patterns, we found that smoking images and then craving occurred usually after moments of accomplishment—for example, finishing an important task, eating a good meal, or a satisfying sexual act with her husband. Research has suggested that stopping smoking is more easily accomplished with persons who smoke as a celebration in contrast to persons who smoke during or following stress or failure. We therefore focused on using aversive imagery involving noxious scenes when smoking fantasies occurred to the patient. She quickly found a reduction in the occurrence of the smoking imagery and subsequent craving. She then on her own substituted just the image of a big sign saying "STOP" and found this abolished the smoking imagery—and the associated craving. Charting her smoking showed that she no longer purchased cigarettes and only occasionally smoked if offered a cigarette by a friend after a lunch or dinner.

REPETITION AND TIME PROJECTION

In my work with clients, I have often combined these two steps proposed independently by Beck and Emery (1985). A patient given to obsessive rumination reported to me that he was about to make an offer on the premises for a new business location. He imagined making a particular financial approach that was actually slightly higher than the asking price but that his business experience told him would assure his winning the property against several competitors. He became extremely anxious as he contemplated the sum he would pay (actually visualizing a check) and, with it, the thought that he might be overpaying. He was encouraged instead to first picture the check and then the scene 3 months later of his taking possession of the premises. After repetitions of this sequence he began to feel less anxious, because the image of moving in was a positive one. He was then encouraged to imagine the check and a scene a year later. As he did so he saw images of a thriving business because the setting and location were really favorable. Repeating this scene a dozen times, he became aware that the original frightening image and its anxious ruminations had faded. Discussing this change, he recognized that on the basis of his business judgment, the seeming overpayment he had made would be trivial compared with the likely profitability of the business within a year's time and his satisfaction with it. He moved quickly to actually make the deal and reported a short time later that his anxious money fantasies had ceased and that his profits had easily erased the check amount of his initial fearful imagery. He saw this as an example of overcoming his tendency for what cognitive psychologists would call *catastrophizing*, or magnifying and intensifying possible problems.

SYMBOLIC IMAGERY AND METAPHOR

Some of the most extensive research and insightful theorizing about the importance of metaphor in thought and language has been generated by George Lakoff. He has shown that in almost all known languages, people rely on analogy and metaphor to reinforce the effect of individual words and to clarify meanings. As he and his collaborator, Mark Johnson, have written,

> Metaphorical imagination is a crucial skill in creating rapport and in communicating the nature of shared experience. This skill consists, in large measure, of the ability to bend your world view and adjust the way you categorize experience. (Lakoff & Johnson, 2003, p. 231)

These authors went on to point out that people are often trapped by unawareness of the limitations of a metaphor they rely on all the time. Communication is usually presented as a *conduit* metaphor, one that involves just moving words to someone else without necessarily any recognition of contextual or traditional cultural differences. They proposed that effective communication is better presented with a *negotiation* metaphor. Much of cognitive therapy is designed to shift the way a patient thinks and acts about problems through encouraging a shift in metaphors. Imagery, as a way of representing situations and events in a fuller context, is especially important in this process.

Beck and Emery (1985) presented an example of the use of metaphor to help a client break out of a writing block. The individual was encouraged to think of her writing as a water-pumping process and to recognize that just as an unused pump may first gush out rust and dirt, keeping the flow going may, before long, yield clean, fresh water (Beck & Emery, 1985, p. 218). She then could write more extensively and not be upset if her early productions did not go well.

I have used a similar metaphor a number of times with patients who were blocked in creative or scholarly writing. I often found that these individuals also were trapped by self-defeating images of great poets or playwrights like Shakespeare, Shelley, Ibsen, or Tennessee Williams looking over their shoulders as they started writing. Clearly, their first productions seemed far below the level of these imagined superhero rivals. An approach I took with one young patient was to encourage him to think of himself more as a gold prospector, sifting a stream and shaking out a large number of rocks until some shiny nuggets appeared. The main goal was to set up an outline for direction, write regularly every morning when he was especially alert, and then work over the material produced. No Tennessee Williams was he, perhaps, but good enough each day to find useful material in the large output he produced. He enjoyed this metaphor and was emboldened to keep working, with some ultimate success.

FLOODING TO CONFRONT AND DEFUSE
CATASTROPHIC THOUGHT

I mentioned earlier the implosive or flooding techniques of behavior modification in connection with persons who are overcome by exaggerated fears. There is always some risk in such a technique (J. L. Singer, 1974), but with judicious use it can be fruitful. Let me describe an approach I have used that might be called a form of triangulation, encouraging a client to consider best- and worst-case scenarios and explore these for a practical image that might lead to a realistic solution.

A young accountant who worked for a high-powered, nationally recognized firm had been in treatment with me to deal with anxieties and self-doubt as he struggled to "make partner" in the practice. As we were engaged in facing up to interpersonal and cognitive distortion issues, he reported that he had in the past weeks developed an increasing fear of walking in his neighborhood. He lived in a part of New York City that had recently been gentrified. Once elegant and later run-down streets of brownstone town houses had now been refurbished and were attracting hundreds of upwardly mobile yuppies like himself. Once or twice as he walked from the subway station to his apartment in a now-elegant town house, he had passed some rather rough-looking boys clustered together and spinning garbage pail covers in some sort of game. He began to imagine that one evening, returning late from work, he was attacked by muggers, robbed, beaten, and left for dead. The thought began to obsess him, and, fortunately, he mentioned it in therapy before it became strongly conditioned.

After some discussion of associations and possible symbolic meanings, we agreed that he would try a series of imagery exercises. First he practiced relaxation; then, in a calm state of mind, he imagined over and over the worst scenes of being surrounded, robbed, and beaten. Then he practiced extremely positive images of scenes of walking by a group who waved and smiled at him. He imagined he was waving back and saying "Hi, there!"

After about 2 weeks of practice in session and at home, the young man reported that the spontaneous catastrophic image was no longer occurring to him. We then talked more analytically about the origin of his concerns, some elements of prejudice that he may have had about poor youth, especially minorities. We also reviewed the reality of his neighborhood. He knew of no instances of muggings or attacks. He realized that he had watched a good deal of violent TV fiction shows recently while relaxing late at night after a stressful workday. Walking home a few days later from the subway stop he saw some boys playing ball against the steps of a brownstone and walked by casually without saying a word. The earlier image recurred without anxiety as he made a mental note to tell me about the incident. The catastrophic image or similar ones did not come spontaneously to his mind again over the next few years in which we were in contact.

IMAGERY IN OBSESSIVE–COMPULSIVE DISORDER AND ITS TREATMENT

Although both psychodynamic and cognitive therapists provided a better understanding of the once baffling link-ups between repetitive bedeviling thoughts and the driven actions such as "checking" and "washing" that followed them, treatment of their extreme forms proved very difficult. In their milder forms, such combinations of thought and seemingly compelled actions often could be incorporated into socially adaptive vocational or hobby activities. Every government bureau has benefited from some pedantic, hard-working persons who keep careful track of forms and records. Psychologists become interested when compulsions seem especially irrational or superstitious, even if they sometimes turn out to be adaptive.

A well-documented example from sports history is the account of the famed Boston Red Sox baseball player Wade Boggs. He believed that his consistent hitting for 20 years depended on his eating chicken before every game, followed by a 5-hour, rigidly pursued practice schedule that involved many ritualistic elements (Vyse, 1997). Although many aspiring boys might gladly accept his compulsions if they could ever hit like Boggs, the reality is that obsessive–compulsive behaviors are often seriously self-defeating and demoralizing.

The research and clinical literature on obsessive–compulsive disorder points not only to the considerable importance of an individual's imagery patterns in the symptomatic picture but also to important ways in which imagery can modify and gradually eliminate the disorder. In a careful analysis, de Silva (1986) identified four forms of imagery that characterize obsessive thought: the obsessional or insistently recurring image, the compulsive image, the disaster image, and the disruptive image. The most frequent forms of compulsive behaviors that follow on these images have generally been categorized by patients who are termed *checkers* and *washers*. Those in the former group respond to recurrent images such as leaving the house with leaking stove gas or with the burglar alarm turned off by endlessly ruminating as they drive away and picturing catastrophe or robbery until they must go back and reenter the house to review the situation. The latter group is characterized by recurrent images of personal smelliness or disease proneness requiring constant hand washing, like the guilt-ridden Lady Macbeth, or, in more severe instances, showering or bathing so often in a day as to be unable to get to work or attend some social function.

Earlier I mentioned Meichenbaum's (1978) proposal of three reasons why imagery may help the troubled patient in a variety of disorder treatments: the recognition of the irrationality and self-defeating nature of the obsessive images; the awareness of how the consequent reaction or compulsion may be useless or ultimately irrelevant; and finally, by the finding that corrective imagery may provide a sense of self-control or emotional regulation (Meichenbaum, 1978). A fairly recent thorough review by Katherine Gapinski has extended this position to show how a therapist can use imagery systematically to eliminate both the obsessive image and its compulsive consequence (Gapinski, 1999–2000). The critical steps in treatment, pioneered by Meyer (1966) and elaborated and extensively researched by Edna Foa and her associates, are the key steps of exposure and response prevention (Foa & Kozak, 1996; Franklin & Foa, 1998). The therapist must find ways to have the patient mentally confront in imagery (or in a real-life situation) the obsessive image followed by some form of prevention of the compulsive follow-up so that gradually, but relatively soon, the two phases, obsessive image and overt act (or its image), become disentangled and the reinforcement effect of the compulsive behavior is no longer operative. Although the research evidence makes it clear that the sequence of exposure and response prevention works best in actual situations (in vivo), such opportunities are often not practical. Using imagery alone may be sufficient in many cases, and controlled experiments show that the imagery method of exposure may have lasting effects on its own without "real world" exposure (Gapinski, 1999–2000). As Gapinski concluded, "It is possible that imaginal exposure may operate long-term by constantly providing a highly accessible process of mental rehearsal as opposed to the more hands-on and less immediate process of live exposure" (1999–2000, p. 361).

EXPLORING MEMORIES AND POSSIBLE FUTURES:
A COGNITIVE MODEL

One often hears that cognitive therapies ignore or minimize memories as influences on current behavior in contrast to more psychodynamic approaches. I propose, however, that the distinction between these two major treatment approaches is based rather on the much greater emphasis by the psychoanalytically derived methods on retrieving very early childhood memories, often going back to the preschool years (pre-Oedipal) in the Melanie Klein or Kohutian object relations or self psychology systems. I suggest, however, that a cognitive–behavioral approach can be integrated to some degree with psychodynamic treatments on the basis of a theoretical model drawn from the script theory of Silvan Tomkins (1995) and its elaboration in a computer science framework by Robert Abelson (Schank & Abelson, 1977; J. A. Singer & Singer, 1994).

The concept of scripts is a form of mental structure generally categorized as part of the schema theory in information processing, as mentioned in chapter 3. *Scripts* are relatively organized outlines that people "carry around" about sequences of events they associate with different environmental physical or social situations. These scripts are based on what they have been told to expect in different situations or, as they mature, on actual sequences of experiences (event memories) in these settings. A 3-year-old taken unprepared to the barbershop for his first haircut is terrified when he is positioned in an unfamiliar chair, covered in a white cloth, and sees a stranger with big scissors coming toward him. After a few painless haircuts, often followed by a lollipop gift, children begin to put together a barbershop or hair salon script that serves them well throughout their lives. They generally know what action sequences to expect and what roles they and the hair-treatment workers are likely to play even in hair salons of hitherto unvisited towns or cities. Human life may well be described as the accumulation of scripts for dozens of settings so that people will not be surprised or greatly confused, even when some details are not fully expected—for example, when as a man one enters a shop to find that the barbers are all women.

The scripts for first dates, for sexual encounters with relative strangers, for the weeks and months of living together that follow the initially well-scripted marriage ceremony or romantic onset of a relationship are far more ambiguous and fraught with uncertainties. People must rely on the categories they have formed for themselves and for other groups of people in an encounter on the basis of an accumulation of episodes from either early life or even relatively recent event memories. In Figure 8.1, the episodes for a particular social script accumulate at the base of the triangle and then are grouped into more general self-defining categories further up the sides. Finally, toward the apex we may find the script synthesized into an abstract "life rule" such as "never marry outside your religion or social class" or "avoid situations in which you might end up humiliated when you try to offer help to strangers." These abstract guiding rules may be efficient in some ways for all of us. Because, however, they ultimately depend on somewhat idiosyncratic life experiences (a combination of actual early episodes in particular families or of one's early misreadings or limited understandings of events), we may all be subject to some self-defeating consequences of following these "rules" too rigidly or applying them to new settings in which they are not really appropriate.

The cognitive–behavioral approaches all seek early on to identify these abstractions that guide many of our social scripts. Albert Ellis, in public demonstrations that I witnessed, used harsh and often profane confrontations with clients who professed beliefs like "never trust a dark-haired woman"

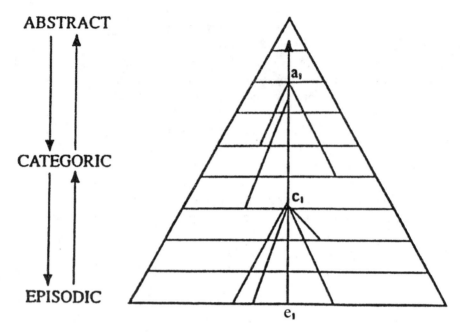

ABSTRACT

CATEGORIC

EPISODIC

a_1

c_1

e_1

Figure 8.1. The evolution of nuclear scripts from the accumulation of critical memory episodes. This diagram suggests how a series of comparable memory episodes—for example, "I was trying to help X when she attacked me"—gradually merge into a categorical belief—"I'm a person who is often hurt when I try to help"—and finally become an abstract script—Don't get involved"—that governs an array of possible events. This visualization was derived from a verbal analysis by Abelson (1981). The assistance of Charles Stinson in the preparation of this figure is gratefully acknowledged. a_1 = Don't get involved . . .; c_1 = I'm a person who is . . . ; e_1 = Episode of being hurt while helping.

or "men won't commit to you unless they really say 'I love you' with warmth and excitement." Beck and his followers may be somewhat gentler but equally firm in guiding patients to recognize the self-defeating or inappropriate nature of these life rules or of the categorized self-beliefs that may underlie them.

However, many clients may not be easily convinced to work to change their relatively abstract or categorical belief systems without the further step of identifying those often very emotional memories of specific events or personal interpretations of episodes from which their scripts were built. The retrieval of the episodes at the base of the triangle in Figure 8.1 almost always involves specific event memories or images. Whether they are truly veridical memories, that is, whether the scenes a patient describes actually occurred with videotape accuracy, seems unlikely from what we know of memory over time. But their vividness and the strong emotions they evoke in the individual provide a sense of importance and reality that can often motivate the person to then reshape the now unworkable self-representations or life rules that were based on these episodes.

A patient I was seeing was troubled because she was engaged to two different men and would meet with both of them regularly within the same week, deftly juxtaposing the two rendezvous. I became aware at some point early in the therapy that she had given me different accounts of her siblings, sometimes mentioning one, sometimes two brothers. After I pointed this out to her at the end of a session, she reported at the next meeting that she had become very emotional after she went home. She was flooded with a series of memories and images from about age 4. A brother was seriously ill, and the whole large family's attention was given over to the boy. Bored and feeling neglected, the little girl went outside and was playing ball alone, throwing the ball against a wall of the house. Her grandmother emerged from the house and shouted angrily, "Stop that banging, Amy. Do you want to be the death of your brother?" Sadly enough, the boy died a few days later.

Several episodes of this type seem to have convinced the girl of her own potential destructiveness or sinfulness and eventually of the risks of a commitment to one person. With the vividness of the recollection, she could recognize that her "no commitment" life rule was inappropriate, and eventually she made a clear choice that eventuated in a long-standing marriage to one of the men.

A case study by the late Rae Carlson (1981), a pioneer in script theory research, provides another example of an early "nuclear" memory or episode that with accumulated analogous incidents led to an abstract life rule about the avoidance of intimacy or involvements in helping others. The female narrator of this incident was a volunteer participant in a life study. She retrieved a memory without coaching, also from about age 4 or 5. She was watching her mother, who was housecleaning and who had climbed a ladder to dust a bookcase. The ladder tipped and the mother fell to the ground. "Call your father in!" she cried to the girl, who ran to fetch him. The father ran in, leaned over the mother to check her injury, and, as the girl watched, he said, "Sit over here on the couch, honey." The little girl (still presumably in the cognitive development stage Jean Piaget called "egocentricism") ran over and sat on the couch. To her confusion and dismay, the father, helping his wife to the couch, snarled at the girl to get out of the way. This episode in which the girl perceived herself as helpful and obedient eventuated in her being rejected and confused. Several other somewhat similar incidents in her life were drawn together into a script and eventually into a set of beliefs about herself (*categorical self-representations*) and eventually into socially isolating abstract life rules.

A clinical case study of a young man who, in an early school grade, was humiliated in class by a teacher who misunderstood his attempt to be helpful was described by J. A. Singer and Singer (1994). Here the memory emerged in a combined psychodynamic and cognitive–behavioral treatment approach when a recurrent transference tendency was being examined.

Encouragement of retrieval of memories or even of the generation of spontaneous imageries is useful in a cognitive approach in helping to clarify belief systems, self-attitudes, or other areas of potential cognitive distortion.

In my own work and in my supervision of therapy by students, I have found that often one can indeed start with the higher levels of the triangle in Figure 8.1, the generalizations about self, the categorical dimension, or the abstract level of life rules. Then one can call for associated memories or simply fantasies and images linked to these schematic belief systems. In the research my colleagues and I conducted as part of the MacArthur Foundation's Program on Conscious and Unconscious Mental Processes, we had trained observers watch videotapes of psychotherapy sessions and score the various instances when patients mentioned what appeared to be their schemas and scripts—for example, "I believe I can't trust people like teachers or bosses—they'll only get you in the end," or, "I feel I'm just not a strong person like my mother was." Such material, often just allowed to go by, even if noticed, in classical analysis, can be quickly recognized, questioned, challenged, and followed up by requests for exemplification or for generation of memories or imagery. Such opportunities were too often missed in the therapy cases we were scoring (Eells et al., 1995).

I hope I have given enough examples of the value of vivid memory material for clarifying cognitive structures. Let me add, finally, that there is an important role for imagery in the final behavior-change feature of a cognitive approach. If the client has identified and clarified the importance and origins of a self-defeating cognitive personal construct or abstract life rule, this individual is still faced with how to implement alternate schematic or script structures through social action. Here, as Beck and Emery (1985) also suggested, one can call for images of a set of future social situations. One can imagine various steps to be taken, various conversations one can have with key individuals, and then rehearse these in the treatment session. The "empty chair" technique, drawn originally from Gestalt therapy, can be used. Through imagery, one imagines oneself trying new ways of talking to a parent, a boss, or another authority figure. Then one moves to imagining that person seated in an empty chair in the room, and one can practice open conversation with the invisible authority while the therapist looks on. One can carry future imagery further in this way by triangulation, assuming best, worst, or "practical-for-oneself" scenarios and work toward what fits best with one's own abilities. Then one can envision a series of possible situations or settings and plan actual encounters in those situations, easy ones first and then some that are more serious. I have already presented the case of a man who, following imagery rehearsal, confronted his feared boss with an important criticism of their business operation. To his surprise, he found his intervention welcomed and implemented. Our capacity for imagery and fantasy can indeed give us a kind of control over possible futures!

9

TOWARD RESEARCH-BASED NEW PSYCHOTHERAPY MODELS: SELF-SYSTEM AND SUCCESSFUL INTELLIGENCE APPROACHES

Throughout my nearly 60 years in psychology, I have sustained a guiding belief that forms of psychotherapeutic intervention may eventually be derived from basic research in the mental and behavioral sciences. Although this book is oriented primarily to assist the clinician in using our human evolution–derived gifts of imagination in the diverse current psychotherapies, I propose in this chapter to call attention to new possibilities of treatment that are founded on basic psychological research and theory in the emotions, cognitive social processes, and personality. The treatment methods I describe have not yet been tested in manualized forms or in comparison studies the way cognitive and interpersonal therapies have, but they have the advantage of reflecting extensive and replicated research on their component processes. My focus, in keeping with the more limited goals of this volume, is especially on how clinicians may apply imagery and narrative skills (their clients' and their own) within the framework of these emergent treatment methods.

SELF-REPRESENTATION AND SELF-SYSTEM THERAPY

The first psychotherapeutic method developed by a psychologist working within a research framework was Carl Rogers's client-centered counseling and psychotherapy (Rogers, 1942, 1951). As Rogers himself told me, he was influenced by exposure to psychoanalysis and, especially, to the relatively jargon-free, patient's "will"-centered modifications introduced by Freud's early but independent-minded close associate, Otto Rank (see Figure 5.1). Rogers eschewed diagnoses based on a medical model and proposed instead that much human distress, as well as growth, emerged from the effort of each person to sustain some sense of congruence in expectations and values, an openness to new experiences, and a capacity for change (Rogers, 1961). The individual's sense of self was at the center of the ongoing challenge and struggle of effective living. Feelings of sadness, incompetence, and anxiety emerged when the person came to believe that one's *actual self* in achievements, skills, or the capacity for understanding and intimacy with significant others was too far removed from some personally constructed or socially expected *ideal self*. An important goal of client-centered counseling is to help the clients through fostering an autonomous searching in the atmosphere of "positive regard" by the therapists. Individuals can identify actual-self and ideal-self discrepancies, perhaps some long-standing false beliefs or inhibitions that sustain either low self-regard or perhaps exaggerated ideal expectations leading to continuing, troubling, and depressing incongruities.

As a psychologist, Rogers was impelled to find methods of measuring self-attitudes and of using these measures to identify the way patient–therapist interactions modified self and ideal-self beliefs in the process of psychotherapy and also as an indicator of the outcome of treatment encounters. Rogers's place in the history of psychology is secure, because he and his collaborators introduced the era of systematic research in psychotherapy and, for social, personality, and clinical psychology, the important research domain of studying self-beliefs, the self-concept, and the significant attitudinal, emotional, and behavioral correlates of the self. By 1975, the range of research methods and research approaches was so extensive as to yield a massive two-volume review by Ruth Wylie (1975).

SOME PERSONAL RESEARCH AND CLINICAL EXPLORATIONS OF THE SELF

Because of my own interest in private experience and imagination, it was natural for me to become involved as early as the 1950s in self research using methods derived from Rogers and his many collaborators. I worked with Rosalea Schonbar, a colleague at Teachers College, Columbia University, and with Vivian McCraven, a former assistant of Ruth Wylie's. We hypothesized, influenced by the interpersonal psychoanalytic theories of Harry Stack Sullivan, that closeness of one's actual self or one's ideal self to one's mother—in the 1930s to 1950s usually the "at home," more storytelling or spiritual parent—would stimulate more inclinations to daydreaming in both females and males. As the great German poet Goethe wrote,

> From Father I learned . . . the serious
> conduct of living . . . From Mother
> came the playfulness and the
> zest for fantasizing. (Goethe, c. 1790; in Trunz, 1988, p. 330; translation
> by J. L. Singer)

Middle-class adults from a variety of ethnic backgrounds responded to questionnaires as their actual selves, as their ideal selves, and then as they thought their fathers or their mothers might answer the same list of questions. By scoring the degree of difference between one's own set of responses and those assumed for the parent, we assessed the degree of identification with a particular parental figure. We found that where one was more closely identified with one's mother, there was a somewhat greater tendency for reporting more daydreaming in both men and women. We also developed a measure in which the discrepancy between self and father in responses to questionnaires was related to the discrepancy between the self and mother so that a simple formula—S-F minus S-M—the greater distance from father and greater closeness to mother—would predict, for example, a positive relationship to reports of daydreaming or creativity. Our findings in general supported the hypothesized relationships (J. L. Singer & McCraven, 1961; J. L. Singer & Schonbar, 1961).

More recently, Tory Higgins (1987) has developed an elaborate and testable theory of self-schemas, or, as he termed them, "self-guides." This work is important because by linking the views of the self with the schemas, one can use the highly efficient retrieval capacity both of schemas and of self-relevant material as well as consider for clinical purposes the biasing effects of self-referential schemas and scripts (J. A. Singer & Singer, 1994; J. L. Singer, 1985; J. L. Singer & Salovey, 1991). The importance of self-focus is manifested in studies of thought sampling and ongoing consciousness (Klos & Singer, 1981; J. L. Singer & Bonanno, 1990). Experiments in memory also attest to the importance of self-relevant material in incidental recall and in autobiographical recollection (Klein & Kihlstrom, 1986; Kreitler & Singer, 1991; J. A. Singer & Salovey, 1993). The motivational role of the ways in which one conceives of possible selves is also shown in the studies of Ruvolo and Markus (1992).

Self-representation is a key product of a schematic memory system and also may be a critical feature of a life narrative. Explicit memories of how one has been treated by other people, of what one wants in different situations, and of how one behaved in dozens of settings form, often enough, an extremely dense and complex network for the general memory associative structure. Self-relevance generally yields a powerful effect in studies of memory. The study by Kreitler and Singer (1991) demonstrated that young adults were more likely to recall self-relevant words compared with words presented as either relevant to another person or under various other controlled conditions. Especially interesting was a personality measure of self-complexity that also correlated with the frequency of word recall under the self-relevant conditions.

It seems likely, as William James (1890/1950) long ago suggested, that one is prone to an awareness more of multiple self-representations than of a single "core" self. James had already identified the actual-self and ideal-self difference, or the actual-self and possible-self representations, in his chapter on the self. The experimental research of Markus and Nurius (1986) on possible selves has shown how some of James's conceptions can be translated into operational forms suitable for experimental and clinical study within a social cognition framework. The research program initiated by Higgins (1987) within a social cognition orientation perhaps operationalizes most effectively some key elements of what might be called *Freud's superego* into the so-called self-guides of actual self, ideal self, and *ought self*, and their relationships. Thus, the actual-self/ideal-self discrepancy (measured by scoring respondents' description of each self-representation) identifies the degree of gap between a currently perceived functioning self and an ideally desired personal representation. This work has been especially effective in demonstrating how discrepancies between the actual- and the ideal-self representations are linked to depression and saddened moods, whereas discrepancies between the actual self and the ought, or socially obligatory, self are linked to agitation and social anxiety (Strauman, 1992, 1994; Strauman & Higgins, 1988). Even more remarkable are Strauman and colleague's dramatic findings linking these discrepancies between actual and ideal or ought selves to the functioning of the "psychologically silent" immune system of the individual (Strauman, Lemieux, & Coe, 1993).

A group of us have sought to examine the concept of discrepancies between various self-representations using the Higgins (1987) method and a great variety of measures of personality and emotion (Garfinkle, 1994; Hart, Field, Singer, & Garfinkle, 1997). We sought in these studies to examine self-representations by exploring the ongoing thought of the individual over a week's time as measured through thought samples.

We initially tested more than 100 young Yale students. The respondents listed the traits or characteristics that they saw as representing their actual selves, their ideal selves, their ought selves, and their undesired selves. By looking at the relationship between the lists of up to 10 traits under each of these categories, we determined how close actual self was to ideal self, to ought self, and to undesired self, and we created a quantitative score. We also asked these individuals to answer a number of other questionnaires designed to measure the so-called Big Five personality traits (Neuroticism, Extraversion, Agreeableness, Conscientiousness, and Openness; Costa & McCrae, 1985, 1987). In addition, we included measures of anxiety, depression, self-esteem, and interpersonal problems that are well standardized and have been widely studied in the research literature.

A unique feature of the study was that in addition to these approaches, we required our participants to carry paging devices for a week's time. They were interrupted randomly during the day and had to complete forms at the point of interruption, describing their situation when interrupted, the specific thoughts they had been having, and their moods associated with the period just at the point of interruption. In this way, we hoped to determine whether the measure of proximities between actual-self and other-self representations such as ideal, ought, or undesired might predict the ongoing thoughts of individuals as sampled over a week's time.

For thought samples, we accumulated the content reports, and these were rated by judges blind to the hypotheses. The judges rated the thoughts and fantasies of the participants for indications that they were sustaining positive evaluations of self. Ratings of the participants' moods and emotions as reported during the same interruptions yielded measures of positive affect, lethargic or depressed affect, and calm affect.

Our data indicated that the proximity between one's actual self-representation and one's ideal representation correlates significantly and negatively with neuroticism scores as well as with scores for anxiety and depression. Proximity between actual and ideal self ratings correlated significantly and positively with scores on an independent scale of self-esteem, developed by M. Rosenberg (1979). Regarding the kinds of interpersonal problems reported by these participants, those who showed a high actual–ideal discrepancy also reported more overall difficulties in interpersonal relationships, particularly with respect to responsibility, intimacy, and submissiveness.

To what degree do proximities between actual and ideal views of self recur in the ongoing thought of the individual? From the accumulation of daily thought samples for participants, there was a clearly significant correlation between these daily reports (which included fantasies of a positive nature involving the self) and the similarity between the actual self and the ideal self as tested weeks before.

Self-ratings of moods during the thought sampling are also consistent with the closeness between actual self and ideal self. There are positive correlations for this closeness with positive emotionality and calm emotionality and negative associations with lethargic or melancholic mood. It might be argued that associations between the self-representations and the personality trait variables, especially Neuroticism and Extraversion, could account for the findings that emerge in thought sampling (i.e., those persons already given to being outgoing or to being neurotic might simply carry over their style of reporting to thought sampling). We conducted various analyses to see if the self-representation measures still correlated with thought samples even when the scores that these participants had obtained on the personality traits were partialed out or dealt with through multiple regression analyses. When the correlations between the actual-self/ideal-self proximity scores and the personality trait variables were considered, the self-representations still contributed significantly to the prediction of ongoing thought patterns (e.g., to greater positive view of self, more daily positive mood states). The actual-self/ought-self proximity predicted positive emotionality, whereas the actual-self/undesired-self proximity predicted agitated rather than calm affect as reported in the participant's daily thoughts.

People are almost continuously engaging in thoughts or daydreams that involve judgments about their own actual traits and, quite possibly, how these relate to ideal or socially expected patterns. One might propose that the actual–ideal self (AI) and actual–ought self (AO) are both forms of the psychoanalytic notion of ego ideal and a punitive superego. Higgins and Strauman (see Strauman, 1992) in their work have indeed related these representations to earlier childhood experiences in which the parent was perceived as either providing positive reinforcement or providing systematic punishment of one kind or another.

Garfinkle (1994) and I tested the hypotheses concerning self-representation and ongoing thought processes. Building on the work of Strauman and Higgins (1993), we proposed that participants whose actual selves were considerably discrepant from either their ideal or their ought selves would be likely to notice negative emotions (dejection and agitation, respectively) more frequently in their day-to-day lives than would participants for whom the actual self is close to the ideal and ought selves. We were especially interested in the continuities across ongoing experiences and therefore sought conditions in which individuals with different discrepancies (compared with yoked controls) would indicate a heightening of an already demonstrated discrepancy through an experimental intervention. Thus, we used groups identified as either *discrepant* or *nondiscrepant* from their actual self, ideal, and ought ratings. Groups were formed of those individuals who showed a high AI discrepancy but a modest AO discrepancy; those who showed a high AO discrepancy and an average AI discrepancy; and finally, those who showed no significant discrepancies at all. These groups were then put into situations in which individuals were asked to imagine a discussion with their "better self" involving a kind of coercive confrontation (e.g., a parent trying to win an argument or expressing disapproval of the person while listening to his or her point of view). If the study involved the parent, the task should have activated the AO mismatch, especially when used in conjunction with an issue raised by a trait word that had been part of each specific participant's mismatch between actual and ought words. In the AO situation, participants should have felt that they had not lived up to the state that a parent and the participant both believed was a personal obligation or duty to fulfill. A series of such simulations occurred.

AI mismatches had to involve the use of an "inner voice" or "part of yourself that is wisest and most insightful." In this way, the AI mismatch trait words used in this self-conversation created a powerful feeling that the individual was not living up to a highly desired state. To create the dialogues as effectively as possible, each trial began with questions such as those posed by a "parent" as read to the participant by an experimenter, beginning with "Why aren't you more _____?" (for an AO mismatch). A self word was inserted here drawn from the participant's own listing so that this question would ring especially true. For the AI mismatch trials, the inner voice began with a question such as "Why is it so important for you to be _____?" where again, a trait chosen from the ideal-self listing of each individual was involved.

On the basis of earlier work by Strauman (1989), eight dialogues were drawn up. The critical dialogues were those in which the respondents imagined an inner voice questioning them about two attributes drawn from their own earlier ideal-self listing that did not coincide with their own actual-self listed attributes. These self-referential AI mismatches presumably heightened the participants' awareness of an actual-self versus ideal-self discrepancy.

For those participants who had no AI mismatches, ideal-self attributes that neither matched nor mismatched any actual-self attributes ("none-match" attributes) were used. In all cases, only attributes unique to the ideal-self state (i.e., not also listed as part of another self-state) were selected. A similar procedure was used for the AO mismatches. For yoked AI mismatches, the participant was presented with attributes that were drawn from the list of a another participant. The attributes had not been included in the target individual's own questionnaire responses. These words were used as primes for an inner voice dialogue. A similar procedure was used for yoked AO mismatches.

The priming trials—that is, the simulated or imagined confrontational dialogues—were presented in random order to control for sequence effects. The experimenter was also blind to each participant's order of presentations. The yoked trials were necessary because it was important to test an alternative hypothesis that priming effects might themselves be due to the specific content of the attributes rather than to the activation of a self-relevant mismatch (Strauman, 1989). After the participants had signed an informed consent, they were asked to complete a mood checklist to estimate emotions just prior to the priming situation. After this, instructions were then repeated, and the role-playing situation began. Immediately following priming, participants were also asked to answer the mood questionnaire. On the next day, they began their 7 days of carrying paging devices with questionnaires on which they entered their mood states. Some also completed dream logs to examine continuity in dream mood as well as in mood of daytime thought. As it turned out, 71% of the 49 experience-sampling record sheets were handed in, with an average of four responses for the seven daily interruption reports required.

A detailed step-by-step analysis of these data made it clear that those individuals who were exposed to a discrepancy between their representations of actual selves and either their ideal or ought selves and who also underwent the priming experience demonstrated clear differences from yoked controls. These participants' daily logs decreased in positive affect reports and indicated increases in more negative, lethargic (depressed) moods as well as decreases in the calm (less agitated) mood state. This was an especially strong effect for those individuals with large AI discrepancies. Over time, they showed consistent increases in negative mood and in more agitation or depressed affect. The AO group generally followed close behind, with both groups tending to be significantly more affected by the priming situation than were the control groups. We debriefed and counseled all of our participants at the end of the week.

These data indicate that the schematic structure of relatively conscious differences experienced between one's actual self-representation and one's ideal-self representation and between one's actual- and one's ought-self representation significantly influence questionnaire ratings of depressed mood or of tendencies toward agitation. These schematic structures, especially when primed, are influential over a week's time period. The ongoing conscious thoughts of individuals, as tapped by the seven daily interruptions over a week's time, do indeed reflect the "chronic" self-representations as measured in the fashion developed by Higgins (1987).

SELF-RATINGS AS A THERAPEUTIC FOCUS: TWO CASE STUDIES

During the period between about 1983 and 1995, I was involved as a senior scientist in the development and in various phases of the execution of the MacArthur Foundation–sponsored program on conscious and unconscious mental processes (directed by Mardi Horowitz at the University of

California, San Francisco School of Medicine). The project included not only experimental and large-scale empirical studies such as that by Hart et al. (1997) but also involved following patients seen in therapy through the use of videotaping and psychophysiological measurement. These records of patient–therapist interaction were then subjected to extensive analyses using Horowitz's role relationship model configural analysis. Descriptions of this work and the general approach have appeared elsewhere (Horowitz, 1991; Horowitz, Eells, Singer, & Salovey, 1995). In the analyses of the therapeutic sessions carried out by teams at Yale and San Francisco, we attempted to identify formal schemas produced by individuals in the course of their conscious presentations to the therapists. Thus, we would score statements such as "I believe I am . . ." or "I think that my parents expected me . . ." or "That's the way people are, they . . . ." These organized belief systems or schemas of self and others were identified and accumulated over five sessions of therapy. Frequency counts provided actual-self representations, forms of ideal-self representations, dreaded selves, or socially expected selves. This work, along with the more large-scale empirical work described earlier, led me to believe that one might increase the effectiveness of therapeutic interactions by having patients complete trait lists of actual, ideal, and ought representations right at the start of therapy.

In a somewhat cognitively oriented therapeutic intervention with a cocaine-dependent patient (Mr. D), Kelly Avants, Arthur Margolin, and I (Avants, Margolin, & Singer, 1994) used not only an initial set of ratings based on self-representations by the client but then used daily logs that were completed during the 10 weeks of therapy and that incorporated the patient's various self-representations. These ranged from desired ideal self to the "addict" self.

Case Example: Mr. D

In one case, the patient, Mr. D, included in his ideal self and ought self attributes such as "being honest with myself and others," "being open and receptive," "feeling centered," "being warm toward others," "setting goals," "being stable and responsible," "communicating my feelings," and "letting people get close." During each therapy session, he worked at making these selected attributes concrete. He did this by identifying specific behaviors that would reflect each of these traits mentioned, and he attempted to role-play how he might manifest such behaviors in situations involving significant people in his environment. This patient kept daily logs and complied with the proposal to engage in specific behaviors that involved reconciling himself with a family member with whom he had quarreled; studying for his high school equivalency examination; arranging to obtain a driver's license; and taking specific steps to maintain his job, which had become endangered by his previous drug use. These behaviors were mentally reenacted by him during the day, even as he engaged in specific overt actions. His daily log documented the steps he took each day and his carrying out of his "homework" of role-playing in preparation for them. At the conclusion of the 10-week treatment, Mr. D was shown the lists of words he had generated early in treatment. He re-rated them on a 5-point scale for his experience of each of the self-representations during the previous week. His sense of being addicted had disappeared, as measured by the rating. It was also verified through toxicology screens and by his exposure to certain "drug triggers." He had returned to school to prepare himself further for his high school examination and had reconciled himself with the estranged family member and was continuing his relationship with this individual. During the previous weeks, he had applied for and obtained a driver's license, and his job performance was being well received.

Considering that this young man had been a drug abuser for 16 years, the progress made in the approximately 3 months of treatment by Kelly Avants was extremely impressive. It strongly suggests that careful attention to the schemas that people carry with them about their various forms of self may be critical in establishing a therapeutic focus.

In my own part-time clinical practice, I began to propose to patients that they list the traits or characteristics that they themselves linked to their actual, ideal, ought, and dreaded selves at the very beginning of their treatment. My patients, admittedly individuals of high intelligence and achievement in business and professional activities, were quite willing to engage in this process. Once they listed these traits (only important ones were requested), one could calculate the proximities or discrepancies between the actual-self and other-self representations. Because of my long experience in encouraging the use of concrete images, memories, and fantasies as part of an ongoing treatment process, the patients were also encouraged to visualize specific scenes or settings in which these behaviors were reflected. The patients were also encouraged to keep daily logs of their awareness of various self-representations in the course of their activities and ongoing thoughts.

Case Example: Mr. L

One example that I offer in disguised form is that of Mr. L, a successful lawyer who was a partner in a specialized but very busy law firm. Mr. L had come to see me because he was experiencing a mixture of both depressive and anxious symptoms, which he attributed chiefly to the stresses of his work and also to a conflictual relationship with the senior partner in the firm.

Mr. L was in his early 30s and had been relatively recently married. He and his wife had two very young children. His wife was supportive throughout treatment, and his personal relationship with her seemed excellent. Mr. L was clearly intelligent and well educated and seemingly gifted in his profession. He had risen quickly to the level of partnership. In the course of his attaining greater prominence in the firm, however, he had become more and more distressed by the continuing pressure for productivity, which he felt often led to some marginally ethical practices on the part of the leadership of the firm.

Mr. L agreed to complete the list of self-representations shown in Exhibit 9.1. He then began by producing a series of memories and fantasies about these various personality traits and characteristics over the 20 sessions that followed. He was the son of a physician who had amassed a sizable fortune through a combination of a very "high-quantity" practice and his keen business skill in real estate investment. After he had filled out the ought-self listing, Mr. L quickly noticed how much pressure he felt from his father to be extremely successful financially. This was also reflected in the dreaded-self representations. In our twice-weekly meetings, Mr. L also associated various memories and fantasies with the self-representations that he had initially provided, and he reported on events occurring daily through the logs he was keeping. Mr. L recognized more and more that the work stress he was experiencing seemed to reflect a transference response from his relationship with his father to the firm's senior partner, a man who shared at least some of the same financially driven qualities that Mr. L perceived in his own father. One can see how Mr. L's insight supports Higgins's views of the agitation associated with AO discrepancies in this circumstance. At the same time, a glance at the ideal-self listings indicates that there was a larger discrepancy between actual and ideal for this man. Especially striking were those aspirations for "respect," "leadership," and "scientist," among others. This discrepancy was reflected also in periodic episodes of sadness in addition to anxiety and agitation. The daily logs presented by this young man called attention primarily to situations in which his own productivity in handling larger numbers of cases was being questioned by his boss and by another partner who was to some extent his rival. The quality of his work was not an issue, but there was increasing pressure on him to handle and to locate more cases than he felt were appropriate to sustain a high quality of performance.

There was a critical turn in the treatment when as he sat working on his log one evening, he also found himself watching a TV movie. The story involved a young man who had been subjected to years of exploitation and public humiliation by an older sibling. The climax of the film came when the younger brother killed his older brother. As he was telling me of this television-viewing experience, Mr. L suddenly began to weep and could not stop for some time.

In talking further about this incident on the following day, Mr. L once again began to weep. Actually, I had seen that same movie on TV the

EXHIBIT 9.1
List of Self Traits by Mr. L at the Outset of Treatment

Actual self	Ideal self	Ought self	Dreaded self
Kind	Respected	Efficient	Failure
Humorous	Leader	Physical/athletic	Bankrupt
Chubby	Intellectual	Financially successful	Unethical
Responsible	Scientist	Good business sense	Stupid
Nervous	Calm	Family leader	Loser
Fearful	Courageous	Devoted son	Weakling
Submissive	Assertive	Fast worker	Disbarred
Loving husband	Family man	Productive	Mediocre
Loving father	Self-assertive	Good team manager	Unable to hold family [together]
Incompetent	Independent	Practical	Clown
Poor business sense	Specialist	Slim	

previous night, so I could appreciate the power of the story itself. What I did not know and what Mr. L revealed to me only later in the session was that this plot was surprisingly similar to a set of experiences that he had had with an older sibling. We had to work through some resistance that he felt in telling me this story, a transference response to me as an authority figure and as a much older man. Once he was able to voice this resistance, he could then tell me about his own recollections of the teasing, physical abuse, and torment that he had received over many years from an older brother. This brother had often mocked him, sometimes actually supported by the patient's father, because Mr. L was at the time obese and also rather timid. What began to emerge as we reviewed these memories and their relation to his sense of self was that he had been systematically suppressing some of his own sense of independent thought and a considerable amount of intellectual curiosity that he had in his specialized law field in the interests of trying to meet the expectations of his father. This suppression was in part a carryover from his brother's bullying and the need to show his brother and father that he could be "strong" by earning a good deal of money. In actuality, his brother was at this point a petty criminal and apparently a long-standing sociopath whose life was at a dead end, in sharp contrast with Mr. L's. Mr. L had not only a successful career but also a satisfying marriage and a very respectable family life.

As Mr. L reviewed his actual- and ideal-self representations through images of various possibilities and waking fantasies, he began to propose that these might be reconciled if he asserted himself more clearly with his boss at the firm. He tried this on a few occasions where he saw a clear-cut issue and found that these efforts yielded good results. To his surprise, he was listened to and not mocked or humiliated. This success led to his reexamining his own intellectual ambitions. He realized that his interests lay more in the theoretical and scholarly aspects of his specialized legal work. He then began to take steps to see if he could move into academic law. When he tried this, he found within a very short time that his skills were quickly appreciated. It took some personal courage and considerable support from his wife for him to consider giving up his more lucrative practice. At the same time, as he moved along toward this new career, he experienced a great sense of autonomy and also a sense of relief that came from what he perceived to be a calmer and more reflective lifestyle.

What finally emerged was that our joint focusing in on his self-representations led this man to experience an increasing proximity between actual and ideal self. At the same time, he realized that his anxiety about the discrepancy between the actual and the ought self was illusory. This discrepancy had been associated with early humiliation and was contrary to his own most cherished personal ideals.

TOWARD A SELF-SYSTEM THEORY-BASED PSYCHOTHERAPY FOR DEPRESSION

I began this chapter by reviewing work by myself and colleagues that led from studying the correlates of self-discrepancies to my own practical applications of self theory in psychotherapy. Independent of this work, Timothy Strauman, now at Duke University, who had worked closely with social psychologist E. Tory Higgins at New York University on the basic research in this area, joined with Angela Vieth at Duke and others at the University of Wisconsin to develop a self-system psychotherapy that has now evolved to a testable model for treatment of depression (Vieth et al., 2003). Let us review here how a basic research conception—here, the role of imagery in the treatment process—can generate a therapy approach.

Vieth et al. (2003) reviewed the research on the role of self-discrepancy theory in self-regulation and how failure in self-control may lead to a persistent depressive distress. They further outlined a treatment approach that they believe can be integrated with, but still differentiated from, cognitive and interpersonal psychotherapy because of its greater emphasis on motivation and the pressure of the actual and ideal self or the actual and ought self as guides to emotion and action. The key principle relates to self-regulation, studied over almost 30 years by Higgins, Strauman, and their coworkers. Four basic principles are enunciated:

1. One's ability to establish and to sustain self-regulation develops in the course of childhood out of basic, perhaps even genetically determined, temperamental characteristics, cognitive growth, and early family and social experiences. Here Vieth et al.'s (2003) approach is related to the tenets of interpersonal and object relations theories but is even more specifically based on research findings that early positive experiences with parental figures or the absence of such supportive experiences are early determinants of the child's views of self and of goals for ideal or socially expected ought behaviors (Bowlby, 1988; Manian, Strauman, & Denney, 1998; Sullivan, 1953).

2. Two motivational processes derived from one's cognitive and motivational efforts determine self-regulation. These are termed *promotion* and *prevention* systems, as described by Higgins (1997). Promotion involves striving for accomplishment, achievement, and autonomy—an attempt, as originally proposed by Tomkins (1962), to maximize the positive emotions of joy and excitement whenever possible. Prevention, on the other hand, involves self-protection, defensiveness, the pressures of security, obligedness, and a somewhat enforced sense

of responsibility—"in everyday terms, striving to keep bad things from happening" (Vieth et al., 2003, p. 246).

One is again reminded of Tomkins's early proposal that the motivational role of the human emotional system involves (a) maximizing positive affect; (b) minimizing negative affect; (c) expressing emotions as fully as possible; and (d) controlling affect expression or adjusting their expression to socially appropriate settings (Tomkins, 1962). Hugs and kisses or praise by parents support the child's experiences of positive outcomes; punishments and humiliating looks or comments convey the absence of positive experience. Promotional experiences foster ideal goals or standards (Freud's ego/ideal revived, one might say). Prevention-oriented self-regulation emerges through early experiences of punishment or harsh criticism and leads to the uncomfortable feeling of "ought," an experience that early on was identified by Freud as the punitive superego and now backed up by the more extensive research evidence demonstrated by Higgins (1989).

3. Self-regulation persists as a kind of existential dialectical struggle throughout the life span, a kind of trade-off between the promotional strivings for accomplishment or effective intimacy and the preventive efforts to avoid failures or the interpretations of limited successes as failures. Vieth et al. (2003) proposed that depression "need not depend upon extreme trauma or deprivation, but rather can emerge over time as a consequence of trade-offs in self-regulation—the relative benefits and costs of an individual's regulatory style" (p. 248).

4. Clinical psychological disorders are a consequence of continuing or catastrophic failures in self-regulation, and these are manifest in promotional defeats that generate depressive moods or in preventive setbacks in which one may observe prolonged agitations or anxieties.

The goal of self-system therapy (SST) for depression is to assist individuals to gain relief through increasing their ability at self-regulation. The treatment emerges from the analysis of the actual-self and ideal-self discrepancies we reviewed in the beginning of the chapter. There is a substantial research basis for self-discrepancy theory, much of it further reviewed in the article by Vieth et al. (2003). Keeping in mind our focus here on the uses of imagery, let us briefly review the main steps of SST as Strauman et al. (2004) have described it.

It should be clear that many features of a treatment based on the principles outlined here would necessarily overlap with cognitive and with interpersonal treatment approaches, as already suggested in my own independently developed treatment efforts. Vieth et al. (2003) did show, however, that SST differs from cognitive therapy because the latter approach does not focus especially on self-knowledge and on modifying self-regulation. They emphasized the motivational as well as the cognitive features of self-knowledge and also the importance of developmental processes, which are less stressed in cognitive approaches. If anything their approach seems closer to interpersonal therapy than to cognitive therapy, except that SST is more oriented to the individual's goals and strivings than to current interpersonal difficulties or confusions. Of particular importance is that although the other approaches emerged largely from clinical experience and speculation, SST is more firmly based on systematic, theory-derived, general psychological research. Here I heartily support their assessment.

The goals of SST include educating the client about symptoms and possible treatment courses, as well as about the ways in which self-regulation may be important in producing and maintaining depression. A major step is to assist the individual in reinstating promotion-focused thought and behavior. This phase also includes seeking to use promotional, forward-striving goals to counter the heavy emphasis on prevention. I used a similar approach in encouraging Mr. L to reconsider his goals for a more scholarly career, which then helped him in moving toward a more realistic reconciliation of the actual and ideal self-guides. SST also calls for ongoing evaluation of the regulation approaches of the clients, their varied psychological and social settings, detailed social interactions, and day-by-day emotional reactivity. Treatment targets are carefully defined on the basis of goals and current situation, and intervention directions are set. When significant self-regulation changes can be accomplished, these are targets of treatment, but if such goals are by the time of therapy not realistic, appropriate compensatory approaches are introduced.

In the case of my own work with Mr. L as described above, his lofty early goals of a scientific career were out of reach by the time he was receiving therapy from me—he was married and had children and financial responsibilities that precluded the intensity of study and immersion in pure research he had longed for early on. He could, however, find ways of sustaining some degree of financial stability as a consultant and draw on his extensive practical experience for particular areas of research that were academically valued. There were trade-offs to be faced. A move to a grander house or elaborate and expensive family vacations had, at least for some years, to be postponed. Fortunately, his wife was supportive in these matters. He recognized that his fantasies of mental planning turned most often to research and law school achievements and were accompanied by strong positive affect. The nagging images of his father's financial expectations for him began to fade.

I hope I have whetted readers' appetites for more intensive exploration of SST. Examination of the carefully outlined procedures shows that they call for a variety of uses of the patient's imagery. Identifying the actual- and ideal-self traits calls for imagining scenes of specific activities, accomplishments or failures, and situations in which one must choose a promotional goal or activity over one that is largely preventive. Although abstract discussions do have a place in this treatment process, they are inevitably followed by planful script building and by images of oneself in a variety of social settings.

Of special interest is the emphasis placed on the use of mindfulness procedures for relaxation, for breaking preventive rigidities, and for learning to focus, at first mentally and then behaviorally, on action sequences. Mindfulness is used also as a means of sustaining gains and avoiding ruminations of a perfectionistic type that only widen the gap between actual and ideal selves. There is already some rigorous cognitive–behavioral research supporting the usefulness of this intriguing imagery-based technique (Vieth et al., 2003, p. 263).

SUCCESSFUL INTELLIGENCE AS THE BASIS FOR A PSYCHOTHERAPEUTIC APPROACH

For the first half of the 20th century, psychologists were best known for their discovery and continuing development of methods for measuring intelligence. Such efforts chiefly began with Binet's attempts to devise procedures for identifying mentally retarded children. Spearman's (1904) statistical analyses of various tests of intellectual capacity led him to propose that intelligence could be formulated as a general human ability for abstract thinking, or g. Terman's standardization of IQ measure based on a battery of tests, the Stanford-Binet, eventually was adapted for use all over the world. The individually administered Stanford-Binet (Terman & Merrill, 1972) and the Wechsler intelligence scales (Wechsler, 1958) were also complemented by large group testing procedures used in military screening, college and professional school admissions, and in civil service and industry employment assessments. Clearly, there emerged a widespread international belief that intelligence, as measured by tests of demonstrated psychometric internal structure and repeat-testing reliability, was predictive of individuals' capacities to perform effectively in meeting minimal life-adjustment standards, in school performance, and in workplace adequacy. Indications from research on the heritability of IQ led to unfortunate excesses such as occurred with the dubious immigration screening in the United States in the 1920s and early 1930s and, more recently, to the claims that the social lagging of certain minority groups reflects genetic limitations in their g factor (Herrnstein & Murray, 1994), an approach critiqued by Sternberg and Grigorenko (2000).

Less known to the public and to many practicing school, clinical, and other applied psychologists have been the continuing research efforts of Thurstone and Thurstone (1941) and of Guilford (1967), among others, that questioned whether effective intelligence is solely measured by tests that emphasize the abstract thought and analytic skills measured by the g factor. Thurstone and Thurstone's work, especially, pioneered the way in demonstrating that a number of components must be combined to judge adaptive intellectual performance and that the standard IQ measures represent only a limited sample of these components.

The past quarter century has been characterized by a striking increase in the recognition that intelligence measurements built around g, or abstract, analytic intelligence, are inadequate predictors of school or more general life achievement and competence. Howard Gardner's (1983, 1999) widely read books *Frames of Mind* and *Intelligence Reframed* convincingly outlined at least seven components of multiple intelligence, including logical/mathematical, musical, and intrapersonal and interpersonal skills. From my vantage point, the triarchic theory of successful intelligence developed by my Yale colleague Robert Sternberg (1985, 1999a, 1999b) has been the most persuasive on two grounds. First of all, it is based, in contrast to Gardner's, on a systematic series of empirical studies and sophisticated statistical analyses that support the conception of three independent forms of measurable intelligence, the analytic (essentially the component of abstract thinking, widely underlying most standardized IQ and college admissions tests), the practical, and the creative. Second, there is an impressive and continuing body of research that indicates that the measures of these three skills not only predict effectiveness in tasks or situations that require specific analytic, practical, or creative ability but that training children or adults in using each component improves academic or daily life achievement (Sternberg, 1999a, 1999b; Sternberg & Grigorenko, 2000).

In view of the scientific support for the notion of three forms of intelligence that can predict a greater variety of life behaviors than just academic grades, Scott Kaufman and I (Kaufman & Singer, 2003–2004) have suggested that perhaps we need to consider whether psychotherapy may be usefully considered as a form of improving a patient's performance in analytic, practical, and creative thought. Sternberg's development of the theory of successful intelligence and his group's demonstrations that performance levels could be improved through formal training included no references to psychotherapy. I propose a challenge to clinicians to consider the value of integrating into the therapy process a tested model for increasing the mental ability of individuals. I also include a case example drawn from my own treatment files in which, well before the emergence of the triarchic theory of multiple intelligences, I was using features of the analytic, creative, and practical components along with imagery in treatment of depressed and anxious clients.

THE COMPONENTS OF SUCCESSFUL INTELLIGENCE

As mentioned above, Sternberg's (1999a, 1999b) extensive psychometric analyses of intelligence consistently yielded three components: analytic, creative, and practical abilities. *Analytic intelligence* is involved when a person analyzes, evaluates, judges, or compares and contrasts stimuli. Analytic intelligence is chiefly what is measured on IQ tests and tends to involves problems that are abstract.

How do the cognitive therapies relate to analytical intelligence? Cognitions that are distortion free may be conceptualized as thoughts that are high in analytical intelligence because of their logical nature. On the other hand, distortions in cognition may be conceptualized as low in analytical intelligence and hence maladaptive. Cognitive therapy is not normally discussed in terms of intelligence, but it does fit within the framework of the theory of successful intelligence. After all, analytic intelligence has an important adaptive function, especially in regard to examining the logic of one's belief systems. A reading of Socrates' defense at his trial more than 2,400 years ago, as presented in Plato's *Apology*, affords one of the earliest examples of human analytic intelligence.

Creative intelligence is involved when an individual creates, explores, imagines, supposes, or synthesizes stimuli. Sternberg's investment theory of creativity (Sternberg & Lubart, 1995) views creativity as a decision in which the creative thinker produces an idea that is initially unpopular ("buys low") and then "sells it" and eventually moves on to the next creative idea once it becomes popular. According to the investment theory, creativity requires six resources: intellectual abilities, knowledge, styles of thinking, personality, motivation, and environment. A great deal of creative intelligence calls for imagery and narrative thinking and activity.

Research has shown support for the investment theory. Sternberg and Lubart (1995) asked 63 people to create various kinds of products, with an infinite variety of responses possible. Individuals were asked to create products in the realm of writing, art, advertising, and science. In writing, they were provided with story titles and were then asked to compose a short story based on that title. In art, participants were asked to produce art compositions with titles such as *The Beginning of Time*. In advertising, they were asked to solve problems such as one asking them how people might detect extraterrestrial aliens among us who are seeking to escape detection. Participants created two products in each domain.

Sternberg and Lubart (1995) found, first, that creativity comprises the resources that were proposed by their investment model of creativity: intelligence, knowledge, thinking styles, personality, motivation, and environment. Second, they found that creativity is relatively, although not completely, domain specific—that is, creativity in fiction writing does not carry over to art. Third, they found that correlations between their measures of creativity and conventional tests of intelligence tended to be higher to the extent that the problems on the conventional tests were novel. These results indicate that even though tests of creative intelligence have some overlap with conventional tests, they also tap skills beyond those measured by conventional tests of intelligence.

Viewing creativity as a decision process has important implications for psychotherapy, because if it is a decision process, it may be possible to teach patients how to make such decisions that could help them in their lives. Strategies to develop creativity have been proposed along with procedures to enhance practical and analytic thinking skills. These strategies were originally proposed to increase intelligence in schoolchildren, but a glance at the strategies should make it clear how these strategies can just as well be applied to an individual's personal life.

Here are some steps in training creative thought:

1. *Question assumptions and encourage others to do so.* Creatively intelligent people question why things are the way they are. Therapists should encourage patients to question assumptions. That way, they will encourage them to think creatively and express their own ideas about the way things are or should be. Certainly this is already a key feature of cognitive therapies, as described in chapter 7. In my private practice, a number of patients who felt intimidated by bosses at work or other authority figures found that when they expressed their differing opinions quietly and clearly but forcefully, they were heeded and not fired or humiliated. This was in contrast to the way they were treated as children, and it allowed them to reexamine their assumptions and latent rage against all authorities. Imagining the situations in which they spoke up and then the various consequences was always useful.

2. *Allow yourself and others to make mistakes.* Making mistakes is an inevitable concomitant of producing creative ideas. The important thing is to teach patients to learn from their mistakes. Clients should realize that they need to be more flexible and that making mistakes is a part of the learning process. Each mistake the patient brings up should be analyzed, and efforts should be made to see how the mistake can be avoided in the future.

3. *Take sensible risks and encourage others to do the same.* Creative individuals will take risks and sometimes fail in doing so. Creative people lean toward taking more risks. Perhaps just the act of taking risks, first in the safety of the therapy session,

can make patients feel refreshed and more in control of their lives. For instance, taking sensible risks in imagery that they would have never thought of taking before may help patients view themselves as more multidimensional. Remember Freud's notion that thoughts can often be viewed as trial actions without necessarily dangerous consequences.

4. *Actively define and redefine problems and help others to do so.* Sometimes people have a problem and see only a few options. This type of thinking leads them to feel pressured and can lead to depression. A way of generating more options is to constantly be redefining the problem. Therapists can allow patients to choose their own ways of solving problems and encourage them to choose again when they learn their selection was mistaken. It is also important here to emphasize to the patient the importance of gathering the proper information before defining a problem.

5. *Understand the obstacles creative people must face and try to overcome them.* Creative people always encounter obstacles and almost always encounter resistance. The question is not whether the person will encounter resistance but whether the person will sulk or will do something about it. The therapist can spend some time working with the patient on building up resilience through role-playing, imagery, or creating pretended dialogues. Emphasis should be placed on how to overcome the obstacle instead of focusing on the obstacle itself. Mentally envisioning specific coping actions may be especially useful.

6. *Recognize the importance of person–environment fit.* Creativity is often an interaction between a person and the environment in which he or she works. Patients should be encouraged to develop their creativity in the areas where they have contributions to make. They need an environment that lets them capitalize on their strengths. Therefore, patients may be advised to consider other environments that may allow them more opportunities to capitalize on their strengths or different social settings that may be a better match to their social style.

During treatment, all these steps can first be practiced in imagination, and possible outcomes considered of behavior attempted in relatively "safe" settings. In effect, then, creative intelligence in Sternberg's theory seems in many ways to overlap with the ways in which therapists have been using imagery and fantasy techniques in cognitive and psychodynamic therapies. Sternberg and his collaborators have good research evidence that even fourth-grade children can be trained to make gains in creative abilities and in insightfulness (Davidson & Sternberg, 1984; Sternberg & Williams, 1996). Independent research by S. Epstein and Pacini (2000–2001) has provided further support for the value of visual imagery training for creative and other intellectual skills.

Practical intelligence is involved when individuals apply knowledge to their daily lives. The key concept Sternberg and his colleagues have used to define practical intelligence is *tacit knowledge*. Tacit knowledge has been conceptualized by Sternberg and his colleagues as a procedural type of knowledge that is acquired implicitly and that is used to achieve personal goals. Tacit knowledge takes the form of a series of "if" clauses that are added to each other to produce a "then" action. I asked a patient of mine to imagine best- and worst-case outcomes of telling his mother he wanted to get his own apartment. After trying imaginary dialogues with his mother, he chose an approach he felt comfortable with. To his delight, his mother was accepting of the move, albeit with some trepidation. Subsequently, she found that she was able to expand her own social life considerably when she and her son did not have to consider each other in planning whom to invite over.

Sternberg and his colleagues have measured tacit knowledge for adults in over two dozen occupations, including management, academia, sales, and the military. Tacit knowledge is typically measured using problems that one might actually encounter on the job. A typical tacit knowledge problem consists of a set of work-related situations. People are asked to rate a set of statements (usually on a scale of either 7 or 9) on how important each statement is for success in a particular situation.

A study of business managers was conducted at the Center for Creative Leadership in Greensboro, North Carolina (Wagner & Sternberg, 1990). In two managerial situations, the test of tacit knowledge was the single best predictor of performance out of a series of measures that included a standard intelligence test, a personality test, a cognitive styles test, a test for preference for innovation, a test of job satisfaction, and a test of orientation in interpersonal relationships. The measure of tacit knowledge also showed a much higher correlation with performance on the job than the IQ measures that were used.

Two studies looked at the tacit knowledge of academic psychology professors. Results showed correlations in the .4 to .5 range between tacit knowledge and the number of citations to the professors' work reported in the *Social Sciences Citation Index* as well as the rated scholarly quality of an individual's departmental faculty (Wagner, 1987).

Tacit knowledge has also been looked at in the domain of sales (Wagner, Sujan, Sujan, Rashotte, & Sternberg, 1999). Correlations in the .3 to .4 range were found between measures of tacit knowledge for sales and sales volume and sales awards. This work made explicit the rules of thumb that salespeople use on the job.

A more recent study looked at the importance of tacit knowledge in military leadership (Hedlund et al., 2003; Sternberg et al., 2000; Sternberg & Hedlund, 2002). A measure of tacit knowledge for military leadership was administered to 562 participants. It was found that their measure of tacit knowledge significantly predicted military effectiveness, whereas scores on a conventional measure of intelligence and on a tacit knowledge test for managers did not.

Research has shown the importance of tacit knowledge not just for success on the job but also for the prediction of mental disorders. Grigorenko and Sternberg (2001) used their measures of analytical, creative, and practical intelligence to predict the mental health of the Russian adults in their study. Mental intelligence was assessed by paper-and-pencil measures of depression and anxiety. It was found that the best predictor of mental health was their measure of practical intelligence, with analytical intelligence and creative intelligence contributing significantly but to a lesser extent to the prediction.

In real-world settings, practical intelligence is important and is demonstrably not the same thing as analytical intelligence. More important for psychotherapy is that it is possible to make explicit these implicit rules for success. This is important because it has been shown that lack of practical intelligence can lead to mental disorders such as depression and anxiety. Many patients having problems dealing effectively with their own personal relationships and school or work situations may be lacking in important tacit knowledge that can be discovered through the use of successful intelligence techniques.

Efforts to teach for practical intelligence have yielded some success. Wendy Williams and her colleagues conducted observations and interviews with middle-school students and teachers in order to determine the tacit knowledge necessary for success in school (Williams et al., 2002). On the basis of their results, they created a program that teaches students the tacit knowledge needed to raise their practical intelligence in school. Sternberg and his colleagues have evaluated the program in a variety of settings and found that students who use the curriculum show better performance in reading, writing, homework, and test-taking ability compared with those not taking the curriculum (Gardner, Krechevsky, Sternberg, & Okagaki, 1994; Sternberg, Okagaki, & Jackson, 1990).

Dowd and Courchaine (1996) have discussed the implications of the experimental research on tacit knowledge for the practice of cognitive therapy. They found evidence that tacit knowledge is often more comprehensive, detailed, and richer than explicit knowledge and that identification of tacit cognitive themes is particularly important to the therapeutic process.

Another closely related construct is that of schemas, which we discussed in earlier chapters. Cognitive therapy has recently been extended to treat personality disorders, and cognitive therapists have posited that schemas are important in the understanding of such disorders (Beck, Steer, Epstein, & Brown, 1990). *Schemas* are cognitive structures that, starting in childhood, are built up over time and are used to process and assign meaning to incoming stimuli. Over the years, schemas can become more and more generalized, often without conscious awareness. The hypothetical constructs of schemas, scripts, prototypes, and stereotypes have become central to most theorizing in cognitive science. They form ways of organizing novel information into rapidly accessible structures that allow for encoding, retention, and retrieval of acquired information when one is confronted with sets of events or signals. New social or environmental data are matched against established schemas. If there is a reasonable fit, the new is assimilated into the older meanings, and emotionally one may experience relief or even enjoyment. If a mismatch occurs, one is first surprised or curious, and exploration may follow until a new schema can be formed, but if a mismatch persists, one may become frightened, angered, or distressed (J. A. Singer & Singer, 1994; J. L. Singer, 1974; J. L. Singer & Salovey, 1991; Tomkins, 1962).

THE THEORY OF SUCCESSFUL INTELLIGENCE IN PRACTICE

Humans possess the ability to reason, to think rationally, and to analyze a situation. However, we also possess the ability to generate novel ideas (or else society would not progress) and the ability to have an understanding (even if at an implicit, tacit level) of how the world works in order to judge whether a novel idea will actually work within the confines of our environment. There are many processes at work when a human attempts to display intelligent behavior. Intelligence is an outcome, after all, not a cause.

This chapter has included an entire section showing that analytical, creative, and practical skills can be increased by professional intervention. This research may have potential for use with patients in a clinical setting. Sometimes the hardest part of therapy can be getting patients to the practical stage—to apply changes made in the psychotherapy session to their own lives.

How could the theory of successful intelligence be applied to a psychotherapy setting? The goal of the patient and therapist would be to (a) work through the various problem-solving cycle stages, (b) using various techniques where appropriate to (c) build skills in analytical, creative, and practical thinking to (d) help patients alter their cognitions and environment in such a way as to alleviate mental health problems.

What are these "problem-solving cycle stages"? For years, psychologists have described the problem-solving process in terms of a cycle (Bransford, 1993; J. R. Hayes, 1989; Sternberg, 1985). These stages include (a) problem recognition, (b) problem definition, (c) formulating a strategy for problem solving, (d) representing information, (e) allocating resources, and (f) monitoring and evaluation.

Within each stage of the analytical problem-solving cycle, different aspects (creative, analytical, and practical) of intelligence should be applied to progress to the next stage. In a psychotherapy setting, a therapist can work with the patient in going through this cycle, applying different aspects of the theory where appropriate. It is important to note, however, that this is a cycle, not a linear set of stages, so it may be necessary for the patient to return to earlier stages.

Stage 1: Problem Recognition

The most important thing for patients to do is recognize that a problem exists. If they do not do that, they will most likely never even go see a therapist.

Stage 2: Problem Definition

Once there is recognition that there is a problem, the next natural step is to figure out the nature of the problem (or combinations of problems). Defining the problem may take a few sessions of psychotherapy and require working through the person's life and pinpointing exactly what the problem is. The patient's analytic intelligence may be an important starting point.

This process may be aided by the use of the *successful intelligence journal*. This is an idea that was modified from a version originally used in the classroom for students to determine their successful intelligence profile. The therapeutic version of the journal allows the patient to keep track of the salient events during the course of a day that lead to feelings of sadness or inadequacy and to recognize how they handled the situation. The patient can keep this list of the strategies used to develop analytical, creative, and practical thinking nearby and can add certain strategies that he or she could have used in the situation to deal with it more effectively. Looking at the journal after a few weeks the patient might notice some patterns that will help to identify exactly where the problem lies and to pinpoint concrete elements that can be worked on in consultation with the therapist with the goal of boosting his or her successful intelligence profile.

Stage 3: Formulating a Strategy for Problem Solving

Whereas Stages 1 and 2 require analytical thinking, Stage 3 involves the application of multiple aspects of intelligence. In this stage, the patient must formulate a strategy for attacking the problem. This stage may include a combination of analytical, creative, and practical thinking. Uses of imagery and fantasy reflect the creative side of thinking. The patient can analytically think of logical solutions, but at this stage ostensibly illogical solutions should not be discounted either. Imagery and make-believe techniques could be used to generate many different options. As suggested above, attention should be directed to the fact that humans do not just have to adapt to their environment but can shape it or select a new one.

Stage 4: Representing Information

Analytical thinking is important in this stage, as patients try to determine whether or not they are representing the problem in a way that is helpful or hurtful to them. For instance, patients may think they are worthless if they do not reach their ideal in every situation. This may prevent them from accurately evaluating information on a case-by-case basis. They may look at every failure as a personal failure in life as opposed to a minor setback in that particular domain. How patients represent this failure is important to their recovery.

Stage 5: Allocating Resources

After strategies are generated and the problem is represented in a different way, strategies can be narrowed down to one practical choice by doing an analysis of the resources that would need to be allocated for each alternative. This is an analytical task but also requires an understanding of what will work in the world, which involves practical skills. A cost–benefit analysis is helpful, as is trying to make the tacit knowledge explicit to modify it or compare it with an expert's tacit knowledge for the same situation. However, creative thinking can also take place here in trying to imagine how a change in environment might accommodate a strategy that would not immediately be accommodated under current environmental circumstances.

Stage 6: Monitoring and Evaluation

This stage is important because the person may come up with multiple practical alternatives for solving the problem even after the narrowing process. This is the time to take risks and to try out these alternatives in the real world. It is important at this point to monitor and evaluate how well the solutions are working and either try another strategy or go back and figure out how a current strategy can be modified (an analytical process).

COMBINING ANALYTIC, PRACTICAL, AND CREATIVE INTELLIGENCE IN PSYCHOTHERAPY: A CASE STUDY

Our discussion of the possible uses of Sternberg's three dimensions of successful intelligence for psychotherapy is obviously speculative. Nevertheless, it may be possible to move toward a real example of how it may operate by searching clinical records for instantiations of therapists' use of the principles we have derived for actual treatment. A search of the records of my practice of psychotherapy over about 50 years turned up a number of cases in which treatment reflected application of facets of the three-dimensional model described, albeit well before the Sternberg theory had even been devised. The following brief case study is one example out of several. Certain background details and, of course, names have been changed to protect privacy.

Herman, a 23-year-old man, had sought therapy because of a mixture of depression and anxiety. He reported right at the outset that he had been enrolled for months in a prestigious university's master of business administration (MBA) program but, without the knowledge of his wife and his parents, he had only attended school for a couple of weeks and was paying no attention to the course content. He would regularly say goodbye to his wife, Louise, when she left for her job as an executive in a merchandising concern, and then head to a large public library to read books unrelated to his schoolwork or else go to the city park, where he would occupy a bench, brood, work on math problems and crossword puzzles, or simply feed the pigeons. He realized that ultimately he would not be able to sustain the deception of his loving wife and admiring parents.

Herman could not explain how he had gotten himself into such a fix. He was obviously a person of high analytic intelligence as indicated by his IQ on traditional tests and by his college grades. The course work to which he had been exposed in his few weeks of the MBA program seemed well within his ability level, but the subject matter could not hold his interest, and his mind wandered to other issues, to mathematics and to political theory and political history. How could he explain to his wife and also to his parents that he seemed to have not the slightest interest in a business career? His wife, though herself very effective in her career, wanted to have children soon, and his parents (successful immigrant shopkeepers) expected Herman, once he obtained the MBA (which they were financing), to move well beyond them to a high-level business career.

Depressed as he was, Herman spoke slowly and sadly. He used many abstractions in his speech and summary statements rather than presenting concrete instances or specific memories. To engage him at all, it became necessary to approach him first through his best-developed form of intelligence, the analytical. I challenged him to join me in attempting to make sense of how he had gotten himself into this situation. I proposed that we both concentrate on an understanding of his cognitive processes and perhaps his belief systems that might be faulty and self-defeating. The importance of eventually concretizing his communications and of allowing himself to speculate or to explore his daydreams or even his night dreams was also stressed. Those might lead to clues as to some of his important but perhaps partly suppressed hopes and goals. In retrospect, one can recognize that although initially focusing on the patient's obvious abstract abilities, my work with this patient was also pointing eventually to the importance of more creative and, ultimately, of more practical skill development as a feature of the treatment process.

Humor played a part in my approach. When the patient would talk at some length in philosophical abstractions about the meaning of life, of Schopenhauer's or Spinoza's theories, I might quietly and gently say, "You get an A in philosophy, but how will this help you get beyond a career as a park pigeon-feeder?" Such approaches, to which the patient seemed responsive, led to an increase in his reporting more specific memories and descriptions of his actual relationships with his family and his experiences in childhood and in college.

To summarize briefly some of the life story that emerged, Herman, an only child, had always experienced great performance pressure from his parents. Their only hope was that he could use the schooling opportunities in America to gain wealth and position beyond the desperate struggles that had characterized their lives running a moderately successful "mom and pop" store with long hours, continual stress, and no opportunities for leisure. At college, Herman was a good student in abstract subjects, skilled in mathematics and sociological and political theories. He had always had good male friends with comparable interests but scarcely noticed these social skills, focused as he was on his seeming ineptitude in practical business matters and his shyness with girls. The family atmosphere at home was strongly puritanical and full of sexual taboos. To his amazement, Herman became the object of the pretty Louise's affection when she saw this good-looking young man, who seemed like a romantic poet to her, excelling on the school debating team. He could not believe that this energetic, sophisticated, very well-dressed girl could really like him. Indeed, she pursued him vigorously, introducing him to sexual activity, and they were married while still in college. Like his parents, she built an image of him in keeping with her own business orientation as a "good provider" as well as a romantic, verbally articulate lover. It seemed quite natural for her to move quickly and effectively into the commercial world to support them while he gained the important business credential of an MBA.

It is not necessary for our purposes here to elaborate on the "dynamics" of Herman's history and psychology. Rather, we are stressing the therapeutic course. Herman, once engaged and challenged intellectually to collaborate with the therapist in "solving the puzzle" of his own self-defeating behavior, began to recount more anecdotes, specific personal history events, and the accumulation of childhood or later life episodes that had led him to denigrating self-categorizations and the unwitting formulation of life rules, such as "One dare not try to act on one's hopes and imaginings when only financial success matters," or "There is no future in pursuing intellectual interests."

When it became clear that Herman was not open to allowing some of his suppressed wishes and fantasies to emerge in the therapy, I encouraged him to use his imaginative abilities to try out a series of alternate life scenarios, modifying his earlier schemas and scripts in a playful, risk-free fashion. This approach, one can see, is an introduction of Sternberg's creative intelligence dimension into the therapeutic setting, although of course not recognized as such by me 40 years ago. Herman found these exercises exciting. His depression began to lift. He realized how much he yearned for opportunities to explore his political science and mathematical interests further through education.

The therapy then moved into questions that now seem clearly relevant to practical intelligence. How important were these goals? What could he do to implement them? How could he approach his wife and parents, first revealing his depression and withdrawal from school and then offering alternatives for his future for them to consider? I encouraged Herman to role-play various encounters with these significant others, sometimes using the Gestalt therapy "empty chair" technique or other forms of imagined dialogues drawn from psychodrama. Here we see a blending of approaches toward practical intelligence, with the client building up tacit knowledge by first using creativity and imaginative resourcefulness.

In the course of these efforts, Herman came to see how he had become intimidated by his continuing exposure early in life to the extreme, almost desperate practicality of his parents and also more recently by his wife's energetic strength and down-to-earth, streetwise realism (hampered, perhaps, by her love-blinded overestimation of Herman's business potential). In the course of these insights, Herman began to consider more carefully what he himself really wanted in life and what it would take to move toward achieving some approximation of his more personal wishes without completely breaking with those persons he genuinely loved.

Herman, after further "rehearsals," was able to confront both Louise and his family with the reality that he had no interest in a business career but did see possibilities for himself to earn a decent living as a teacher of either mathematics or political science. He asked for their support in pursuing such a career and took the practical step first of obtaining work as a part-time mathematics instructor in a community college. To his surprise, his wife and parents, at first shocked by his revelation, soon turned their practical abilities to helping him move toward his goals.

Herman found that his math skills combined with the creative, imaginative resources he had practiced in therapy made him an extremely effective teacher of a difficult subject. With family support, he went on to a master's degree in political science, and he was able to secure a permanent position, decently paid, as a community college instructor combining his mathematics and social science background. His depressing thoughts faded, and he found new resources of energy, enjoying his teaching, administration, and college politics. His relationship with his wife grew even closer as they began their family. A follow-up some years later showed that he was a respected academic who continued his philosophical discourses with colleagues and students and was well remunerated for his teaching and administrative roles (albeit certainly not rich). With an academic schedule, there were opportunities for vacations and travel as well as for sharing child care with Louise. His lifestyle was truly gratifying, after all, to his parents and their hopes for him. Clearly, this was an instance of therapy that served to enhance the young man's successful intelligence, even though the therapist had no awareness during the treatment process that the approach used might someday fit well within the scope of the as yet undiscovered Sternberg theory!

SOME CONCLUDING REMARKS

Let me again remind the reader of the speculative aspect of my inclusion of this section on successful intelligence. My case example demonstrates how some of my own psychotherapeutic work used features that may have anticipated Sternberg's theory of successful intelligence with its analytic, practical, and creative components. But I had no idea at that time that concepts drawn from the psychometric research on intelligence might be relevant to the psychotherapy process. At this writing, no systematic treatment manual has been developed for applying notions of human intelligence to treatment of relationship problems or emotional distress. I believe that if one does emerge, stimulated I hope by this chapter or by the more technical article by Kaufman and Singer (2003–2004), it will then be available for training use and formal evaluation of the treatment process.

It may be desirable to add the concept of emotional intelligence as a human ability to the analytic, practical, and creative components. The initial work of Peter Salovey and John Mayer (1990) has led to a rapidly accumulating research literature supporting the emotional intelligence construct and its value as a predictor of social and vocational adaptation (Lopes, Salovey, & Straus, 2003; Salovey, Mayer, Caruso, & Lopes, 2003). The literature demonstrating that these three or four forms of human ability are teachable and that they can serve to train clients not only to overcome current distress but to prevent recurrences or to guide individuals into effective social relations is encouraging. From the perspective of the current work, what seems clear enough is how critical the use of the patients' imagery is as part of the treatment process.

I began this chapter with a discussion of the self and of the Strauman group's work on self-system therapy. In that case, a treatment manual is already developed and being tested (Strauman et al., 2004). It is my hope that the two new developing methods described can stimulate clinicians to recognize that basic psychological research in cognition, emotion, personality, and social psychology may yield impressive possibilities for more sophisticated and effective forms of psychotherapy. What I want to stress once more is the extent to which uses of imagery occur again and again in the training of therapists (or teachers, in the Sternberg approach) as well as in the various stages of the treatment process. I turn in the next chapter to how imagery may prove useful as a skill for clients more generally as well as for therapists themselves.

10

EXPANDING IMAGERY IN PATIENT AND THERAPIST

I began this book with a brief account of my early professional career and have throughout the volume mentioned instances from my own life experience as well as my professional practice. My purpose is to encourage clinicians to engage in some degree of self-reflection about their treatment efforts. We need to recognize that although we may use techniques and methods as professionals, we are more than technicians, and our patients are more than clusters of *Diagnostic and Statistical Manual of Mental Disorders* symptoms. It should be apparent that a unifying feature of my professional career as a researcher, educator, and clinician has been my early-developed interest in the variations and complexity of our human imagination and our conscious thought. One's life is, of course, more complex, and I have spared the reader details of my personal relationships; family; friends; early loves; economic concerns; political beliefs; religious orientation; sports preferences; involvements with sons, their wives, and grandchildren; and possible futures for my wife and myself.

When modern psychotherapy emerged at the start of the 20th century under the leadership of Sigmund Freud, it began as a symptom-oriented, ostensibly medical treatment—but before long, psychoanalysts attracted both clients and practitioners because it offered a unique opportunity to study human lives in their vicissitudes and complexities. In the final third of the 20th century, the seemingly limited impact of psychoanalysis as treatment occasioned the emergence of the shorter, demonstrably more effective behavior modification and cognitive therapies. One could, after all, measure symptom changes fairly precisely compared with evaluating the vague lifestyle, interpersonal behavior, or "id–ego–superego reorganizations" sought for in the psychodynamic therapies. Although Albert Bandura, as an early leader in the theory and spread of behavior therapies, often urged psychologists to emphasize the educational rather than the symptom-relief, medical-model features of their efforts, economic and insurance pressures dominated. The manual-based empirically assessed therapies have now "taken over." And yet, despite the research evidence of the effectiveness of such therapies, surveys show that the majority of persons in clinical treatment are characterized by multiple-symptom and multiple-problem patterns. Practitioners are regularly confronted with people who are seeking to make sense of their life experiences and to change their relationship styles as well as to overcome specific, narrowly defined symptoms (Beutler, 2004; Westen & Morrison, 2001).

WHY SHOULD CLINICIANS TAKE IMAGERY SERIOUSLY?

Earlier in this volume, I provided some indication that there is an important emerging scientific body of research on the adaptive role of narrative processes and on how self-defining memories and one's efforts at forming integrated life stories may shape personality. My focus here, however, is on the narrower subject of uses of our imagery capacities as part of that broader ongoing human striving for meaningfulness in a complex, overstimulating, and often confusing flurry of economic survival, hard work, and the subtleties of relationships. We have been gifted through evolution with the capacity to produce what we see, hear, smell, touch, or taste in mental images, representations that we can sustain over time and manipulate into novel forms and connections. We have the potential through imagery to control our past and future, admittedly in limited ways but with considerable possibility for modifying our emotions, a capacity that offers us hope; practical suggestions; and, ultimately, opportunities for taking effective actions. If we examine the exciting bodies of research on narrative (Green, Strange, & Brock, 2002), the life story and autobiographic memory (McAdams, 1993; J. A. Singer, 2004), constructive thinking (S. Epstein & Brodsky, 1993; S. Epstein & Meier, 1989), positive illusions (S. E. Taylor, 1989), learned optimism (Seligman, 1991), hardiness (Maddi & Kobasa, 1991), and the Sternberg group's work on successful intelligence discussed in chapter 9 (Sternberg & Grigorenko, 2000), we see again and again how often such processes are reflected in specific imagery, event memories, and projected future scenes and interactions.

Seymour Epstein, for example, who has conducted significant experimental research on the cognitive–experiential self system and its role in health and social adaptation, has provided some vivid examples of how even vivid, dreamlike waking fantasy can play an adaptive role in constructive thought (S. Epstein, 1999). Epstein's wife, Alice, had been diagnosed with an untreatable cancer and was informed that she only had 3 months to live. The Epsteins decided to use psychological means to fight this outcome. Alice began psychotherapy with an outside therapist and, informally, with her husband. What emerged quickly was that despite a life of successful personal and work relations, she was a deeply pessimistic person because of childhood experiences. To speed therapy, they tried guided fantasy that often yielded vivid quasi-mythological images. Along with meditation and relaxation, the sequence of images helped Alice overcome her ingrained pessimism and sense of helplessness and hopelessness. Her mood changed to a more positive one and, amazingly, within a few months, her cancer receded and disappeared on all tests. She herself wrote a vivid and poignant account of her experience (A. H. Epstein, 1989). An e-mail message I received in 2004 along with some professional communications from Seymour Epstein indicated that Alice continues to be well and cancer free more than 15 years after the supposedly fatal diagnosis.

Seymour Epstein has proposed that fantasy imagery may produce changes in personality and health. What he calls "the experiential mind" often encodes and stores our life events in symbolic or imagery forms, using the religious and cultural legends with which we've grown up and their constant re-presentation to us in our reading and (perhaps even more so) in television features or commercials ("put a tiger in your tank," "drive a Jaguar," etc.). As S. Epstein and Brodsky (1993) wrote,

> This information is associated with feelings (emotions, vibes, and moods), which, in turn, are associated with bodily functions, including the functioning of the endocrine and immune system. Thus, accessing the experiential mind through fantasy can produce changes not only in feelings, but also in bodily functions that are critically related to health. (p. 254)

S. Epstein and Brodsky (1993) also mentioned the instance of a famous 20th-century political columnist, Max Lerner, who described how he had fought off very dangerous illnesses by inventing an imaginary helper or "guide." This figment of his thought served as a kind of fantasy personal god with whom he had intense mental conversations during long walks. Many therapists interested in helping patients to use imagery will encourage clients to draw on ideal figures from religion, legend, or their own past to use as "wise guides" in troubled periods of life stress. The connection to formal and informal religious practices of talking to one's deity or to patron saints or other such figures is obvious. A systematic scientific study of whether the imagery used in such resorts to religious symbols by believers can have measurable impact would be worthwhile (Vyse, 1997).

In the course of writing the above account of Alice Epstein's use of fantasy imagery in confronting her allegedly fatal illness, I was reminded of a personal experience with illness and imagery that occurred at roughly the same time as hers. I had received a diagnosis following intensive examination of a noncancerous colon blockage that would probably require surgery. The specialist and I agreed to take a month to reexamine the situation while I tried using an austere diet and a period of rest. I did not tell the physicians but set up a series of imagery exercises for myself that involved regular engagement in imagery of peaceful, relaxing scenes (generally of nature settings) and positive imagery meditation. I have no personal interest in or patience for established, religion-derived methods like yoga or Zen. Mindfulness was not then on our psychological horizon (see Bishop et al., 2004). Listening to classical music is perhaps my best source of relaxation (even if the music itself is dramatic or tragic), and my thoughts when listening are replete with images. I arranged more opportunities to listen to recordings or to the radio during that month. When I returned for my medical check-up with the gastroenterologist, the Yale specialist actually used the term *miracle* as he told me that the obstruction had disappeared and no surgery or further treatment was necessary. In my opinion, the only miracle involved was the result of our evolution, in which humans have developed the brain capacity to use complex abstract thought and language and also to sustain memory and possible future images and combine such images creatively into ongoing narrative forms. Because we are indeed fully organismic, our thought processes may be linked, as in the S. Epstein and Brodsky quote above, to important bodily function systems. Impressive research evidence on the association of imagery and health may be found in the handbooks edited by Anees Sheikh and colleagues (Sheikh, 1983; Sheikh, Kunzendorf, & Sheikh, 1989).

Imagery is important because it can have a significant constructive impact on one's overt behavior as well as on one's bodily functioning. I must, however, offer two caveats, or at least scientific questionings, about the assumption that encouraging imagistic thought is inherently valuable for human health or for effective social interactions. One area that needs more systematic research involves the distinction between more abstract thought and imagery. Most clinicians believe, and I obviously include myself in that group, as is evident from previous chapters, that purely abstract verbalizations in spoken communication and in thought have less emotional and bodily impact than sensory-like images. Remember Mrs. Vogel, whom I described at the start of this book? Had she simply said, "I'm troubled because I believe I'm no longer playing a central role in our family," would that remark have had the same emotional, and ultimately, behavior-changing impact as her dreamlike fantasy image of the Siamese twins, one older and one younger man attached at the hip? We need more research lest we assume that only imagistic thought matters. I would argue—and here I believe I would have the support of Bruner, Epstein, Sternberg, and others emphasizing the importance of logical–sequential and abstract–analytical thought processes—that both forms, the concrete and the abstract, are essential for effective functioning (see also Sadoski & Paivio, 2001).

Perhaps, for therapeutic purposes, the critical issue is one of sequence. The bare verbal statement alone, however widely generalizable and however important the ultimate implications contained in its phrasing, may lack the impact (note how one uses a sensory metaphor) of an imagery representation. Think of the physicists at the secret Los Alamos laboratory during the early 1940s working out the implicit consequences of Einstein's abstract $e = mc^2$ formula. Only when they saw the gigantic mushroom cloud at the first atom bomb test did many, like the project director Robert Oppenheimer, fully appreciate the enormity and world-shaking possibilities of nuclear weapons.

I remember, while stationed in a combat zone in the Philippine Islands, receiving the news of the American atomic bombs dropped on the Japanese cities of Hiroshima and Nagasaki. My fellow intelligence agents and I welcomed this news because it meant that the war might end soon and we would not face the further danger of an invasion of Japan. A few months later, as a member of the first group of U.S. occupation troops traveling on an assignment in Japan, I found myself on a hill overlooking the vast ruins of the city of Hiroshima, and the real meaning of the power of a single nuclear-energy bomb began to penetrate. Even then, I tried, as so many did, to avoid thinking often or in detail about the implications of this event. A few years later, when I was safely a graduate student in America, I read newspaper reports that the Soviet Union had developed its own atom bomb, a potential threat to our country. The image of the ruined Hiroshima recurred to me. That night I had a vivid and elaborate dream that atom bombs had accidentally exploded both in Russia and in America aboard a ship on which I was apparently serving as an officer. Following various adventures, both U.S. and Russian troops threw down their arms and refused to guard atomic weapons installations so that (in my apparent wishful thinking) the abandoning of nuclear armaments would now be negotiated. After that dream, I could sustain an abstract generalization of the danger and world implications of nuclear weaponry, and this generalization has guided my thoughts and some of my political behavior ever since.

In psychotherapy, the specificity of one's memories or of one's fantasies may produce an emotional, bodily impression that convinces clients that a particular area of life needs attention and may be deeply significant. I have proposed that this may be in part because when one is imagining a specific past event or a possible future situation, one temporarily inhabits the context of that event, and one's thoughts are more likely to involve further relevant, perhaps long dissociated, incidents or implications (J. L. Singer, 1974; J. L. Singer & Pope, 1978). In psychoanalytic or cognitive–behavioral therapies, it seems to be critical to establish guiding beliefs, schemas, or scripts and, to some degree, to reconstruct the origins of these in specific earlier experiences or interpretations of these experiences. Following implications in the script theory of Silvan Tomkins (1995), one can diagram the link between specific event memories; their gradual organization into categorical self-schemas as discussed in the beginning of chapter 9; and, eventually, creation of abstract guiding life rules (see Figure 8.1).

In most theories of emotional distress or neurotic behavior, a critical feature of treatment involves identifying and then dispelling the faulty abstractions about relationships or self-schemas that guide actions in particular social domains. At the base of the triangle in Figure 8.1 are sample specific event memories of episodes in one's life that because of repetition or similarities in seeming origins and consequences lead a person to form a nuclear script, an organized belief about oneself in relation to others or to specific situations. From an accumulation of earlier episodes, one may eventually form a categorical belief about oneself and eventually (as at the apex of the triangle) a guiding abstract rule about how one ought to behave. These beliefs can then form a semi-abstract category such as "I'm the kind of person who . . ." or "people expect me to . . . ." With time and some further reinforcements of behavior based on such a categorization, the individual may then unwittingly form a grand abstract generalization or life rule (at the apex of the triangle) such as "one can never really trust people," or (for a woman) "men are only out for one thing," or (for a man) "never show women what you really feel." These guiding beliefs in the various social domains of experience, however they may have originated in actual earlier experiences or in one's often faulty interpretation of particular episodes, may lead to inappropriate or self-defeating behaviors in situations that only superficially resemble the early episodes at the triangle's base.

The experiences and belief systems of a patient of Jefferson Singer are represented in the diagram. This young man, Tom, had early in childhood tried to be helpful and curious in a classroom situation, but when he accidentally broke a pencil his teacher humiliated him before the whole class and made him stay in a clothes closet at the back of the class. This early misadventure became the template against which he measured other unfortunate events in his life so that he accumulated enough episodes to lead to a categorical formulation, "I'm someone who is hurt when I try to be helpful or curious." Then he moved eventually to the formulation of a kind of life rule: "Don't get involved." This led him as an adult to unnecessary isolation or failures to be helpful in situations where such behavior would actually have been valuable for him and appreciated by others (J. A. Singer & Singer, 1992, p. 526).

SPECIFICITY AND THE FORMS OF IMAGINAL THOUGHT

The important feature of imagery usage in both psychodynamic and cognitive–behavioral therapies is that one must assist the patient in producing specific self-defining memories such as Tom's about the classroom episode. Various psychoanalytic "schools" may emphasize the critical importance of memories that date to very early childhood, even the baby and toddler years. Cognitive therapists are less likely to strive for the patient to produce very early childhood memories but will still seek the clusters of specific event memories from any age period if they will help the patient to grasp the source of maladaptive categorical or abstract beliefs. An accumulating body of personality research on narrative identity and meaning formulations through the adult life span has emerged, supporting the critical role for self-understanding and positive development of the ability to evoke specific autobiographical memories and connect these to coherent narrative accounts of one's life (Blagov & Singer, 2004; J. A. Singer, 2004). The usefulness of specific vivid imagery is certainly evident.

I mentioned at the outset of this section two caveats or concerns about the value of imagery in the therapy process. The way that imagery episodes, even when they are painful, can be constructively used is apparent. But what of recurrent unpleasant imagery or ruminative thought that has been associated with depression and posttraumatic stress syndromes (Borkovec, Shadick, & Hopkins, 1991; Nolen-Hoeksema, 2000)? In my own research, with collaborators including John Antrobus and George Huba (Huba, Aneshensel, & Singer, 1981; J. L. Singer & Antrobus, 1972), I developed psychometric scales of imaginal processes and have consistent evidence of three independent dimensions that characterize the ongoing thought of hundreds of individuals. These can be labeled *positive constructive daydreaming*, the generally upbeat, wishful, or planful fantasies of everyday life; *guilty dysphoric fantasy*, images of failed achievement efforts or of hurting intimates or friends; and *poor attentional control*, characterized by much wandering of the mind, fantasies of disaster and catastrophe, and boredom or distractibility. All of these kinds of fantasy styles occur in the thought streams of normal individuals, but the latter two are more likely to be predominant in the consciousness of anxious, obsessive, or depressed persons (J. A. Singer, Singer, & Zittel, 2000).

As I read the research literature, however, and the detailed accounts of the thought processes of depressed individuals, severe neurotics, or borderline personalities, I am impressed that their inner thoughts are characterized mostly by poor attentional control—by verbal phrases of hopelessness, guilt, or anger. They seem, often, to lack the ability to understand the special features of their thought stream, to be unable to apply self-regulation or even detachment to use their mental associations for playfulness, sheer distraction and self-entertainment, or effective planfulness through imagined possible actions. I think again of the children we have observed in pretend play, just learning how to control and vary make-believe worlds, who show again and again greater smiling, joy, curiosity, self-control, and creativity than the children who show little evidence of pretend play (D. Singer & Singer, 1990; see chap. 4). I am strongly inclined to believe that the ruminations and repetitive thoughts of depressives, the chronically anxious, and the obsessed are reflections, in part, of a failure to develop the rich and varied imagery skills that have emerged in our factor analyses as positive constructive daydreaming. My faith in humanity suggests (as I wrote in my first book, *Daydreaming*, in 1966) that daydreaming is a cognitive skill, one that can be developed in favorable childhood circumstances but that we can also train in psychotherapy. My presentation of Sternberg's successful intelligence model (Sternberg, 1999a, 1999b) and Seymour Epstein's constructive thinking approach (outlined both in technical articles and in a popular book entitled *You're Smarter Than You Think*; S. Epstein & Brodsky, 1993), reflects my belief that as therapists we can educate our clients to control their negative thoughts and improve their understanding and skill in using their fundamental human imagery capacity.

An intriguing development in the past 2 decades has been the "discovery" by committed cognitive–behaviorists that effective long-term therapeutic gains of their interventions can be sustained by training patients in mindfulness. Individual tough-minded researchers I know like Alan Marlatt, Zindel Segal, John Teasdale, Timothy Strauman, Jean Kristeller, and, to some degree, Stephen Hayes have all conducted studies and presented positive clinical arguments for therapists to consider variations of mindfulness as a feature of an ongoing therapy. Scott Bishop and collaborators have proposed a unifying operational definition of mindfulness in an impressive paper followed by useful commentaries (Bishop et al., 2004). Mindfulness (in contrast to mindlessness) was first introduced in the 1980s as a potentially constructive feature of psychological consciousness by Ellen Langer (2005). More recently, it has been promoted as an outcome of meditative training by Kabat-Zinn (1993), traceable to ancient Zen Buddhist practices. In discussing the constructive possibilities of imagery, I want chiefly to emphasize that *learned mindfulness skills*, in Bishop et al.'s (2004) terminology, involve a self-regulation of attention, an ability to monitor and to control one's ongoing thought—indeed, a so-called *metacognitive* skill—that implies an understanding and appreciation of one's thought stream. The authors proposed two components to mindfulness, self-regulation of attention and acceptance and openness to experience, which the authors linked to the so-called Big Five personality trait of Openness, to curiosity, and to receptivity toward one's imagery as well as to one's external experiences. In research on the Imaginal Processes Inventory, T. Zhiyan and I (Zhiyan & Singer, 1997) found that the Costa and McCrae (1987) Big Five trait of Openness was indeed correlated with the Positive–Constructive Daydreaming Scale (Zhiyan & Singer, 1997), whereas self-regulation of attention would correspond to our scale of positive mental control. The scale of positive mental control did correlate with the Big Five trait of Conscientiousness. Langer's (2005) recent work demonstrated the links between mindfulness and emergent artistic creativity.

Although mindfulness grew out of a meditation procedure and is still largely trained through meditation, it is possible to regard it, as S. Hayes and Shenk (2004) have done, in more general terms. They proposed a variety of nonmeditative training procedures, some involving imagery, others more purely cognitive, that essentially accomplish some of the goals of mindfulness without relying solely on some of the ritualistic and time-consuming features of mindfulness meditation. The next section considers more concretely ways in which we as therapists can help patients enhance their imagery skills, in part to increase their abilities to use imagery in their treatment but also, as suggested in chapter 9, to increase their intelligence in the practical and creative domains.

HELPING A CLIENT DEVELOP AND IMPROVE IMAGERY

As should be apparent from previous chapters, many patients may initially have difficulty in generating imagery. To some degree, the problems of many patients who are caught up in rumination, obsessive worry, or even hallucinatory experiences stem from a lifelong history of failure to identify imagery in their thought stream, to recognize its occasional random or trivial quality, or to master and guide their imagery, whether for self-entertainment or for effective planning purposes. Research on children has suggested that parental reading, storytelling, and direct play with children fosters imaginative play and early signs of flexible thought and creativity in the young (D. Singer & Singer, 1990, 2005). We cannot assert with certainty from long-term longitudinal research that adult problems with producing imagery in psychotherapy are traceable to early failures of experience with pretend play, but retrospective reports and case studies do suggest this likelihood. There is a further possibility that certain individuals have early on acquired tendencies for what has been called *repressive defensiveness*. They fear that allowing themselves to relax and to experience naturally occurring waking images may lead to an emergence of threatening or frightening memories or experiences of past shames or guilts. They in effect practice avoidant mental activities, focusing on external stimuli, on clichélike thoughts, and on putting aside emerging imagery (Blagov & Singer, 2004; Bonanno & Singer, 1990). As Korn (1983) has written, "Any system or ability that is not nurtured tends to atrophy. When we do not utilize the birthright of imagery experience, we eventually 'forget' the experience entirely" (p. 62).

I believe that *forget* is perhaps too strong a term. Korn himself, by developing a series of exercises for athletes and others seeking to use imagery to enhance physical performance, has implicitly acknowledged that the capacity for imagery may seem absent, but more likely it is dissociated or set aside unwittingly for very limited contexts and hence it can be revived and expanded by overcoming resistances and by training (Korn, 1994; Sheikh & Korn, 1994).

Let me present some examples of how one can help clients who report that they show very little imagery and rarely daydream, or, if they do have speculative thoughts about possible futures, their mental activity seems largely verbal or, at best, extremely lacking in vivid sensory qualities. I draw to a great extent on my own experience but also on the imagery research literature (Korn, 1994; Sheikh & Korn, 1994; J. L. Singer, 1974). I also propose that one outcome of meditation exercises like yoga and mindfulness is that a participant learns to notice, to accept, and to understand the "naturalness" of passing fantasies without either avoidant or overly emotionally involved reactions. A method free of some of the religious baggage of meditation approaches is S. Hayes and Shenk's (2004) acceptance and commitment therapy exercise. Individuals who have trouble with imagery may even try to resolve simple physical problems by expressing them in purely verbal language.

Relaxation

It is apparent that one key to helping a patient capture the imagery experience is a state of relative relaxation. It seems no accident that so many therapy approaches, from the behaviorists' systematic desensitization to the panoply of guided imagery "trips" (Leuner, 1978; J. L. Singer, 1974), begin with some form of relaxation exercise. The most commonly used method that depends predominantly on kinesthetic feedback is the Jacobsen (1938) progressive relaxation technique. On theoretical grounds, the relaxation exercises seem crucial only in relation to Wolpe's (1958) theory of reciprocal inhibition, or *counterconditioning*. In the desensitization method, presumably the degree of relaxation should provide an inhibiting element for the anxiety aroused by the phobic images.

The evidence suggested by the results of van Egeren, Feather, and Hein (1971) and others seems, on the whole, to be contrary to the original notion of the counterconditioning effect of the relaxation. If anything, the data suggest, as Mathews (1971) concluded, that "relaxation may augment both vividness and the autonomic effects of imagery, while at the same time maximizing the response decrement with repeated presentations" (p. 88). In other words, there is some slight support for the fact that there are autonomic changes associated with various relaxation exercises and varieties of autogenic training (Geissman & Noel, 1961), but the task demands of the situation and the relationship to the therapist seem equally crucial. There is also the likelihood that concentration and the reduction of external stimulation that characterize the relaxation instructions produce a situation conducive to the occurrence or awareness of imagery and ongoing daydreaming (Antrobus, 1968; Antrobus, Singer, & Greenberg, 1966).

The demand characteristics of the situation and the attribution process raise serious questions about the specific theory of desensitization in relation to relaxation. At the same time, it seems reasonable to suppose that a major consequence of the relaxation instructions is to establish conditions that enhance attention to one's own ongoing imagery processes. Relaxation should also reduce hyperalertness to external stimulation that would blur the vividness of imagery and overload the visual system, which must handle both imagery derived from long-term memory and incoming stimulation. Wilkins (1971) was inclined to conclude that an attribution model based on the subject's self-perception and relabeling of his or her experience may be more critical in producing reduction of phobic reactions than the inhibition of anxiety by relaxation. The relaxation exercises seem to be part of a gradual introduction of patients to circumstances that allow them to experience their imagery vividly. The relaxation experience permits patients to engage in the imagery under controlled conditions and to become aware that they can indeed confront this situation.

Viewed in this context, then, relaxation exercises appear to be valuable primarily as inducements to the production of imagery and to helping the patient develop a sense of capacity for control over imagery. In addition, the relaxation procedures themselves involve a distraction from the press of external stimulation. Relaxation comes close, in this way, to many of the goals of various meditation exercises. If we ignore the complex superstructure of religious belief and mysticism associated with various approaches to meditation, we can see how systematic attention to one's own breathing, repetition of certain phrases, and the exercises in various forms of meditation may lead to systematic reduction of the external stimuli that have to be processed and also to the reduction of repetitive internal formulas associated with fear and avoidance responses.

In our ordinary waking life, we are often acutely aware of a flood of external information, whether generated by work demands or communications from others or by noises and shifts in temperature, smells, and other sensory signals. We are also subject to awareness of a pressure from unfinished business, or, as studied by Eric Klinger, current concerns that often come to mind as verbal commands to action (Klinger, 1978, 1990a, 1990b). One thinks of the sonnet by William Wordsworth that begins,

> The world is too much with us; late and soon,
> Getting and spending, we lay waste our powers. (Hartman, 1980, p. 172)

Maupin (1965) found evidence that subjects with considerable fantasy capacity and awareness of their own ongoing imagery were most likely to be good candidates for Zen meditation. Furthermore, Linden (1971) found that schoolchildren trained in meditation became more field independent, that is, more capable of ignoring the flood of natural external stimulation.

A more probable value of the relaxation, in addition to its establishment of conditions conducive to imagery and control of thought processes, is that it may also play a role in enhancing alertness to one's ongoing feedback processes from autonomic and muscular systems. This emphasis on the control of autonomic responses and capacity to control brain rhythms, such as the alpha rhythms, has some apparent relationship to relaxation and, in certain subjects, occurrence of imagery as well (Antrobus, Antrobus, & Singer, 1964).

Confronting and Appreciating One's Ongoing Consciousness

It behooves psychotherapists to be attentive to the fact that they can help patients, through relaxation exercises or related methods, to become aware and capable of discriminating among their various affective states (Izard, 1972) and also to become aware of the nature of their ongoing imagery processes. In my own view, it appears unnecessary to include the many elaborate, rather mystical notions drawn from some Asian philosophy or based on pseudoscientific elaborations in order to justify this relatively simple kind of exercise in self-awareness. It is one thing to acknowledge some of the philosophical implications of various ideologies or quasi-religious orientations and to appreciate aesthetically their contributions to art and culture. It is a different matter to overload the already confused client with this kind of superstructure when the processes of self-awareness and behavioral control are grasped relatively easily in relation to reasonably well-defined operations of the imagery and daydreaming capacities with which humans are all endowed.

If it is true that we have available as a basic resource the ongoing processing of our brain, which is actively dealing with a variety of stored materials by a continuous transformation, then the set of attitudes we take toward our own imagery may be a critical factor in ultimate control of this process. One of the major biofeedback methods available to us is a heightened sensitivity to our ongoing fantasy processes. By covert rehearsal, discrimination of different images, and the use of positive images as a distraction and shift away from recurring frightening scenes, there is the likelihood that we can increasingly master our social and physical world through a more effective resort to our storehouse of experience.

For many patients, the first step—realizing that thoughts do not necessarily lead to actions—may be a significant therapeutic entryway. One patient of mine became aware of a series of thoughts that she might harm her children. It was possible to show her that such thoughts came when there were situations with her husband or family that had made her extremely angry. The thoughts reflected her anger rather than any likelihood of overt action against the children. Once realizing this, she was, on the one hand, greatly relieved and, on the other, quicker to ignore such thoughts if they occurred. The patient also learned to use the thoughts as signals that there was something troubling in her interpersonal situation that ought to be addressed. The more frightening notion that she was psychotic and that thoughts were as dangerous as actions (a belief that could be traced back to early childhood experiences in her family setting) was dispelled relatively quickly. This case is a simple example of the combination of an attribution therapy with the development of a cognitive schema for recognizing and regulating thought available to the patient so that she could then assimilate these thoughts more effectively and be less likely to experience distress or negative affect when they occurred.

An important first step, then, in psychotherapeutic application of imagery techniques involves the establishment of conditions in which patients can identify their ongoing streams of thought, perceive them as *egosyntonic*, that is, a natural part of their own development, and learn that they can begin to use, to some extent, the material presented for some type of self-understanding or self-control. This awareness was probably one of the major factors in the attraction to psychoanalysis on the part of so many young intellectuals. The therapist's reinforcement of the recall of dreams and fantasies and the possibility that these could be analyzed were extremely exciting. Indeed, the almost narcissistic gratification associated with extensive examination of one's daily dreams and fantasies may have led to the prolongation of analyses when only limited external improvement was occurring.

As I suggested earlier, the controlled awareness of one's ongoing stream of thought provides an interesting alternative stimulus field, which, because it introduces only moderately complex material, arouses the affect of interest and, as it is examined and reformulated, leads to a reduction of this arousal and the occurrence of the affect of joy (Tomkins, 1962). McGhee (1971), in his review of the development of humor, also seemed to present evidence and increasingly consistent theoretical indications for a position similar to the one I am proposing concerning the combination of the affects of interest and joy in dealing with novel materials of moderate complexity. By its very nature as an extremely diverse processing system, the brain is capable of providing us with a set of outputs that create variety and novelty to an amazing degree. Our attention to these processes, provided we have been prepared for their strangeness and seemingly metaphoric and symbolic qualities, can be an important addition to our behavior repertory.

There are ample indications that persons who have already developed gifts for introspection or for elaborate development of fantasy and imaginative or philosophical thought have been able to tolerate long periods of social isolation reasonably well. A number of significant philosophical works have been composed in prison. One thinks, for example, of Bertrand Russell's productivity during his imprisonment during World War I or Cervantes's composition of *Don Quixote* in prison. A distinguished architect and planner, Herman Field, told me about his prolonged imprisonment as a presumed American agent by the then Communist Czechoslovak government in the 1950s under conditions of severe social and sensory deprivation. He managed to pass the time and resist his captors' efforts to extract a false confession by mentally composing a novel based on his experiences. He also engaged in elaborate imagination of the captors' thoughts and expectations so that he could gradually win certain rights from them, including access to pen and paper.

Helping an "Imageless" Patient Generate and Appreciate Imagery

Supposing a patient tells you that he or she does not experience imagery, that the pictures or sounds in the "mind's eye" or "mind's ear" are too vague or lack vividness, or even that all thinking is purely in verbal sentences or abstractions. I have encountered such individuals occasionally in treatment. Surveys year after year in my large undergraduate classes generally turned up less than a tenth of students reporting such lack of imagery. In one instance, a graduate student, now an influential researcher and clinician, reported that all his thought was in verbal sentences. A fellow student of his who later became a prominent contributor to imagery in therapy studies, volunteered to work informally with him. Within a couple of months the first student began to experience imagery and came to see that his earlier "lack" of this ability was partly a result of his extreme demands for camera-like vividness and partly a consequence of his personality trait of repressive defensiveness.

One can approach a therapy client who makes the claim of lacking imagery by first asking for a few "easy" memories, drawn from that day's events, "What was breakfast like?"; "Who was encountered at work?"; or, the classic imagery research question, "How many windows are there in your apartment or house?" Some imagery will almost usually emerge, because, for example, unless you have recently ordered new shades or drapes for every window, you're not likely to have ever counted your windows and stored the number in your memory. To answer the question you must mentally stroll from room to room picturing the windows in each.

A next step, still focusing on memory images, would involve recall of recent or even early vacations, trips to museums or classical music or rock concerts, parties, or other positive events. Gradually, more vivid and specific event memories may emerge. Recall of films or TV programs may work well also. One can then encourage fantasies of possible future events and their various consequences. The use of more fanciful "imagery trips" in the pattern of the European guided waking dream approach can follow with selected clients (J. L. Singer, 1974). For many purposes, in the more focused cognitive therapies, it may be sufficient to practice new future responses in different variations.

The considerable power of covert rehearsal has been supported in some careful experiments by McFall and Twentyman (1973) in studying so complex a behavior as assertiveness. It is likely that many of the important benefits accruing from a variety of mental imagery techniques, as well as behavior modification methods, relate to the fact that conditions have been established whereby the patient not only can identify more clearly a specific area of difficulty and can entertain it mentally but then is provided with a certain amount of "coaching" (McFall & Twentyman, 1973) in the form of suggested alternative behaviors, which can be used in both covert and overt rehearsal to modify behavior.

A closer scrutiny of the rambling, somewhat romantic, or seemingly mystical character of many mental imagery techniques may indicate that their effectiveness depends on the following:

1. The patients can discriminate more clearly their own ongoing fantasy processes.
2. They can get some clues from the therapist as to alternative ways of approaching these situations.
3. They can become aware within this area of imagery situations that they have avoided.
4. They are encouraged in a variety of fashions to engage in covert rehearsal of alternatives.
5. They ultimately are less afraid to make overt approaches to these situations.

Associated with these activities is an increase in the generally positive affective state. The novelty of the fantasy activity, the sense of mastery of difficult situations, the joy of recognition when symbolic material can be translated into recognizable current interpersonal dilemmas—all of these lead to increased positive affect and a sense of self-control.

Opening the Way to Greater Vividness and Creativity

I have thus far emphasized helping patients overcome their seemingly limited potential for or aversion to sensory-like imagery in the visual, auditory, tactile, gustatory, and olfactory domains. Using relaxation and memory images works well with most patients for the cognitive–behavioral approaches as described in chapter 8. However, there is good evidence that many of the complexities of our lives are continuously retrieved and reshaped in novel storytelling, metaphoric, and symbolic forms in our conscious thought streams as daydreams or in the ongoing mentation we engage in during sleep. Freud became one of the most famous scientists of the 20th century because he opened the way for thousands of patients as well as novelists, playwrights, critics, and historians to recognize how interesting and seemingly meaningful their nocturnal dreams could be. It would take us too far afield to go into the research literature on night dreaming at this point, but let me mention some ways in which calling attention to dreamlike experiences can be helpful to clients.

Many patients who at first claim they have little imagery can be encouraged to keep track of their night dreams. At first some will claim they never dream at all. If they are encouraged to lie quietly on a regular basis when they awaken in the morning, or if by chance they are awakened during the later hours of sleep, when the sleep cycle is characterized by more time spent in the rapid eye movement, Stage 1 phase, they will certainly remember vivid dreams. We know from sleep mentation research how replete our dreams are with visual imagery and story characteristics. Once patients are aware of these naturally occurring phenomena, they become more willing to use imagery in cognitive as well as psychodynamic treatment.

I do not wish to argue here that dream interpretation is, as psychoanalysts once believed, a critical feature of the therapeutic process, Freud's "royal road to the unconscious." As interesting as our dreams are, I believe that they were "oversold" for treatment purposes. There seems to be little research evidence of dream interpretation having specific value in producing symptom relief or personality change. There are many practitioners who can report anecdotes in which a patient's reexperiencing and narrating a dream in a therapy session yielded important insights and the excitement of discovery, which hastened behavior change. Certainly this appeared to be the case for my patient with the "transference dream" of confronting her mother in the office of the "goat-therapist" (described in chap. 7). If one's goal in having patients keep track of their dreams and link them to current concerns, unfinished intentions, and the odd thoughts of the previous day (Freud's "day residues") is primarily personality study, then dreams can be useful. If one's goal is personality change or symptom reduction, spending much time on dream interpretation, however intriguing, may not be an efficient use of the limited time and expense of psychotherapy. Too often dream interpretations seem more like asking patients to look at inkblots or thematic apperception cards and to produce associations that may bear little relation to either the patients' early childhood or to the "unconscious."

I realize that my position may seem shocking to therapists trained in a psychoanalytic perspective. I am myself someone who recalls dreams regularly and, at my age, when one must urinate more frequently during the night, often several dreams for every night's sleep. My dreams can be very interesting, colorful, and also troubling, but they are generally easily related to current concerns about members of my family, issues relating to my psychological role and aspirations as a recent retiree, and to the inevitable fears of some loss of my physical and mental powers because of my advanced age. What is most striking about my dreams is the extent to which they draw on my waking fantasies, the metaphors I have used in my recent stream of thought, movies or TV shows seen recently, and books or articles read in previous days. They generally are formed into interesting narratives, an indication of the creativity with a small c that researchers in creativity describe. Well-prepared artists, writers, or scientists may occasionally use dreams or waking fantasies as starting points for significant big-C creative achievements, but one must be really expert in a domain for such occurrences to yield actual creative achievements (Sternberg, Grigorenko, & Singer, 2004).

For our purposes in this chapter, I simply encourage clinicians faced with clients who have trouble generating imagery to alert the patients to become more aware of their night dreams, which we know are vivid and frequent. One can also then encourage patients to try to generate waking dreams—shutting their eyes and allowing the reverberatory nature of their natural thought stream to operate, as was the case with Mrs. Vogel and her Siamese twins image.

An instance from my own practice involving a middle-aged woman I'll call Mrs. Renfrew exemplifies the use of guided waking dreams in fostering more imagery use and in circumventing a repetitious, difficult verbalization pattern. Mrs. Renfrew, the wife of a distinguished scientist, was referred to me by a physicians' group because she was perceived by the doctors as a hypochondriac, constantly returning with a variety of physical complaints for which they could find no medical basis. This intelligent, well-educated woman during session after session recounted her list of body aches and pains along with a list of increasingly disabling phobias. One could see in a few sessions why her various doctors were exasperated by her recounting of her numerous visits to different physicians, her detailing of symptoms, and her inability to generate more than some abstractions about her personal history or her relationships.

I confess that I experienced a mounting frustration and contemplated suggesting that Mrs. Renfrew move on to another therapist. Instead, I decided to level with her and to present my concerns. I also suggested that we try a different approach, a form of the European guided imagery therapy in which patients, after a relaxation exercise, imagine that they are walking in a meadow, climbing a hill, or following a stream. Mrs. Renfrew, who had appreciated my candor and my obvious eagerness to help her, agreed to try. After using the Jacobsen (1938) relaxation procedure, with eyes shut she imagined herself to be in a meadow and allowed herself to experience a series of images in which she walked through fields, noticed the flowers and their colors, and from time to time encountered strangers who shared her appreciation of the beauty of the nature settings. After a few sessions of such "trips," Mrs. Renfrew reported feeling increasingly refreshed, and we both were surprised by the vividness of her imagery, her sensitivity to color and shape, the nuances of light at different times of day in these fields and forests. This woman suddenly seemed more "alive." The robotic recitals of doctors' visits and ailments ceased, and she began to talk of her childhood and adolescent love of nature and art. She mentioned the Impressionist paintings of Monet, such as his series of haystacks. Her memories led her to remember how she had (surprisingly, like the aforementioned Mrs. Vogel) majored in art history, and she realized that she had let those interests slide once she married her energetic and research-inspired husband. She began to recognize a kind of yearning to find a way to create some sort of art career. In her travels with her husband to various science meetings, she had collected large numbers of slides of paintings and sculptures from around the world, and she thought she might start out by giving lectures to senior citizen groups. She consulted a famous art historian at the university and mapped out a plan. The problem, of course, was her phobias; she was too anxious to drive or to walk alone on city streets and was moderately agoraphobic. It became possible to use more structured cognitive and behavior therapy methods to help her with these fears, because she was much more open to using her imagery as part of the process. With systematic desensitization, exposure treatment, and covert modeling, she was able to move about more freely, to give the art lectures at senior citizen centers, and to arrange personal meetings with local artists. After 2 years of therapy that also included some analysis of interpersonal issues in her current life situation, Mrs. Renfrew began to build a career as an agent for artists and opened a small gallery to exhibit modern painting and sculpture. It was gratifying to me as her former therapist to receive notes in the mail about some of the exhibits she organized and especially to meet her occasionally at university-sponsored social events or in local department stores or shops. The whole issue of her physical ailments seemed to have faded.

In summary, it should be clear that our human capacity for imagery can be unlocked through recourse to specific memories and the encouragement of awareness of one's nocturnal or waking dream experiences. Such imagery can then become a useful tool in cognitive and behavioral therapies as well as in the exploration of a client's relevant interpersonal transactions. Sheikh, Sheikh, and Moleski (1994) have brought together a whole series of methods and some supporting research that document many ways to help clients develop and heighten their effective awareness, vividness, and uses of imagery. These include some of the methods I have already mentioned as well as other techniques, some drawn from ancient Buddhist or yoga approaches, many based on fundamental psychological research on concentration, awareness of one's breathing, one's sensory experiences, and one's stream of consciousness. These range from having clients pretend to be reporters describing news events or scientists describing what they see under microscopes or in tropical rain forests to manipulating colored cubes mentally and describing their colors on different sides. I would add to their suggestions by encouraging clients to become aware of the vast numbers of images that make up our linguistic resource of metaphors, as Lakoff and Johnson (2003) have shown, imagining a person "busy as a bee" or using Shakespeare's great supply. Think of *King Lear* and phrases like "sharper than a serpent's tooth it is to have a thankless child," or "as flies to wanton boys are we to the gods, they kill us for their sport." Phrases we take for granted, like "a stitch in time saves nine," can become sources of vivid imagery and alert clients to their own capacity for imagination.

THE IMPORTANCE OF THE CLINICIAN'S IMAGERY

One of the rewards of the career of a psychotherapist is the opportunity to peer into the lives of strangers, to imagine the settings from which they have come, to picture their fantasies or the situations in which some of their beliefs or family myths developed. Curiosity alone cannot be a sufficient rationale for undertaking the often lonely life of the mental health worker. It would lead only to a prurient voyeurism if there were not also motives of helping the suffering and, as in Freud's case, contributing to the science of mental life. Can a therapist be effective, however, without the ability to construct sensory-like representations of the events and experiences reported by a client?

At a recent symposium during the 2004 Convention of the American Psychological Association I heard four clinicians who were also researchers on the psychotherapy process discuss the objectives and limitations of the use of very strict treatment manuals as features of empirically assessed therapies (Goodhart, Levant, Westen, & Wampold, 2004). A beginning therapist following such a set of instructions might indeed provide guidance to a patient with a specific phobia or a difficulty in assertiveness without having to engage in imagining much about the patient's life events, social situations, or fantasies. The research evidence presented makes it clear that the great majority of clients seeking help suffer from multiple symptoms. In such cases, a sequential application of different manualized therapies would seem to be called for. Because many patients also show personality difficulties, these would necessitate attention by the therapist to their clients' life stories or to their social relationships. If psychotherapy could be dispensed only through manuals or by provision of specific medications, who would be attracted to professions like clinical psychology or psychiatry?

A fascinating study reexamined the well-known results of the National Institute of Mental Health's study comparing interpersonal, cognitive, clinically managed medication, and clinically managed placebo treatments of depression in a randomized clinical trial (Blatt, Sanislow, Zuroff, & Pilkonis, 1996). Blatt and his colleagues focused on the contributions and effectiveness of the therapists rather than on either the treatment techniques or the patient characteristics. They found that the therapists who had the greatest positive impact on the improvement of the depressed patients were more psychologically minded, less interested in purely biological interventions in their own practice, and more likely to expect psychotherapy to have a longer duration. These findings cut across the specific treatments with indications that the qualities of the therapists make a difference even in the "medication with clinical management" conditions. The authors called attention to the fact that although the psychologist therapists generally obtained the best outcomes, the single most effective treater was a female psychiatrist working either with imipramine medication or with placebo whose clinical management consisted of offering a psychologically supportive approach including optimism, sensitivity, reassurance, and hope. Although we need many more studies like this, it seems likely to me that efficacious therapy is dependent on a therapist's personal qualities of attentiveness, optimism, and ability to use his or her psychological mindedness and imagery capacity in work with the client.

Though there are few systematic data on the imagery styles of psychotherapists, it is probably that persons who choose the profession are strongly inclined toward imaginative thought. Still, there may be would-be therapists who have not fully developed their skills in imagery or who may overuse such skills indiscriminately with little effort to match their own mental representations to those of the client. Let us turn, then, to a brief consideration of how therapists can best use their imagery in the service of a client and also identify situations in which imagery may have negative countertransferential implications.

As Freud soon came to recognize once he had identified the phenomenon of transference, there is a real possibility that the same problems that lead to a patient's distortions of beliefs about the therapist and significant others in his or her life may also beset a therapist, resulting in countertransference with respect to a client. I was once supervising a therapist who was a candidate in a psychoanalytic institute. This individual often spoke of his early scholastic difficulties, his graduation from a relatively unprestigious college and graduate school, and his feeling that he was unappreciated even now in his postdoctoral institute. One could picture the well-known comedian Rodney Dangerfield and his signature complaint, "I get no respect!"

As it turned out, the patient referred to him for treatment was a graduate student in psychology from a nationally respected university where admission to clinical psychology training was extremely competitive. One day the young patient, who was a few minutes late for his therapy hour, began talking at once about his distress when he couldn't fully grasp a technical concept in statistics necessary for his research. He had begun to relate his strong emotional reaction to an earlier experience of humiliation by a sibling when the therapist interrupted him by saying, "Why are you so angry with me today?" The patient was confused and said, "I'm not angry." The therapist persisted, mentioning the lateness for the session, which was actually just a few minutes and easily attributable to a traffic tie-up. The patient, after explaining, started again on the troubling issue in his current situation at school, but again the therapist accused him of avoiding facing his strong feelings of anger toward the therapist. The patient now said,

> I don't see what you're getting at, but I am annoyed now. I came in really troubled about something which I wanted to share with you and get some help with but you seem certain I was angry. Well, maybe I'll explore my anger but I really was distressed about this problem about my research and how I might have overreacted because my older brother used to make fun of my schoolwork.

I explored the situation further with the therapist as we listened again to the recorded session. It became clear that the therapist's own imagery as he listened to this bright young patient talking about the complex statistical problem reflected his own confusion about statistics and research; his resentment of his young client, whom he had pictured as "this snotty nerd snob"; and his envy over the elite school whose "ivy" doors, as he imagined them, were shut to him. Clearly, the therapist had projected his own anger onto this young man who had entered the session obviously trusting the therapist and eager for his help, not in statistics but in the persisting personal problem that had evoked an emotional overreaction.

Another form of countertransference one can observe was reviewed in an article that my colleagues and I published some years ago (J. L. Singer, Sincoff, & Kolligian, 1989). We explored the broader literature on the phenomenon but also called attention to the ways in which one's theoretical orientation, inculcated often with the intensive training of an institution, may lead one's imagery in a direction that misses the simple reality of a situation. In one instance, a client who was doing well in treatment and was very appreciative brought the analyst a Christmas fruitcake, only then to be queried intensively about why this particular gift. Was she implying the therapist was crazy (a "fruitcake") or a homosexual (a "fruit," then a widely used term)? The well-meaning patient pleaded that she baked fruit-cakes for all her most important friends at Christmastime. Clearly, this therapist was caught up too much in the theoretical necessity of exploring possible transferences and lacked the imagination to recognize a simple gift.

Often problems arise because the therapist has not taken the extra steps of trying to capture the particular culture of a given patient or has not taken the trouble to explore in reading or in direct inquiry of the patient special features of a client's social, cultural, or religious background. In my own practice, I found it of great value to explore in various ways the settings to which my patients referred and to look up issues of culture to which they seemed attached. Sometimes this meant asking patients to provide more detailed descriptions of their childhood homes, neighborhoods, or schools. Because my clients, before coming to New York or Connecticut, had grown up in many different places, this was a matter of persisting concern as I tried in my imagery to follow a narrative about family relations or traumatic events in places as disparate as What Cheer in Iowa, Teheran in Iran, Bakersfield in California, Parkersburg in West Virginia, or Savannah in Georgia. I was privately amused by the disproportionate number of my patients who hailed from the many small cities of Ohio and would often smile as I thought of the song in a Broadway musical, *Wonderful Town*, with the lyrics, "Why, oh why, oh why, oh/Did I ever leave Ohio?"

Obviously no therapist can be well traveled and well read enough to be able to imagine vividly the scenes patients describe that have occurred in homes in Massillon, Ohio, or an Armenian refugee church in Damascus, Syria. Still, travel and a wide reading of literature can ease the task for clinicians and avoid the provincialism of mentally setting patients' accounts in one's own background of Flatbush in Brooklyn, Pacific Grove in California, or Highland Park near Chicago. We must level with our clients and ask their help when it seems useful to them so that we are able to mentally characterize the neighborhood or cultural setting they describe.

Can we as clinicians ever share our images or fantasies with our clients? I believe that one must be circumspect about such efforts lest we inflict our countertransferences and personal quirkinesses on people seeking our help for their dilemmas and relationship difficulties. In a gem of a book, the interpersonal psychoanalysts Edward Tauber and Maurice Green (1959) examined the fleeting imagery and barely conscious thoughts in the ongoing experience of a psychoanalyst. They pointed to situations in which it may be useful to share one's imaginings with a client, subject, however, to careful introspection about one's own transference distortions.

Here is an example from my own experience that reflects Tauber and Green's (1959) approach to clinicians' uses of their imagery with patients. A young man who was ordinarily articulate and likely to begin talking of significant issues in his life opened a session slowly with much starting and stopping. Then he talked of recent basketball scores and the likelihood that his favorite team would get to the playoffs. He slowed down and then started talking again in a hesitant fashion of some recent news events, mostly the doings of celebrities one reads about in supermarket checkout counter newspapers or magazines. As he slowed down again, a vivid image came to my mind. It was of a giant Galapagos Island tortoise, slowly moving along under its large black shell. I thought for a few moments about this image and decided that it was not reflective of personal problems but rather of my immediate experience of the patient's hesitancy and, probably, evasion and defensiveness. I then interrupted him to tell him of the picture that had come to me as he spoke. He was momentarily taken aback and then laughed. "You're right," he said.

> Something happened to me today that was very shameful and humiliating. As I was on my way to your office I realized that I should tell you about it and try to make sense of the situation. But then I was too embarrassed, and when I walked into the office I saw you and I just couldn't bring myself to talk about it the way I ordinarily would. You must have felt like I was shuffling along like a big turtle.

He then was able to recount the awkward incident and to explore in the session why he had allowed himself to become involved in it.

In summary, our imaginative potential can become useful to us as therapists for grasping the details of patients' narratives, for occasionally identifying their false beliefs or self-defeating schemas or scripts, and also for helping patients overcome their hesitancies and defensive evasions. We must constantly be on guard against our own countertransferential tendencies, and for therapists no longer subject to supervision, regular meetings to review cases with colleagues in small groups may be a valuable and indeed an ethical procedure. Finally, let me again assert my belief that with the proper controls against prurience or exploitation, the excitement of learning about the lives and inner thoughts of people from all walks of life is an important reward in the practice of all forms of psychotherapy.

IMAGERY'S ROLE IN ENHANCING PERSONAL CREATIVITY AND AESTHETIC APPRECIATION

In closing, I have tried to suggest throughout this volume how what I, as a secular humanist, still refer to as the "evolutionary miracle of human imagery" can not only enrich the psychotherapy treatment process but also the extramural personal lives of both patients and therapists. I refer to the likelihood that the increased awareness of imagery and willingness to use it on the part of the patient as a consequence of its effective use in the treatment may also open up a new aesthetic dimension for many persons who have, in the past, ignored the variety and colorful quality of private experiences. This can include enhanced creativity. By *creativity* I do not necessarily mean the capacity to produce a great work of art or science. There are many creative ways of relating in normal human interaction, which can be heightened by sensitivity to fantasy and the transformations of dreams or daydreams. Just the ability to use imagery in expressing oneself or the possibility of mentally trying out a variety of unusual alternatives prior to some social situation may lead to a unique or interesting approach by the patient in that new situation. Here we deal with the kind of creativity also fostered by someone like Gordon (1961) in his development of *synectics*—an approach particularly oriented toward scientists and engineers to help them develop original orientations to problem solutions.

Self-disclosure in imagery form can also be a meaningful way of communicating with another person and suggesting deeper feeling. Remember the song "You Tell Me Your Dream, I'll Tell You Mine"? The awareness of imagery and greater control in the use of one's own daydreams and fantasies make it possible for a subtler appreciation of many aspects of art and culture.

Much of the significant literature in Western civilization has been produced by introspective individuals who, in poetry, fiction, or philosophical essays, have paid considerable attention to their own ongoing streams of thought. The person whose sensitivity to imagery has been deepened will more quickly experience the shock of recognition and the associated affect of joy in reading material from many of the great classic writers as well as the sensitive new novelists or poets. Much of the world's art represents either in fairly direct or abstract form some attempt to capture private experience and present it in a form that is reasonably recognizable to members of a particular culture. Greater sensitivity to one's own imagery will increase awareness of what painters or sculptors may have been striving to communicate as drawn from their own experience.

Much humor is closely related to taboo subjects such as sex or excretory functions. The greatest humor, however, has a somewhat different orientation and is built more on an arousal of an expectation and then a shift from it, sometimes even with a hint of sadness—recall the Charles Addams cartoon of the lone unicorn gazing wistfully after the departing Noah's ark. Wild shifts of focus, such as those appearing in some of the Charlie Chaplin or Woody Allen movies, represent similar examples of play with divergent processes leading to a situation that is humorous by its very dramatic shift from a conventional expectation. For the person not much given to playing with his or her own thoughts and fantasies, some of this kind of humor will not seem at all funny. It will, if anything, seem so complex as to arouse some fear or a startle reaction without any opportunity to match this up against one's own previous established schema for outlandish thoughts. The more active fantasizer, given to playing with a variety of possibilities in his or her own thoughts, will be more prepared for the wild shift of focus of a great comedian and, although startled momentarily by the shift, can then make a connection and reduce the aroused condition so that the experience of joy or laughter follows.

In Chaplin's *Modern Times*, the little tramp sees a red flag fall off a passing construction truck. He picks it up and runs after the truck, waving. Suddenly a Communist parade comes around the corner just behind him, and since he seems to be leading the procession, he becomes embroiled in a melee with the waiting police. In Woody Allen's *Bananas*, the hero, under pursuit from police, inadvertently picks up a cross-shaped tire tool and joins a religious procession that is passing, thus managing to avoid detection. The scene is funny in its own right, but even funnier if one can make the additional match to the Chaplin scene before it, which Allen clearly had in mind.

Our ability to generate imagery goes well beyond the appreciation of humor. It is central to the ways in which we make sense of our world more generally. It opens the way to creative thought and action either in the modest ways of effective ordinary life, as Robert Sternberg's research on successful intelligence demonstrates (see chap. 9), or in the significant new productions of artists and scientists, as the research of Michelle and Robert Root-Bernstein demonstrates. As Silvan Tomkins, my favorite psychological theorist, has written,

> Afferent sensory information is not directly transformed into a conscious report. What is consciously perceived is *imagery* which is created by the organism itself. The world we perceive is a dream we learn to have from a script we have not written. (Tomkins, 1962, p. 13)

Our imaginative world, as Tomkins suggested, is as real to us as humans as the broader outside world described by physicists and biologists. It goes beyond just making cognitive sense of our immediate surroundings or our memories of past events. Because of the continuous representation of our experiences to us in our waking and dreaming stream of consciousness we continue to try to organize and reshape the sometimes seemingly random conjunctions of memories and novel connections. If we are sensitive to them and motivated to use them to change our lives, the creativity they generate may often help us in our personal relationships as well as helping the specially gifted to produce novels, poems, works of art, or scientific discoveries. As clinicians, through our uses of imagery we can teach our clients new ways of dealing with their problems and new strengths for effective living, and we professionals can also gain from this effort. In the words attributed to Socrates by Plato:

> Beloved Pan and all you other gods who haunt this place, give me beauty in the inward soul; and may the outward and the inward person be at one. (Plato, *Phaedrus*)

REFERENCES

Abelson, R. P. (1981). Psychological status of the script concept. *American Psychologist, 36,* 715–729.

Ahern, D. K. (1981). Operant conditioning of heart rate increases with partial experimental control of respiration. *Dissertation Abstracts International, 42*(3-B), 1221–1222.

Angyal, A. (1965). *Neurosis and treatment: A holistic theory.* New York: Wiley.

Ansbacher, H. L., & Ansbacher, R. R. (Eds.). (1970). *The individual psychology of Alfred Adler.* New York: Basic Books.

Antrobus, J. S. (1968). Information theory and stimulus-independent thought. *British Journal of Psychology, 59,* 432–430.

Antrobus, J. S. (1993). Thinking away and ahead. In H. Morowitz & J. L. Singer (Eds.), *The mind, the brain, and complex adaptive systems* (pp. 155–174). New York: Addison-Wesley.

Antrobus, J. S. (1999). Toward a neurocognitive processing model of imaginal thought. In J. A. Singer & P. Salovey (Eds.), *At play in the fields of consciousness: Essays in honor of Jerome L. Singer* (pp. 3–28). Mahwah, NJ: Erlbaum.

Antrobus, J. S., Antrobus, J., & Singer, J. L. (1964). Eye movements accompanying daydreaming, visual imagery, and thought suppression. *Journal of Abnormal and Social Psychology, 69,* 244–252.

Antrobus, J. S., Singer, J. L., & Greenberg, S. (1966). Studies in the stream of consciousness. *Perceptual and Motor Skills, 23,* 399–417.

Ashem, B., & Donner, L. (1968). Covert sensitization with alcoholics: A controlled replication. *Behaviour Research and Therapy, 6,* 7–12.

Avants, K., Margolin, A., & Singer, J. L. (1994). Self-reevaluation therapy: A cognitive intervention for the chemically dependent patient. *Psychology of Addictive Behaviors, 8,* 214–222.

Baars, B. (1988). Momentary forgetting as a "resetting" of a conscious global workspace due to the competition between incompatible contexts. In M. J. Horowitz (Ed.), *Psychodynamics and cognition* (pp. 269–293). Chicago: University of Chicago Press.

Baars, B. (1997). *In the theater of consciousness: The workspace of the mind.* New York: Oxford University Press.

Bakan, D. (1966). *The duality of human existence.* Chicago: Rand McNally.

Bakan, P. (1969). Hypnotizability, laterality of eye-movements and functional brain asymmetry. *Perceptual and Motor Skills, 28,* 927–932.

Bandura, A. (1977). Self-efficacy: Toward a unifying theory of behavioral change. *Psychological Review, 84,* 191–215.

Bandura, A. (1982). Self-efficacy mechanism in human agency. *American Psychologist, 37,* 122–147.

Bandura, A. (1986). Fearful expectations and avoidant actions as coeffects of perceived self-inefficacy. *American Psychologist, 41,* 1389–1391.

Barlow, D. H., Leitenberg, H., & Agras, W. S. (1969). Experimental control of sexual deviation through manipulation of the noxious scene in covert sensitization. *Journal of Abnormal Psychology, 74,* 596–601.

Bauer, J. J., & McAdams, D. P. (2004). Personal growth in adults' stories of life transitions. *Journal of Personality, 72,* 573–602.

Beck, A. T. (1967). *Depression: Clinical, experimental, and theoretical aspects.* New York: Harper & Row.

Beck, A. T. (1976). *Cognitive therapy and the emotional disorders.* New York: International Universities Press.

Beck, A. T., & Emery, G. (1985). *Anxiety disorders and phobias: A cognitive perspective.* New York: Basic Books.

Beck, A. T., Rush, A. J., Shaw, B. F., & Emery, G. (1979). *Cognitive therapy of depression.* New York: Guilford Press.

Beck, A. T., Steer, R. A., Epstein, N., & Brown, G. (1990). Beck Self-Concept Test. *Psychological Assessment, 2,* 191–197.

Betts, G. H. (1909). *Distribution and functions of mental imagery.* New York: Columbia University Press.

Beutler, L. E. (2004). The empirically supported treatments movement: A scientist–practitioner's response. *Clinical Psychology: Science and Practice, 11,* 225–229.

Bishop, S., Lau, M., Shapiro, S., Carlson, L., Anderson, N., Carmody, J., et al. (2004). Mindfulness: A proposed operational definition. *Clinical Psychology, 11,* 230–241.

Blagov, P. S., & Singer, J. A. (2004). Four dimensions of self-defining memories (specificity, meaning, content, and affect) and their relationships to self-restraint, distress, and repressive defensiveness. *Journal of Personality, 72,* 481–512.

Blatt, S. (1990). Interpersonal relatedness and self definition: Two personality configurations and their implications for psychopathology and psychotherapy. In J. L. Singer (Ed.), *Repression and dissociation* (pp. 299–335). Chicago: University of Chicago Press.

Blatt, S. J., Auerbach, J. S., & Levy, K. N. (1997). Mental representations in personality development, psychopathology, and the therapeutic process. *Review of General Psychology, 1,* 351–374.

Blatt, S. J., Sanislow, C. A., III, Zuroff, D. C., & Pilkonis, P. A. (1996). Characteristics of effective therapists: Further analyses of data from the National Institute of Mental Health Treatment of Depression Collaborative Research Program. *Journal of Consulting and Clinical Psychology, 64,*1276–1284.

Blatt, S., & Schichman, S. (1983). Two primary configurations of psychopathology. *Psychoanalysis and Contemporary Thought, 6,* 187–254.

Blatt, S. J., Straynor, D. A., Auerbach, J. S., & Behrends, R. S. (1996). Change in object and self-representations in long-term, intensive, inpatient treatment of seriously disturbed adolescents and young adults. *Psychiatry, 59,* 82–107.

Bogen, J. E. (1995a). On the neurophysiology of consciousness: I. An overview. *Consciousness and Cognition, 4,* 52–62.

Bogen, J. E. (1995b). On the neurophysiology of consciousness: II. Constraining the semantic problem. *Consciousness and Cognition, 4,* 137–158.

Bonanno, G. A., & Singer, J. L. (1990). Repressive personality style: Theoretical and methodological implications for health and pathology. In J. L. Singer (Ed.), *Repression and dissociation* (pp. 435–470). Chicago: University of Chicago Press.

Borelli, J. L., & David, D. H. (2003–2004). Attachment theory and research as a guide to psychotherapy practice. *Imagination, Cognition and Personality, 23,* 257–288.

Borkovec, T. D., Shadick, R., & Hopkins, M. (1991). The nature of normal and pathological worry. In R. Rapee & D. H. Barlow (Eds.), *Chronic anxiety: Generalized anxiety disorder and mixed anxiety–depression* (pp. 29–51). New York: Guilford Press.

Bornstein, R. F. (2001). The impending death of psychoanalysis. *Psychoanalytic Psychology, 18,* 2–20.

Bower, G. H. (1990). Awareness, the unconscious, and repression: An experimental psychologist's perspective. In J. L. Singer (Ed.), *Repression and dissociation* (pp. 209–231). Chicago: University of Chicago Press.

Bowlby, J. (1988). *A secure base: Parent–child attachment and healthy human development.* London: Routledge.

Bransford, J. (1993). The Jasper Series: Theoretical foundations and data on problem solving and transfer. In L. A. Penner & G. M. Batsche (Eds.), *The challenge in mathematics and science education: Psychology's response* (pp. 113–152). Washington, DC: American Psychological Association.

Breger, L., & McGaugh, J. L. (1965). Critique and reformulation of "learning-theory" approaches to psychotherapy and neurosis. *Psychological Bulletin, 63,* 338–358.

Broadbent, D. (1958). *Perception and communication.* Oxford, England: Pergamon Press.

Bruner, J. (1986). *Actual minds, possible worlds.* Cambridge, MA: Harvard University Press.

Cantor, N., & Kihlstrom, J. F. (1987). *Personality and social intelligence.* Englewood Cliffs, NJ: Prentice-Hall.

Carlson, R. (1981). Studies in script theory: I. Adult analogs of a childhood nuclear scene. *Journal of Personality and Social Psychology, 40,* 501–510.

Cautela, J. R. (1966). Treatment of compulsive behavior by covert sensitization. *Psychological Record, 16,* 33–41.

Cautela, J. R. (1967). Covert sensitization. *Psychological Reports, 20,* 459–468.

Cautela, J. R. (1970a). Covert negative reinforcement. *Journal of Behavior Therapy and Experimental Psychiatry, 1,* 273–278.

Cautela, J. R. (1970b). Covert reinforcement. *Behavior Therapy, 1,* 33–50.

Cautela, J. R. (1970c). Treatment of smoking by covert sensitization. *Psychological Reports, 26,* 415–420.

Cautela, J. R. (1971). Covert extinction. *Behavior Therapy, 2,* 192–200.

Cautela, J. R. (1976). Covert response cost. *Psychotherapy: Theory, Research and Practice, 13,* 397–404.

Chalmers, D. J. (1996). *The conscious mind: In search of a fundamental theory.* New York: Oxford University Press.

Chappell, M. N., & Stevenson, T. I. (1936). Group psychological training in some organic conditions. *Mental Hygiene, 20,* 588–597.

Chen, A. C. (1991). Cognitive neuropsychophysiology of thought imagery versus imagination imagery. *International Journal of Neuroscience, 60,* 65–77.

Christianson, S. A. (Ed.). (1992). *The handbook of emotion and memory.* Hillsdale, NJ: Erlbaum.

Ciba Foundation. (1993). *Ciba Foundation Symposium: No. 174. Experimental and theoretical studies of consciousness.* Chichester, England: Wiley.

Costa, P. T., & McRae, R. R. (1985). *The NEO Personality Inventory manual.* Odessa, FL: Psychological Assessment Resources.

Costa, P. T., & McCrae, R. R. (1987). On the need for longitudinal evidence and multiple measures in behavioral-genetic studies of adult personality. *Behavioral and Brain Sciences, 10,* 22–23.

Crits-Christoph, P., & Singer, J. L. (1980). Imagery in cognitive–behavior therapy: Research and application. *Clinical Psychology Review, 1,* 19–32.

Crits-Christoph, P., & Singer, J. L. (1983). An experimental investigation of the use of positive imagery in the treatment of phobias. *Imagination, Cognition and Personality, 3,* 305–323.

Cunningham, W. A., Preacher, K. J., & Banaji, M. R. (2001). Implicit attitude measures: Consistency, stability, and convergent validity. *Psychological Science, 121,* 163–170.

Davidson, J. E., & Sternberg, R. J. (1984). The role of insight in intellectual giftedness. *Gifted Child Quarterly, 28,* 58–64.

de Silva, P. (1986). Obsessional–compulsive imagery. *Behaviour Research and Therapy, 24,* 333–350.

Dollard, J., & Miller, N. E. (1950). *Personality and psychotherapy: An analysis in terms of learning, thinking, and culture.* New York: McGraw-Hill.

Domhoff, G. (1996). *Finding meaning in dreams.* New York: Plenum Press.

Dowd, E. T., & Courchaine, K. E. (1996). Implicit learning, tacit knowledge, and implications for stasis and change in cognitive psychotherapy. *Journal of Cognitive Psychotherapy, 10,* 163–180.

Dyckman, J. M., & Cowan, P. A. (1978). Imaging vividness and the outcome of in vivo and imagined scene desensitization. *Journal of Consulting and Clinical Psychology, 46*, 1155–1156.

Edelman, G. M. (1989). *The remembered present: A biological theory of consciousness.* New York: Basic Books.

Eells, T. D., Horowitz, M. J., Singer, J. L., Salovey, P., Daigle, D., & Turvey, C. (1995). The role-relationship models method: A comparison of independently derived case formulations. *Psychotherapy Research, 5*, 154–168.

Ekman, P., & Davidson, R. (Eds.). (1994). *The nature of emotion: Fundamental questions.* New York: Oxford University Press.

Ellis, A. (1989). Rational psychotherapy. *TACD Journal, 17*, 67–80.

Ellman, S. J., & Antrobus, J. S. (Eds.). (1991). *The mind in sleep: Psychology and psychophysiology* (2nd ed.). New York: Wiley.

Ellmann, R. (1990). *A long the riverrun: Selected essays.* New York: Random House/Vintage.

Engell, J. (1981). *The creative imagination: Enlightenment to romanticism.* Cambridge, MA: Harvard University Press.

Epstein, A. H. (1989). *Mind, fantasy, and healing.* New York: Bantam Dell.

Epstein, S. (1994). Integration of the cognitive and the psychodynamic unconscious. *American Psychologist, 49*, 709–724.

Epstein, S. (1997). This I have learned from over 40 years of personality research. *Journal of Personality, 65*, 3–32.

Epstein, S. (1999). The interpretation of dreams from the perspective of cognitive–experiential self-theory. In J. A. Singer & P. Salovey (Eds.), *At play in the fields of consciousness: Essays in honor of Jerome L. Singer* (pp. 51–82). Mahwah, NJ: Erlbaum.

Epstein, S., & Brodsky, A. (1993). *You're smarter than you think: How to develop your practical intelligence for success in living.* New York: Simon & Schuster.

Epstein, S., & Meier, P. (1989). Constructive thinking: A broad coping variable with specific components. *Journal of Personality and Social Psychology, 57*, 332–350.

Epstein, S., & Pacini, R. (2000–2001). The influence of visualization on intuitive and analytical information processing. *Imagination, Cognition and Personality, 20*, 195–216.

Erdelyi, M. H. (1985). *Psychoanalysis: Freud's cognitive psychology.* New York: Freeman.

Erikson, E. H. (1950). *Childhood and society.* New York: Norton.

Estes, W. K. (Ed.). (1975). *Handbook of learning and cognitive processes* (Vols. 1–2). Hillsdale, NJ: Erlbaum.

Farah, M. J. (1985). Psychophysical evidence for a shared representational medium for mental images and percepts. *Journal of Experimental Psychology: General, 114*, 91–103.

Fenichel, O. (1945). *The psychoanalytic theory of neurosis.* New York: Norton.

Finke, R. A. (1989). *Principles of mental imagery*. Cambridge, MA: MIT Press.

Fishbein, M., & Ajzen, I. (1975). *Belief, attitude, intention, and behavior: An introduction to theory and research*. Reading, MA: Addison-Wesley.

Foa, E. P., & Kozak, M. J. (1996). Obsessive–compulsive disorder. In C. G. Lindemann (Ed.), *Handbook of the treatment of the anxiety disorders* (2nd ed., pp. 139–171). Northvale, NJ: Jason Aronson.

Fonagy, P., Gergely, G., Jurist, E., & Target, M. (2002). *Affect regulation mentalization and the development of the self*. New York: Other Press.

Franklin, M. G., & Foa, E. P. (1998). Cognitive behavioral treatments for obsessive–compulsive disorder. In P. E. Nathan & J. J. Gorman (Eds.), *A guide to treatments that work* (pp. 367–386). London: Oxford University Press.

Freud, S. (1958). Fragment of an analysis of a case of hysteria. In J. L. Strachey (Ed. & Trans.), *The standard edition of the complete psychological works of Sigmund Freud* (Vol. 7, pp. 3–132). London: Hogarth Press. (Original work published 1905)

Freud, S. (1962a). Creative writers and daydreaming. In J. L. Strachey (Ed. & Trans.), *The standard edition of the complete psychological works of Sigmund Freud* (Vol. 9, pp. 141–154). London: Hogarth Press. (Original work published 1908)

Freud, S. (1962b). Formulations regarding the two principles of mental functioning. In J. L. Strachey (Ed. & Trans.), *The standard edition of the complete psychological works of Sigmund Freud* (Vol. 12, pp. 218–226). London: Hogarth Press. (Original work published 1911)

Freud, S. (1962c). The interpretation of dreams. In J. L. Strachey (Ed. & Trans.), *The standard edition of the complete psychological works of Sigmund Freud* (Vol. 4, pp. 1–626). London: Hogarth Press. (Original work published 1900)

Freud, S. (1964). New introductory lectures on psychoanalysis. In J. A. Strachey, (Ed. & Trans.), *The standard edition of the complete psychological works of Sigmund Freud* (Vol. 22, pp. 3–184). London: Hogarth Press. (Original work published 1933)

Fromm, E. (1941). *Escape from freedom*. New York: Rinehart.

Fromm, E. (1955). *The sane society*. New York: Rinehart.

Gapinski, K. D. (1999–2000). Imagery in obsessive–compulsive disorder: Implications for symptoms and treatment. *Imagination, Cognition and Personality, 19*, 351–365.

Gardner, H. (1983). *Frames of mind: The theory of multiple intelligences*. New York: Basic Books.

Gardner, H. (1999). *Intelligence reframed: Multiple intelligence for the 21st century*. New York: Basic Books.

Gardner, H., Krechevsky, M., Sternberg, R. J., & Okagaki, L. (1994). Intelligence in context: Enhancing students' practical intelligence for school. In K. McGilly (Ed.), *Classroom lessons: Integrating cognitive theory and classroom practice* (pp. 105–127). Cambridge, MA: MIT Press.

Garfinkle, J. R. (1994). *Discrepant representations of self: Relations to personality, emotion and continuous mood.* Unpublished doctoral dissertation, Yale University, New Haven, CT.

Geissman, P., & Noel, C. (1961). EEG study with frequency analysis and polygraphy of autogenic training. *Proceedings of the 3rd World Congress of Psychiatry, 3,* 468–472.

Geller, J., Cooley, R., & Hartley, D. (1981–1982). Images of the psychotherapist: A theoretical and methodological perspective. *Imagination, Cognition and Personality, 1,* 123–146.

Glassman, N. S., & Andersen, S. M. (1999). Activating transference without consciousness: Using significant-other representations to go beyond what is subliminally given. *Journal of Personality and Social Psychology, 77,* 1146–1162.

Golla, F. L., & Antonovitch, S. (1929). The respiratory rhythm in its relation to the mechanisms of thought. *Brain, 52,* 491–509.

Goodhart, C., Levant, R., Westen, D., & Wampold, B. (2004, July–August). *Best psychotherapy based on the integration of research evidence, clinical judgment, and patient values.* Plenary session symposium conducted at the 112th Annual Convention of the American Psychological Association, Honolulu, HI.

Gordon, W. J. J. (1961). *Synectics: The development of creative capacity.* New York: Harper.

Gould, R. (1972). *Child studies through fantasy: Cognitive–affective patterns in development.* New York: Quandrangle Books.

Grayson, J. B., & Borkovec, T. D. (1978). The effects of expectancy and imagined response to phobic stimuli on fear reduction. *Cognitive Therapy and Research, 2,* 11–24.

Green, M. C., Strange, J. J., & Brock, T. C. (Eds.). (2002). *Narrative impact: Social and cognitive foundations.* Mahwah, NJ: Erlbaum.

Greene, R. J., & Reyher, J. (1972). Pain tolerance in hypnotic analgesic and imagination states. *Journal of Abnormal Psychology, 79,* 29–38.

Grigorenko, E. L., Jarvin, L., & Sternberg, R. J. (2002). School-based tests of the triarchic theory of intelligence: Three settings, three samples, three syllabi. *Contemporary Educational Psychology, 27,* 167–208.

Grigorenko, E. L., & Sternberg, R. (2001). Analytic, creative, and practical intelligence as predictors of self-reported adaptive functioning: A case study in Russia. *Intelligence, 29,* 57–73.

Guilford, J. P. (1967). *The nature of human intelligence.* New York: McGraw-Hill.

Haier, R. J., Siegel, B. V., MacLachlan, A., Soderling, E., Lottenberg, S., & Buchsbaum, M. S. (1992). Regional glucose metabolic changes after learning a complex visuospatial/motor task: A positron emission tomographic study. *Brain Research, 570,* 134–143.

Haier, R. J., Siegel, B. V., Tang, C., Abel, L., & Buchsbaum, M. S. (1992). Intelligence and changes in regional cerebral glucose metabolic rate following learning. *Intelligence, 16,* 415–426.

Harris, P. (2000). *The work of the imagination*. Oxford, England: Blackwell Publishers.

Hart, D., Field, N. P., Garfinkle, J. R., & Singer, J. L. (1997). Representations of self and others: A semantic space model. *Journal of Personality, 65*, 77–105.

Hartman, G. (Ed.). (1980). *The selected poetry and prose of Wordsworth*. New York: New American Library.

Hartmann, E. (1998). *Dreams and nightmares: The new theory on the origin and meaning of dreams*. New York: Plenum Press.

Hartmann, H. (1958). *Ego psychology and the problem of adaptation*. New York: International Universities Press.

Hassin, R. R., Uleman, J. S., & Bargh, J. A. (Eds.). (2005). *The new unconscious*. New York: Oxford University Press.

Hayes, J. R. (1989). Cognitive processes in creativity. In J. A. Glover & R. R. Ronning (Eds.), *Handbook of creativity: Perspectives on individual differences* (pp. 135–145). New York: Plenum Press.

Hayes, S., & Shenk, C. (2004). Operationalizing mindfulness without unnecessary attachments. *Clinical Psychology, 11*, 249–254.

Hedlund, J., Forsythe, G. B., Horvath, J. A., Williams, W. M., Snook, S., & Sternberg, R. J. (2003). Identifying and assessing tacit knowledge: Understanding the practical intelligence of military leaders. *Leadership Quarterly, 14*, 117–140.

Herrnstein, R. J., & Murray, C. A. (1994). *The bell curve: Intelligence and class structure in American life*. New York: Free Press.

Higgins, E. T. (1987). Self-discrepancy: A theory of relating self and affect. *Psychological Review, 94*, 319–340.

Higgins, E. T. (1989). Continuities and discontinuities in self-regulatory and self-evaluative processes: A developmental theory relating self and affect. *Journal of Personality, 57*, 407–444.

Higgins, E. T. (1997). Beyond pleasure and pain. *American Psychologist, 52*, 1280–1300.

Hill, B. (1968). *Gates of horn and ivory: An anthology of dreams*. New York: Taplinger.

Hobbes, T. (1968). *Leviathan* (C. B. MacPherson, Ed.). Harmondsworth, England: Penguin. (Original work published 1651)

Hobbes, T. (1972). *Elementa philosophica de cive*. Garden City, NJ: Anchor Books. (Original work published 1642)

Holt, R. R. (1964). Imagery: The return of the ostracized. *American Psychologist, 19*, 254–264.

Horan, J. J. (1973). "In vivo" emotive imagery: A technique for reducing childbirth anxiety and discomfort. *Psychological Reports, 32*, 1328.

Horney, K. (1939). *New ways in psychoanalysis*. New York: Norton.

Horney, K. (1945). *Our inner conflicts, a constructive theory of neurosis*. New York: Norton.

Horowitz, M. J. (1977). *Image formation and cognition.* New York: Appleton-Century-Crofts.

Horowitz, M. J. (1978). Controls of visual imagery and therapist intervention. In J. L. Singer & K. S. Pope (Eds.), *The power of human imagination* (pp. 37–50). New York: Plenum Press.

Horowitz, M. J. (Ed.). (1991). *Person schemas and maladaptive interpersonal patterns.* Chicago: University of Chicago Press.

Horowitz, M. J. (1997). *Formulation as a basis for planning psychotherapy treatment.* Washington, DC: American Psychiatric Press.

Horowitz, M. J., Eells, T., Singer, J. L., & Salovey, P. (1995). Role relationship models for case formulation. *Archives of General Psychiatry, 52,* 625–632.

Huba, G., Aneshensel, C., & Singer, J. L. (1981). Development of scales for three second-order-factors in inner experience. *Multivariate Behavioral Analysis, 16,* 181–206

Humphrey, R. (1954). *The stream of consciousness in the modern novel.* Berkeley: University of California Press.

Hurlburt, R. T. (1990). *Sampling normal and schizophrenic inner experience.* New York: Plenum Press.

Izard, C. E. (1972). *Patterns of emotions.* New York: Academic Press.

Izard, C. E. (1977). *Human emotions.* New York: Plenum Press.

Izard, C. E. (1991). *The psychology of emotions.* New York: Plenum Press.

Jacobsen, E. (1938). *Progressive relaxation.* Chicago: University of Chicago Press.

James, W. (1950). *The principles of psychology.* New York: Holt. (Original work published 1890)

Janis, I. L. (1958). *Psychological stress: Psychoanalytic and behavioral studies of surgical patients.* New York: Wiley.

Johnson, M. K., & Multhaup, K. (1992). Emotion and MEM. In S. A. Christianson (Ed.), *The handbook of emotion and memory* (pp. 33–66). Hillsdale, NJ: Erlbaum.

Joyce, J. (1934). *Ulysses.* New York: Random House.

Jung, C. G. (1971). *Psychological types.* New York: Pantheon. (Original work published 1921)

Kabat-Zinn, J. (1993). *Wherever you go, there you are: Mindfulness meditation in everyday life.* New York: Hyperion.

Kahneman, D., Slovik, P., & Tversky, A. (Eds.). (1982). *Judgment under uncertainty: Heuristics and biases.* Cambridge, England: Cambridge University Press.

Kahneman, D., & Tversky, A. (1973). On the psychology of prediction. *Psychological Review, 80,* 237–251.

Kaufman, S. B., & Singer, J. L. (2003–2004). Applying the theory of successful intelligence to psychotherapy training and practice. *Imagination, Cognition and Personality, 23,* 325–355.

Kaufmann, W. (Ed. & Trans.). (1968). *Basic writings of Nietzsche.* New York: Modern Library.

Kazdin, A. E. (1973). Covert modeling and the reduction of avoidance behavior. *Journal of Abnormal Psychology, 81*, 87–95.

Kazdin, A. E. (1974). Covert modeling, model similarity, and reduction of avoidance behavior. *Behavior Therapy, 5*, 325–340.

Kazdin, A. E. (1975). Covert modeling, imagery assessment, and assertive behavior. *Journal of Consulting and Clinical Psychology, 43*, 716–724.

Kazdin, A. E. (1976). Effects of covert modeling, multiple models, and model reinforcement on assertive behavior. *Behavior Therapy, 7*, 211–222.

Kazdin, A. E. (1978). *History of behavior modification: Experimental foundations of contemporary research*. Baltimore: University Park Press.

Kazdin, A. E. (1979). Effects of covert modeling and coding of modeled stimuli on assertive behavior. *Behaviour Research and Therapy, 17*, 53–61.

Kazdin, A. E. (Ed.). (1998). *Methodological issues and strategies in clinical research* (2nd ed.). Washington, DC: American Psychological Association.

Kazdin, A. E. (2000). *Psychotherapy for children and adolescents: Directions for research and practice*. New York: Oxford University Press.

Kazdin, A. E. (2001). *Behavior modification in applied settings* (6th ed.). Belmont, CA: Wadsworth.

Kazdin, A. (2005). *Parent management training: Treatment for oppositional, aggressive and antisocial behavior in children and adolescents*. New York: Oxford University Press.

Kazdin, A. E., & Wilcoxon, L. A. (1976). Systematic desensitization and nonspecific treatment effects: A methodological evaluation. *Psychological Bulletin, 83*, 729–758.

Kelly, G. (1955). *The psychology of personal constructs* (Vols. 1–2). New York: Norton.

Kiesler, D. J. (1996). *Contemporary interpersonal theory and research*. New York: Wiley.

Kihlstrom, J. F. (1987, September 18). The cognitive unconscious. *Science, 237*, 1445–1452.

Kihlstrom, J. F. (1990). The psychological unconscious. In L. Pervin (Ed.), *Handbook on personality: Theory and research* (pp. 445–464). New York: Guilford Press.

Kinsbourne, M. (1993). Integrated cortical field model of consciousness. In *Ciba Foundation Symposium: No. 174. Experimental and theoretical studies of consciousness* (pp. 43–60). Chichester, England: Wiley.

Kirkpatrick, L. A., & Epstein, S. (1992). Cognitive–experiential self-theory and subjective probability: Further evidence for two conceptual systems. *Journal of Personality and Social Psychology, 63*, 534–544.

Klein, S., & Kihlstrom, J. F. (1986). Elaboration, organization and the self-reference effect in memory. *Journal of Experimental Psychology, 115*, 26–38.

Klinger, E. (1978). Modes of normal conscious flow. In J. L. Singer & K. S. Pope (Eds.), *The stream of consciousness* (pp. 226–258). New York: Plenum Press.

Klinger, E. (1990a). *Daydreaming*. Los Angeles: Tarcher.

Klinger, E. (1990b). Thought flow: Properties and mechanisms underlying shifts in content. In J. A. Singer & P. Salovey (Eds.), *At play in the fields of consciousness: Essays in honor of Jerome L. Singer* (pp. 29–50). Mahwah, NJ: Erlbaum.

Klos, D. S., & Singer, J. L. (1981). Determinants of the adolescent's ongoing thought following simulated parental confrontations. *Journal of Personality and Social Psychology, 41*, 975–987.

Korn, E. H. (1983). *Visualization: Uses of imagery in the health professions*. Homewood, IL: Dow, Jones, Irwin.

Korn, E. H. (1994). Mental imagery in enhancing performances: Theory and practical exercises. In A. A. Sheikh & E. H. Korn (Eds.), *Imagery in sports and physical performance* (pp. 201–203). Amityville, NY: Baywood.

Kosslyn, S. M. (1976). Can imagery be distinguished from other forms of internal representation? Evidence from studies of information retrieval times. *Memory and Cognition, 4*, 291–297.

Kosslyn, S. M. (1995). Mental imagery. In S. M. Kosslyn & D. N. Osherson (Eds.), *Visual cognition: An invitation to cognitive science* (2nd ed., Vol. 2, pp. 267–296). Cambridge, MA: MIT Press.

Kreitler, H., & Kreitler, S. (1976). *Cognitive orientation and behavior*. New York: Springer Publishing Company.

Kreitler, H., & Kreitler, S. (1990). *Cognitive foundations of personality traits*. New York: Plenum Press.

Kreitler, S., & Singer, J. L. (1991). The self-relevance effect in incidental memory: Elaboration, organization, rehearsal and self-complexity. *Imagination, Cognition and Personality, 10*, 167–194.

Kunzendorf, R. G. (Ed.). (1991). *Mental imagery*. New York: Plenum Press.

Kunzendorf, R. G., & Sheikh, A. A. (Eds.). (1990). *Psychophysiology of mental imagery: Theory, research, and application*. Amityville, NY: Baywood.

Lakoff, G., & Johnson, M. (2003). *Metaphors we live by*. Chicago: University of Chicago Press.

Lane, J. B. (1977). Problems in assessment of vividness and control of imagery. *Perceptual and Motor Skills, 45*, 363–368.

Lang, P. J. (1977). Imagery in therapy: An information processing analysis of fear. *Behavior Therapy, 8*, 862–886.

Lang, P. J. (1979). A bio-informational theory of emotional imagery. *Psychophysiology, 16*, 495–512.

Langer, E. J. (2005). *On becoming an artist: Reinventing yourself through mindful creativity*. New York: Ballantine Books.

Lazarus, A. A. (1971). *Behavior therapy and beyond*. New York: McGraw-Hill.

Lazarus, A. A. (1981). *The practice of multimodal therapy*. New York: McGraw-Hill.

Leahey, T. H. (1992). The mythical revolutions of American psychology. *American Psychologist, 47*, 308–318.

Leahey, T. H. (1994). Is this a dagger I see before me? Four theorists in search of consciousness. *Contemporary Psychology, 39,* 575–581.

LeDoux, J. (1996). *The emotional brain.* New York: Simon & Schuster.

Leibniz, G. W. (1981). *New essays on human understanding* (P. Remnant & J. Bennett, Trans. & Eds.). Cambridge, England: Cambridge University Press. (Original work published 1705)

Leslie, A. M. (1987). Pretense and representation: The origins of "theory of mind." *Psychological Review, 94,* 412–426.

Leuner, H. (1978). Basic principles and therapeutic efficacy of guided affective imagery (GAI). In J. Singer & K. S. Pope (Eds.), *The power of the human imagination* (pp. 125–166). New York: Plenum Press.

Lewin, I. (1986–1987). A three dimensional model for the classification of cognitive products. *Imagination, Cognition and Personality, 6,* 43–52.

Lewin, K. (1935). *A dynamic theory of personality.* New York: McGraw-Hill.

Lewis, N. (1996). *The interpretation of dreams and portents in antiquity.* Wanaconda, IL: Bolchazy-Carducci.

Libet, B. (1993). *Neurophysiology of consciousness: Selected papers and new essays by Benjamin Libet.* Boston: Birkhäuser.

Linden, W. (1971). *Meditation, cognitive style, and reading in elementary school children.* Unpublished doctoral dissertation, New York University, New York.

Lopes, P. N., Salovey, P., & Straus, R. (2003). Emotional intelligence, personality, and the perceived quality of social relationships. *Personality and Individual Differences, 35,* 641–658.

Luborsky, L., & Crits-Christoph, P. (1990). *Understanding transference: The core conflictual relationship theme method.* New York: Basic Books.

Luria, A. R. (1932). *The nature of human conflicts.* New York: Liveright.

Maddi, S. R., & Kobasa, S. C. (1991). The development of hardiness. In A. Monat & R. S. Lazarus (Eds.), *Stress and coping: An anthology* (3rd ed., pp. 245–257). New York: Columbia University Press.

Mahoney, M. J. (1974). *Cognition and behavior modification.* Cambridge, MA: Ballinger.

Mandler, G. (1984). *Mind and body.* New York: Norton.

Manian, N., Strauman, T. J., & Denney, N. (1998). Temperament, recalled parenting styles, and self-regulation: Testing the developmental postulates of self-discrepancy theory. *Journal of Personality and Social Psychology, 75,* 1321–1332.

Marks, D. F. (1973). Visual imagery differences in the recall of pictures. *British Journal of Psychology, 64,* 17–24.

Markus, H. (1977). Self-schemata and processing information about the self. *Journal of Personality and Social Psychology, 35,* 63–78.

Markus, H. (1983). Self-knowledge: An expanded view. *Journal of Personality, 51,* 543–565.

Markus, H. R., & Nurius, P. (1986). Possible selves. *American Psychologist, 41,* 954–969.

Marlatt, G. A., & Kristeller, J. L. (1999). Mindfulness and meditation. In W. R. Miller (Ed.), *Integrating spirituality into treatment: Resources for practitioners* (pp. 67–84). Washington, DC: American Psychological Association.

Mathews, A. M. (1971). Psychophysiological approaches to the investigation of desensitization and related procedures. *Psychological Bulletin, 76,* 73–91.

Maupin, E. W. (1965). Individual differences in response to a Zen meditation exercise. *Journal of Consulting Psychology, 29,* 139–145.

McAdams, D. P. (1985). *Power, intimacy, and the life story: Personological inquiries into identity.* Homewood, IL: Dorsey Press.

McAdams, D. P. (1987). A life-story model of identity. In R. Hogan & W. H. Jones (Eds.), *Perspectives in personality* (Vol. 2, pp. 15–50). Greenwich, CT: JAI Press.

McAdams, D. P. (1989). *Intimacy: The need to be close.* New York: Doubleday.

McAdams, D. (1990). *The person.* San Diego, CA: Harcourt Brace Jovanovich.

McAdams, D. P. (1993). *Stories we live by: Personal myths and the making of the self.* New York: Morrow.

McFall, R. M., & Twentyman, C. T. (1973). Four experiments on the relative contributions of rehearsal, modeling, and coaching to assertion training. *Journal of Abnormal Psychology, 81,* 199–218.

McGhee, P. (1971). Development of the humor response: A review of the literature. *Psychological Bulletin, 76,* 328–348.

McGuire, W. J. (1973). The yin and yang of progress in social psychology: Seven koan. *Journal of Personality and Social Psychology, 26,* 446–456.

McLeod, J. (1997). *Narrative and psychotherapy.* Thousand Oaks, CA: Sage.

Meichenbaum, D. (1974). *Cognitive behavior modification.* Morristown, NJ: General Learning Press.

Meichenbaum, D. (1977). *Cognitive–behavior modification: An integrative approach.* New York: Plenum Press.

Meichenbaum, D. (1978). Why does using imagery in psychotherapy lead to change? In J. L. Singer & K. S. Pope (Eds.), *The power of human imagination* (pp. 381–394). New York: Plenum Press.

Meins, E. C., Fernyhough, R., Wainwright, D., Clark-Carter, M., Das Gupta, M., Fradley, E., & Tuckey, M. (2003). Pathways to understanding mind: Construct validity and predictive validity of maternal mind-mindedness. *Child Development, 74,* 1194–1211.

Menand, L. (2001). *Marketplace of ideas.* New York: American Council of Learned Societies.

Messer, S. B., & Warren, C. S. (1995). *Models of brief psychodynamic therapy.* New York: Guilford Press.

Meyer, V. (1966). Modifications of expectations in cases with obsessional rituals. *Behavior Research and Therapy, 4,* 273–280.

Mitchell, S. A. (1988). The intrapsychic and the interpersonal: Different theories, different domains, or historical attractions? *Psychoanalytic Inquiry, 8,* 472–496.

Nolen-Hoeksema, S. (2000). The role of rumination in depressive disorders and mixed anxiety/depressive symptoms. *Journal of Abnormal Psychology, 109,* 504–511.

Paivio, A. (1971). *Imagery and verbal processes.* New York: Holt, Rinehart & Winston.

Pamuk, O. (2005, March 7). The Pamuk apartments. *The New Yorker,* 34–41.

Partiot, A., Grafman, J., Sadato, N., Wachs, J., & Hallett, M. (1995). Brain activation during the generation of non-emotional and emotional plans. *Neuroreport, 6,* 1397–1400.

Piaget, J. (1962). *Play, dreams, and imitation in childhood.* New York: Norton.

Pope, K. S. (1978). How gender, solitude, and posture influence the stress of consciousness. In K. S. Pope & J. L. Singer (Eds.), *The stream of consciousness* (pp. 259–299). New York: Plenum Press.

Pope, K. S., & Singer, J. L. (Eds.). (1978). *The stream of consciousness.* New York: Plenum Press.

Posner, M. I. (1994). Neglect and spatial attention. *Neuropsychological Rehabilitation, 4,* 183–187.

Reyher, J. (1978). Emergent uncovering psychotherapy: The use of imagoic and linguistic vehicles in objectifying psychodynamic processes. In J. L. Singer & K. S. Pope (Eds.), *The power of human imagination* (pp. 51–94). New York: Plenum Press.

Richardson, A. (1969). *Mental imagery.* New York: Springer Publishing Company.

Richardson, A. (1984). *The experiential dimension of psychology.* St. Lucia, Queensland, Australia: University of Queensland Press.

Richardson, A. (2000). Individual differences in visual imagination imagery. In R. G. Kunzendorf & B. Wallace (Eds.), *Individual differences in conscious experience: Advances in consciousness research* (pp. 125–146). Philadelphia: Benjamins.

Rodin, J., & Singer, J. L. (1976). Eye-shift, thought, and obesity. *Journal of Personality, 44,* 594–610.

Rogers, C. R. (1942). *Counseling and psychotherapy: Newer concepts in practice.* Boston: Houghton Mifflin.

Rogers, C. R. (1951). *Client-centered therapy: Its current practice, implications, and theory.* Boston: Houghton Mifflin.

Rogers, C. R. (1961). *On becoming a person: A therapist's view of psychotherapy.* Boston: Houghton Mifflin.

Rorschach, H. (1942). *Psychodiagnostics.* (P. Lemkau & B. Kronenburg, Trans.). Berne, Switzerland: Hans Huber Press.

Rosen, C. (1995). *The romantic generation*. Cambridge, MA: Harvard University Press.

Rosenberg, B. A. (1980). Mental-task instructions and optokinetic nystagmus to the left and right. *Journal of Experimental Psychology: Human Perception and Performance, 6*, 459–472.

Rosenberg, H. S. (1987). *Creative drama and imagination*. New York: Holt, Rinehart & Winston.

Rosenberg, M. (1979). *Conceiving the self*. New York: Basic Books.

Rubin, D. C. (2005). A basic-systems approach to autobiographical memory. *Current Directions in Psychological Science, 14*, 79–83.

Russ, S. W. (2004). *Play in child development and psychotherapy*. Mahwah, NJ: Erlbaum.

Russ, S. W., Robins, A. L., & Christiano, B. A. (1999). Pretend play: Longitudinal prediction of creativity and affect in fantasy in children. *Creativity Research Journal, 12*, 129–139.

Ruvolo, A. P., & Markus, H. R. (1992). Possible selves and performance: The power of self-relevant imagery. *Social Cognition, 10*, 95–124.

Sadoski, M., & Paivio, A. (2001). *Imagery and text: A dual code theory of reading and writing*. Mahwah, NJ: Erlbaum.

Safran, J. D. (1990). Towards a refinement of cognitive therapy in light of interpersonal theory: II. Practice. *Clinical Psychology Review, 10*, 107–121.

Salovey, P., & Mayer, J. D. (1990). Emotional intelligence. *Imagination, Cognition and Personality, 9*, 185–211.

Salovey, P., Mayer, J. D., Caruso, D., & Lopes, P. N. (2003). Measuring emotional intelligence as a set of abilities with the Mayer–Salovey–Caruso Emotional Intelligence Test. In S. J. Lopez & C. R. Snyder (Eds.), *Positive psychological assessment: A handbook of models and measures* (pp. 251–265). Washington, DC: American Psychological Association.

Salovey, P., & Singer, J. A. (1991). Cognitive behavior modification. In F. H. Kanfer & A. P. Goldstein (Eds.), *Helping people change: A textbook of methods* (4th ed., pp. 361–395). New York: Pergamon Press.

Sarason, I. G. (1975). Test anxiety and the self-disclosing coping model. *Journal of Consulting and Clinical Psychology, 43*, 148–153.

Sarbin, T. R. (1986). Prediction and clinical inference: Forty years later. *Journal of Personality Assessment, 50*, 362–369.

Schachtel, E. G. (1959). *Metamorphosis*. New York: Basic Books.

Schank, R. C., & Abelson, R. P. (1977). *Scripts, plans, goals and understanding: An inquiry into human knowledge structures*. Hillsdale, NJ: Erlbaum.

Schultz, J. H. (1978). Imagery and the control of depression. In J. L. Singer & K. S. Pope (Eds.), *The power of human imagination* (pp. 281–308). New York: Plenum Press.

Schultz, J. H., & Luthe, W. (1969). *Autogenic training: A psychophysiologic approach to psychotherapy*. New York: Grune & Stratton.

Schwartz, G. E. (1975). Biofeedback, self-regulation, and the patterning of physio-logical processes. *American Scientist, 63,* 314–324.

Schwartz, G. E., Fair, P. L., Salt, P., Mandel, M. R., & Klerman, G. L. (1976, April 30). Facial muscle patterning to affective imagery in depressed and nondepressed subjects. *Science, 192,* 489–491.

Schwartz, G. E., Weinberger, D. A., & Singer, J. A. (1981). Cardiovascular differen-tiation of happiness, sadness, anger, and fear following imagery and exercise. *Psychosomatic Medicine, 43,* 343–364.

Schwebel, D., Rosen, C., & Singer, J. L. (1999). Preschoolers' pretend play and theory of mind: The role of jointly conducted pretense. *British Journal of Developmental Psychology, 17,* 333–348.

Searle, J. R. (1995). *The mystery of consciousness.* New York: New York Review of Books.

Segal, J. S. (Ed.). (1971). *Imagery: Current cognitive approaches.* New York: Aca-demic Press.

Segal, Z. V., Williams, J. M. G., & Teasdale, J. D. (2002). Mindfulness-based cognitive therapy for depression. *Psychotherapy and Psychosomatics, 71,* 363.

Seligman, M. E. P. (1991). *Learned optimism.* New York: Knopf.

Shallice, T. (1978). The dominant action-system: An information processing ap-proach to consciousness. In K. S. Pope & J. L. Singer (Eds.), *The stream of consciousness* (pp. 117–158). New York: Plenum Press.

Sheikh, A. A. (Ed.). (1983). *Imagery: Current research, theory, and application.* New York: Wiley.

Sheikh, A. A., & Korn, E. H. (Eds.). (1994). *Imagery in sports and physical perfor-mance.* Amityville, NY: Baywood.

Sheikh, A. A., Kunzendorf, R. G., & Sheikh, K. S. (1989). Healing images: From ancient wisdom to modern science. In A. A. Sheikh & K. S. Sheikh (Eds.), *Eastern and Western approaches to healing* (pp. 470–515). New York: Wiley.

Sheikh, A. A., Sheikh, K. S., & Moleski, L. M. (1994). Improving imaging abilities. In A. A. Sheikh & E. H. Korn (Eds.), *Imagery in sports and physical performance* (pp. 201–230). Amityville, NY: Baywood.

Shepard, R. N. (1978). The mental image. *American Psychologist, 33,* 125–137.

Shepard, R. N. (1984). Ecological constraints on internal representation: Resonant kinematics of perceiving, imagining, thinking, and dreaming. *Psychological Review, 91,* 417–447.

Short, P. L. (1953). The objective study of mental imagery. *British Journal of Psychology, 44,* 38–51.

Singer, D. G. (1993). *Playing for their lives.* New York: Free Press.

Singer, D. G. (1998). The use of children's imagery in play therapy. *International Medical Journal, 5,* 83–91.

Singer, D. G., Cohen, P., & Tower, R. (1978). A developmental study of animistic thinking: Preschoolers through the elderly. In R. Weismann, R. Brown, P. J.

Levinson, & P. A. Taylor (Eds.), *Piagetian theory and the helping professions: Seventh annual conference* (pp. 237–243). Los Angeles: Children's Hospital of Los Angeles.

Singer, D. G., & Kornfeld, B. (1973). Conserving and consuming: A developmental study of abstract and action choices. *Developmental Psychology, 8, 314.*

Singer, D. G., & Singer, J. L. (1990). *The house of make-believe: Children's play and the developing imagination.* Cambridge, MA: Harvard University Press.

Singer, D. G., & Singer, J. L. (Eds.). (2001). *Handbook of children and the media.* Thousand Oaks, CA: Sage.

Singer, D. G., & Singer, J. L. (2005). *Imagination and play in the electronic age.* Cambridge, MA: Harvard University Press.

Singer, D. G., Singer, J. L., Plaskon, S. L., & Schweder, A. E. (2003). A role for play in the preschool curriculum. In S. Olfman (Ed.), *All work and no play: How educational reforms are harming our preschoolers* (pp 59–101). Westport, CT: Greenwood.

Singer, J. A. (1997). *Message in a bottle: Stories of men and addiction.* New York: Free Press.

Singer, J. A. (2004). Narrative identity and meaning making across the lifespan: An introduction. *Journal of Personality, 72,* 437–460.

Singer, J. A., & Salovey, P. (1993). *The remembered self: Emotion and memory in personality.* New York: Free Press.

Singer, J. A., & Salovey, P. (Eds.). (1999). *At play in the fields of consciousness: Essays in honor of Jerome L. Singer.* Mahwah, NJ: Erlbaum.

Singer, J. A., & Singer, J. L. (1992). Transference in psychotherapy and daily life: Implications of current memory and social cognition research. In J. W. Barron & M. N. Eagle (Eds.), *Interface of psychoanalysis and psychology* (pp. 516–538). Washington, DC: American Psychological Association.

Singer, J. A., & Singer, J. L. (1994). Social–cognitive and narrative perspectives on transference. In J. M. Masling & R. F. Bornstein (Eds.), *Empirical perspectives on object relations theory* (pp. 157–193). Washington, DC: American Psychological Association.

Singer, J. A., Singer, J. L., & Zittel, C. (2000). Personality variations in autobiographical memories, self-representations and daydreaming. In R. G. Kunzendorf & B. Wallace (Eds.), *Individual differences in conscious experience* (pp. 351–373). Philadelphia: John Benjamins.

Singer, J. L. (1973). *The child's world of make-believe.* New York: Academic Press.

Singer, J. L. (1974). *Imagery and daydream methods in psychotherapy and behavior modification.* New York: Academic Press.

Singer, J. L. (1984). *The human personality.* New York: Harcourt Brace Jovanovich.

Singer, J. L. (1985). Transference and the human condition: A cognitive–affective perspective. *Psychoanalytic Psychology, 2,* 189–219.

Singer, J. L. (Ed.). (1990). *Repression and dissociation.* Chicago: University of Chicago Press.

Singer, J. L. (1995). William James, James Joyce and the stream of thought. In R. Fuller (Ed.), *Seven pioneers of psychology, behavior, and mind* (pp. 21–46). London: Routledge.

Singer, J. L. (1999). Imagination. In M. Runco & S. Pritzker (Eds.), *Encyclopedia of creativity* (Vol. 2, pp. 13–25). San Diego, CA: Academic Press.

Singer, J. L., & Antrobus, J. S. (1972). Daydreaming, imaginal processes, and personality: A normative study. In P. Sheehan (Ed.), *The function and nature of imagery* (pp. 175–202). New York: Academic Press.

Singer, J. L., & Bonanno, G. (1990). Personality and private experience: Individual variations in consciousness and in attention to subjective phenomena. In L. Pervin (Ed.), *Handbook of personality* (pp. 419–444). New York: Guilford Press.

Singer, J. L., & Lythcott, M. A. (2002). Fostering school achievement and creativity through sociodramatic play in the classroom. *Research in the Schools, 9,* 41–50.

Singer, J. L., & McCraven, V. (1961). Some characteristics of adult daydreaming. *Journal of Psychology, 51,* 151–164.

Singer, J. L., & Pope, K. S. (1978). *The power of human imagination.* New York: Plenum Press.

Singer, J. L., & Salovey, P. (1991). Organized knowledge structures and personality: Person schemas, self-schemas, prototypes and scripts. In M. V. Horowitz (Ed.), *Person schemas and maladaptive interpersonal patterns* (pp. 33–79). Chicago: University of Chicago Press.

Singer, J. L., & Schonbar, R. (1961). Correlates of daydreaming: Dimensions of self-awareness. *Journal of Consulting Psychology, 25,* 1–17.

Singer, J. L., Sincoff, J. G., & Kolligian, J., Jr. (1989). Countertransference and cognition: Studying the psychotherapist's distortions as consequences of normal information-processing. *Psychotherapy, 26,* 344–355.

Slade, A. (2002). Moments of regulation and the development of self-narratives. *Journal of Infant, Child, and Adult Psychotherapy, 2,* 1–15.

Smith, M. L., & Glass, G. V. (1977). Meta-analysis of psychotherapy outcome studies. *American Psychologist, 32,* 752–760.

Snyder, C. R., Ilardi, S., Michael, S. T., & Cheavens, J. (2000). Hope theory: Updating a common process for psychological change. In C. R. Snyder & R. E. Ingram (Eds.), *Handbook of psychological change: Psychotherapy processes and practices for the 21st century* (pp. 128–153). New York: Wiley.

Sorabji, R. (1972). *Aristotle on memory.* Providence, RI: Brown University Press.

Spearman, C. (1904). "General intelligence" objectively determined and measured. *American Journal of Psychology, 15,* 201–293.

Sperry, R. W. (1976). Changing concepts of consciousness and free will. *Perspectives in Biology and Medicine, 20,* 9–19.

Spurgeon, C. (1935). *Shakespeare's imagery and what it tells us.* Cambridge, England: Cambridge University Press.

Stampfl, T. G., & Levis, D. J. (1967). Essentials of implosive therapy: A learning theory–based psychodynamic behavioral therapy. *Journal of Abnormal Psychology, 72*, 496–503.

Sternberg, R. J. (1985). *Beyond IQ: A triarchic theory of human intelligence*. New York: Cambridge University Press.

Sternberg, R. J. (1997). Educating intelligence: Infusing the triarchic theory into school instruction. In R. J. Sternberg & E. L. Grigorenko (Eds.), *Intelligence, heredity, and environment* (pp. 343–362). New York: Cambridge University Press.

Sternberg, R. J. (1999a). Looking back and looking forward on intelligence: Toward a theory of successful intelligence. In M. Bennett (Ed.), *Developmental psychology: Achievements and prospects* (pp. 289–308). Philadelphia: Psychology Press.

Sternberg, R. J. (1999b). The theory of successful intelligence. *Review of General Psychology, 3*, 292–316.

Sternberg, R. J., Forsythe, G. B., Hedlund, J., Horvath, J. A., Wagner, R. K., Williams, W. M., et al. (2000). *Practical intelligence in everyday life*. New York: Cambridge University Press.

Sternberg, R. J., & Grigorenko, E. L. (2000). *Teaching for successful intelligence*. Arlington Heights, IL: Skylight Training & Publishing.

Sternberg, R. J., & Grigorenko, E. L. (2002). *Dynamic testing: The nature and measurement of learning potential*. New York: Cambridge University Press.

Sternberg, R., Grigorenko, E., & Singer, J. L. (Eds.). (2004). *Creativity: From potentiality to realization*. Washington, DC: American Psychological Association.

Sternberg, R. J., & Hedlund, J. (2002). Practical intelligence, g, and work psychology. *Human Performance, 15*, 143–160.

Sternberg, R. J., & Lubart, T. I. (1995). *Defying the crowd: Cultivating creativity in a culture of conformity*. New York: Free Press.

Sternberg, R., Okagaki, L., & Jackson, A. (1990). Practical intelligence for success in school. *Educational Leadership, 48*, 35–39.

Sternberg, R. J., Torff, B., & Grigorenko, E. L. (1998). Teaching triarchically improves school achievement. *Journal of Education Psychology, 90*, 374–384.

Sternberg, R. J., & Williams, W. M. (1996). *How to develop student creativity*. Alexandria, VA: Association for Supervision and Curriculum Development.

Strauman, T. J. (1989). Self-discrepancies in clinical depression and social phobia: Cognitive structures that underlie emotional disorders. *Journal of Abnormal Psychology, 98*, 14–22.

Strauman, T. J. (1992). Self-guides, autobiographical memory, and anxiety and dysphoria: Toward a cognitive model of vulnerability to emotional distress. *Journal of Abnormal Psychology, 101*, 87–95.

Strauman, T. J. (1994). Introduction: Social cognition, psychodynamic psychology, and the representation and processing of emotionally significant information. *Journal of Personality, 62*, 451–458.

Strauman, T. J., & Higgins, E. T. (1988). Self-discrepancies as predictors of vulnerability to distinct syndromes of chronic emotional distress. *Journal of Personality*, 56, 685–707.

Strauman, T. J., & Higgins, E. T. (1993). The self-construct in social cognition: Past, present, and future. In Z. Siegel & S. Blatt (Eds.), *Self in emotional distress* (pp. 3–40). New York: Guilford Press.

Strauman, T. J., Lemieux, A., & Coe, C. (1993). Self-discrepancy and natural killer cell activity: Immunological consequences of negative self-evaluation. *Journal of Personality and Social Psychology*, 64, 1042–1052.

Strauman, T. J., Vieth, A. Z., Kolden, G. G., Klein, M. H., Woods, T. E., & Michels, J. (2004). *Self-system therapy for depression: Research treatment manual.* Unpublished manuscript.

Strupp, H. H., & Binder, J. L. (1984). *Psychotherapy in a new key: A guide to time-limited psychotherapy.* New York: Basic Books.

Sullivan, H. S. (1953). *The interpersonal theory of psychiatry.* New York: Norton.

Switras, J. E. (1978). An alternate-form instrument to assess vividness and controllability of mental imagery in seven modalities. *Perceptual and Motor Skills*, 46, 379–384.

Tauber, E., & Green, M. (1959). *Prelogical experience.* New York: Basic Books.

Taylor, M. (1999). *Imaginary companions and the children who create them.* Oxford, England: Oxford University Press.

Taylor, S. E. (1989). *Positive illusions: Creative self-deception and the healthy mind.* New York: Basic Books.

Terman, L. M., & Merrill, M. A. (1972). *Stanford-Binet Intelligence Scale: Manual for third revision.* Boston: Houghton-Mifflin.

Thurstone, L. L., & Thurstone, T. C. (1941). *Factorial studies of intelligence.* Chicago: University of Chicago Press.

Tomkins, S. S. (1962). *Affect, imagery, consciousness* (Vol. 1). New York: Springer Publishing Company.

Tomkins, S. S. (1963). *Affect, imagery, consciousness* (Vol. 2). New York: Springer Publishing Company.

Tomkins, S. S. (1995). Script theory. In E. V. Demos (Ed.), *Exploring affect: The selected writings of Silvan S. Tomkins* (pp. 296–312). New York: Cambridge University Press.

Tondo, T. R., & Cautela, J. R. (1974). Assessment of imagery in covert reinforcement. *Psychological Reports*, 34, 1271–1280.

Tower, R. B., & Singer, J. L. (1981). The measurement of imagery: How can it be clinically useful? In P. Kendall & S. Hollon (Eds.), *Assessment strategies for cognitive–behavioral interventions* (pp. 119–159). New York: Academic Press.

Trunz, E. (Ed.). (1988). *Goethes Werke* (Vols. 1–14). Hamburg, Germany: Wegner.

Tulving, E. (1998). Brain/mind correlates of human memory. In M. Sabourin, F. Craik, & M. Robert (Eds.), *Advances in psychological science: Vol. 2. Biological and cognitive aspects* (pp. 441–460). Hove, England: Psychology Press.

Turk, D. C. (1980). *Cognitive–behavioral techniques for the control of pain: A skills-training manual*. Washington, DC: American Psychological Association.

Tversky, A., & Kahneman, D. (1983). Extensional versus intuitive reasoning: The conjunction fallacy in probability judgment. *Psychological Review, 90,* 293–315.

Twain, M. (1876). *Tom Sawyer*. New York: Harper & Brothers.

van Egeren, L. F., Feather, B. W., & Hein, P. L. (1971). Desensitization of phobias: Some psychophysiology propositions. *Psychophysiology, 8,* 213–228.

Velmans, M. (1996). (Ed.). *The science of consciousness: Psychological, neuropsychological, and clinical reviews*. New York: Routledge.

Vieth, A. Z., Strauman, T. J., Kolden, G. G., Woods, T. E., Michels, J. L., & Klein, M. H. (2003). Self-system therapy (SST): A theory-based psychotherapy for depression. *Clinical Psychology: Science and Practice, 10,* 245–268.

Vygotsky, L. S. (1966). Play and its role in the mental development of the child. *Soviet Psychology, 12,* 62–76.

Vygotsky, L. S. (1978). *Mind in society: The development of higher mental processes*. Cambridge, MA: Harvard University Press.

Vyse, S. A. (1997). *Believing in magic: The psychology of superstition*. New York: Oxford University Press.

Wagner, R. K. (1987). Tacit knowledge in everyday intelligent behavior. *Journal of Personality and Social Psychology, 52,* 1236–1247.

Wagner, R. K., & Sternberg, R. J. (1990). Street smarts. In K. E. Clark & M. B. Clark (Eds.), *Measures of leadership* (pp. 493–504). West Orange, NJ: Leadership Library of America.

Wagner, R. K., Sujan, H., Sujan, M., Rashotte, C. A., & Sternberg, R. J. (1999). Tacit knowledge in sales. In R. J. Sternberg & J. A. Horvath (Eds.), *Tacit knowledge in professional practice: Researcher and practitioner perspectives* (pp. 155–182). Mahwah, NJ: Erlbaum.

Wechsler, D. (1958). *The measurement and appraisal of adult intelligence* (4th ed.). Baltimore: William & Wilkins.

Weinberger, D. A. (1990). The construct validity of the repressive coping style. In J. L. Singer (Ed.), *Repression and dissociation* (pp. 337–386). Chicago: University of Chicago Press.

Westen, D. (2001). Diagnosing personality disorders. *American Journal of Psychiatry, 158,* 324–325.

Westen, D., & Morrison, K. (2001). A multidimensional meta-analysis of treatments for depression, panic, and generalized anxiety disorder: An empirical examination of the status of empirically supported therapies. *Journal of Consulting and Clinical Psychology, 69,* 875–899.

Wilkins, W. (1971). Desensitization: Social and cognitive factors underlying the effectiveness of Wolpe's procedure. *Psychological Bulletin, 76,* 311–317.

Williams, W. M., Blythe, T., White, N., Li, J., Gardner, H., & Sternberg, R. J. (2002). Practical intelligence for school: Developing metacognitive sources of achievement in adolescence. *Developmental Review, 22,* 162–210.

Wilson, S. C., & Barber, T. X. (1978). The Creative Imagination Scale as a measure of hypnotic responsiveness: Applications to experimental and clinical hypnosis. *American Journal of Clinical Hypnosis, 20*, 235–249.

Witkin, H. A., Lewis, H. B., & Weil, E. (1968). Affective reactions and patient–therapist interactions among more differentiated and less differentiated patients early in therapy. *Journal of Nervous and Mental Disease, 146*, 193–208.

Wolpe, J. (1958). *Psychotherapy by reciprocal inhibition*. Stanford, CA: Stanford University Press.

Wylie, R. C. (1975). *The self-concept*. Lincoln: University of Nebraska Press.

Zhiyan, T., & Singer, J. L. (1997). Daydreaming styles, emotionality, and the Big Five personality dimensions. *Imagination, Cognition and Personality, 16*, 399–414.

AUTHOR INDEX

Ellman, S. J., 27
Ellmann, R., 53
Emery, G., 105, 118–121, 128
Engell, J., 22, 23
Epstein, A. H., 163
Epstein, N., 152
Epstein, S., 45–48, 55–57, 59, 150, 162,
    163, 168
Erdelyi, M. H., 38
Erikson, E. H., 29

Fair, P. L., 112
Farah, M. J., 57
Feather, B. W., 171
Fenichel, O., 70
Field, N. P., 26, 132
Finke, R. A., 57
Fishbein, M., 26
Foa, E. P., 124
Fonagy, P., 62
Franklin, M. G., 124
Freud, S., 22, 70, 83, 86, 90
Fromm, E., 74

Gapinski, K. D., 124
Gardner, H., 146, 151
Garfinkle, J. R., 26, 132, 134
Geissman, P., 171
Geller, J., 86, 103
Gergely, G., 62
Glass, G. V., 110
Glassman, N. S., 96
Goethe, J. W., 131
Golla, F. L., 116
Goodhart, C., 180
Gordon, W. J. J., 184
Gould, R., 62
Grafman, J., 28–29
Grayson, J. B., 108
Green, M. C., 162, 183
Greenberg, S., 57, 171
Greene, R. J., 111
Grigorenko, E. L., 56, 64, 146, 151, 162,
    177
Guilford, J. P., 146

Haier, R. J., 39
Hallett, M., 29

Harris, P., 26
Hart, D., 26, 132, 137
Hartley, D., 86, 103
Hartman, G., 13, 23
Hartmann, E., 98
Hassin, R. R., 9, 26, 38, 54
Hayes, J. R., 153
Hayes, S., 169, 170
Hedlund, J., 151
Hein, P. L., 171
Herrnstein, R. J., 145
Higgins, E. T., 91, 131, 132, 134, 136,
    142, 143
Hill, B., 19
Hobbes, T., 20
Holt, R. R., 57
Hopkins, M., 167
Horney, K., 74
Horowitz, M. J., 50, 58, 86, 91, 92, 137
Huba, G., 116, 167
Humphrey, R., 36
Hurlburt, R. T., 35

Ilardi, S., 83
Izard, C. E., 27, 53, 172

Jackson, A., 151
Jacobsen, E., 170, 178
James, W., 8, 24, 34, 132
Janis, I. L., 108
Johnson, M., 121, 179
Joyce, J., 35, 36
Jung, C. G., 21
Jurist, E., 62

Kabat-Zinn, J., 168
Kahneman, D., 47
Kaufman, S. B., 146, 158
Kaufmann, W., 68
Kazdin, A. E., 67, 74, 88, 97, 105, 107–
    110, 113, 115, 118
Kelly, G., 56, 68, 77, 79, 106
Kiesler, D. J., 27, 74
Kihlstrom, J. F., 26, 38, 54, 131
Kinsbourne, M., 27
Kirkpatrick, L. A., 48
Klein, S., 131
Klerman, G. L., 112

Uleman, J. S., 9, 26, 38, 54

van Egeren, L. F., 171
Velmans, M., 28
Vieth, A. Z., 142–145
Virel, A., 72
Vygotsky, L. S., 23, 28
Vyse, S. A., 47, 123, 164

Wachs, J., 29
Wagner, R. K., 150
Wampold, B., 180
Warren, C. S., 103
Wechsler, D., 145

Weil, E., 83
Weinberger, D. A., 27, 101
Westen, D., 80, 162, 180
Wilcoxon, L. A., 111
Wilkins, W., 88, 107, 111, 171
Williams, J. M. G., 107
Williams, W. M., 149, 151
Wilson, S. C., 116
Witkin, H. A., 83
Wolpe, J., 87, 110, 170
Wylie, R. C., 130

Zhiyan, T., 169
Zittel, C., 85, 167
Zuroff, D. C., 180

SUBJECT INDEX

Catastrophizing, 120
Categorical self-representations, 127
Catharsis, 71
Cave drawings, 19
CBTs. *See* Cognitive–behavioral
therapies
Center for Creative Leadership, 150
Cervantes, Miguel de, 174
Chalmers, D. J., 32
Changed meaning, 107
Chaplin, Charlie, 37, 185
"Checkers," 123
Child development, 28–30, 47–48
Childhood memory(-ies), 10–11
Children's play, 58–64
Classical psychoanalysis, 70
Client-centered psychotherapy, 70–73,
130
Clinical psychology, 5–6
Clinician's imagery, 179–184
Cognitive–behavioral therapies (CBTs),
105–128
and assessing imagery/fantasy capacities, 116–117
and catastrophic thought, 122–123
covert conditioning, 112–115
emergence of, 106–107
and imagery enhancement, 117–118
implosive imagery/flooding, 115
importance of imagery in, 107–110
and maladaptive belief identification, 119
memories/futures in models of, 124–
128
modifying images/subsequent belief
systems, 119
and OCD, 123–124
positive imagery, 111–112
repetition/time projection, 120
role of imagery in, 118
stress/pain inoculation, 115
symbolic imagery/metaphor in, 121
systematic desensitization, 110–111
turning off unwanted fantasy with,
119–120
Cognitive–experiential self system,
163
Cognitive therapy, 56, 70, 76–77, 79,
106–107, 118, 144
Cognitive unconscious, 38
Coleridge, Samuel, 23

Communication, 84
imagery's role in, 3–4
and metaphor, 121
Communion, 33–34
Conduit metaphors, 121
Conscientiousness trait, 169
Conscious experience, 7
Conscious imagery, 32
Consciousness, 25–52
cognitive–affective formulation of,
29–34
and modern psychology, 26–29
ongoing, 172–174
properties of, 37–43
role of, 8
stream of, 35–37
three-dimensional structure of,
49–52
two-dimensional structure of, 43–49
Consciousness and Cognition (journal), 7
Context establishment, 43
Contrastive phenomenology, 38–43
Control, 42, 107
Core conflictual relationship, 91, 97
Counterconditioning, 170, 171
Countertransference, 181–183
Courchaine, K. E., 151
Covert aversive conditioning, 113–114
Covert conditioning, 113–115
Covert extinction, 114
Covert modeling, 109–110, 114–115
Covert rehearsal, 173, 175
Covert reinforcement, 114
Covert sensitization, 113
Cowan, P. A., 116
Creative Imagination Scale, 116
Creative intelligence, 56, 147–150
Creativity, 184–186
Crick, Francis, 9
Crits-Christoph, P., 91, 96, 97, 108, 109,
111, 112, 118
Csikszentmihalyi, Mihaly, 9
Culture, 28, 182
Cuneiform, 19

Dangerfield, Rodney, 181
Daydreaming, 51, 167, 168
Daydreaming (J. L. Singer), 168
Decision making, 42

Defense mechanisms, identification of, 95–96
Desensitization, systematic, 110–111, 171
De Silva, P., 123
Desoille, Robert, 72, 95, 101
Dewey, John, 74
Directedness, 50
Dollard, John, 70, 76
Don Quixote (Cervantes), 174
"Dora" (case study), 83
Dowd, E. T., 151
Dreams
    as imaginative experiences, 51
    interpretation of, 19
    night, 176–177
    transference emerging through
        content of, 98–100
Dyckman, J. M., 116

EEG (electroencephalograph), 28
Egocentrism, 127
Ego psychology, 70
Egosyntonic thought, 173
Egypt, ancient, 19
Electroencephalograph (EEG), 28
Elements of Philosophy (Hobbes), 20
Ellis, Albert, 56, 68, 77, 106, 118, 125
Ellmann, R., 53
Embeddedness affect, 33
Emergent uncovering psychotherapy, 94
Emery, G., 118–121, 128
Emotional intelligence, 158
Emotional system, 53
Emotive imagery, 111
Empty chair technique, 128
Enlightenment, 22
Epstein, Alice, 163
Epstein, Seymour, 45–47, 49, 55, 150, 163
Erickson, Milton, 71
Erikson, Erik, 93
Error identification, 42–43
Evaluation stage (problem solving), 154
Expectations, 83, 109–110
Experiential thinking, 45–47, 55, 163
Exposure and response prevention, 124
Eye movements, 116, 117

Facial muscle responses, 112, 116, 117
Fair, P. L., 112
Fairbairn W. R. D., 70
Fantasy games, 11
Faulkner, William, 24
Fear behavior, 108–109
Feather, B. W., 171
Feedback, 21, 172
Fenichel, O., 70
Ferenczi, Szandor, 70
Field, Herman, 174
Field dependence, 83
Field independence, 83, 172
Film, 37
Flooding, 115, 122
Foa, Edna, 124
Fonagy, P., 62
Forehead muscle tension, 112
Frames of Mind (Gardner), 146
Free association, 85–86, 94
Free-floating imagery, 79–80
Fretigny, Andre, 72
Freud, Anna, 70
Freud, Sigmund, 12, 68–72
    as classical psychoanalyst, 70
    and Dollard and Miller, 75
    and Dora case study, 83
    on dreams, 78, 98
    and free association, 94
    and hypnosis, 71, 86
    on id and ego, 90
    as leader of modern psychotherapy, 161
    and modern cognitive psychology, 38
    and nocturnal dreams, 176
    on preconscious thought, 43
    and primary process, 47
    on thoughts as trial actions, 149
    and transference, 96, 181
    and unconscious motivation, 37
Fromm, Erich, 74
Functional psychology, 74

Gaming industry, 49
Gapinski, Katherine, 124
Gardner, Howard, 146
Gazzaniga, Michael, 9
Geller, Jesse, 103
General semantics, 76

Imagination research, 6
Immune systems, 132
Implicit Attitudes Test, 38
Implosive imagery, 115
Individual Differences Questionnaire, 116
Individual psychology, 73
Induced imagery, 118
Information processing, 39, 40, 116
Information representation stage, 154
Inkblot test, 12, 13
Intelligence. *See* Successful intelligence
Intelligence Reframed (Gardner), 146
Interpersonal psychoanalysis, 73–74, 78, 93
The Interpretation of Dreams (Freud), 86
Interventionist psychotherapists, 83
Introjective dimension, 32, 33
Investment theory of creativity, 147–148
IQ measures, 145
Irrational thinking, 46–47, 49
Izard, C. E., 53

Jacobsen progressive relaxation technique, 170
Jacob's ladder, 19
James, William, 7, 8, 24, 27, 33, 37, 132
Janet, Pierre, 37
John Carter of Mars (Burroughs), 12
Johnson, Marcia, 30
Johnson, Mark, 121, 179
Joseph's dreams, 19
Joyce, James, 35–37, 46
Jung, Carl, 21, 37, 38, 71–72, 79, 95

Kabat-Zinn, J., 168
Kafka, Kurt, 75
Kaufman, Scott, 146
Kazdin, Alan, 80, 88, 105, 109, 110, 115, 118
Kelly, George, 56, 68, 77, 78, 79, 106, 118
Kiesler, D. J., 74
Kihlstrom, John, 9, 38
Klein, Melanie, 70, 124
Klerman, G. L., 112
Klinger, Eric, 9, 172
Kobasa, S. C., 34

Köhler, Wolfgang, 75
Korn, E. H., 170
Korzybski, Alfred, 76
Kosslyn, Stephen, 9
Kreitler, H., 30
Kreitler, S., 30, 132
Kris, Ernst, 70
Kristeller, Jean, 168

Lakoff, George, 121, 179
Lang, P. J., 108–109, 117
Langer, Ellen, 168, 169
Language, 54, 76
Lateral eye movements, 116, 117
Lazarus, Arnold, 75, 90, 105, 111
Learned mindfulness skills, 168
Learning theory, 5, 75–76
Leibniz, Gottfried Wilhelm, 21–22
Lerner, Max, 163
Leuner, Hans-Carl, 72, 79, 95, 101
Leviathan (Hobbes), 20
Levis, D. J., 115
Lewin, Isaac, 49–50
Lewin, Kurt, 12, 75
Lewis, Helen Block, 83
Lexical system, 49
Life rules, 125, 166
Lifespan crises, 93
Linden, W., 172
Loewenstein, Rudolph, 70
Logical intelligence, 64
Logical thinking, 49
Lubart, T. I., 147
Luborsky, L., 91, 96, 97
Luthe, H., 72

MacArthur Foundation, 92, 128, 136
Maddi, S. R., 34
Magnetic resonance imaging (MRI), 28
Mahoney, Michael, 80, 105
Make-believe, 11
Maladaptive beliefs, 119
Mandel, M. R., 112
Mandler, G., 53
Marcel, Anthony, 9
Margolin, Arthur, 137
Markus, H. R., 132
Marlatt, Alan, 168

Massage, 71
Mastery imagery, 109
Mathews, A. M., 117, 171
Maupin, E. W., 172
Mayer, John, 158
McAdams, D., 33
McCraven, Vivian, 131
McFall, R. M., 175
McLeod, J., 91
Mead, George, 74
Meaning structure, 30
Meditation, 170, 172
Meichenbaum, Donald, 80, 105, 107–108, 115, 124
Meins, E. C., 62
Memory(-ies)
    and cognitive model, 124–128
    and imagination, 20
    and self-representations, 131
    short-/long-term encoding of, 31
Memory image, 18
Menninger Foundation, 83
Mental disorders prediction, 151
Mentalization, 62
Messer, S. B., 103
Metaphorical imagination, 121
Miller, Neal, 70, 76
Mindfulness, 145, 168–169
Mind-mindedness, 62
Minnesota Multiphasic Personality Inventory, 5
Mistakes, learning from, 148
"Mister Rogers' Neighborhood" (TV show), 59
M&M study, 48
Modern Times (film), 185
Moleski, L. M., 179
Monitoring stage (problem-solving), 154
Mood, 133–134
Motivation, 142–143
Motivational structure, 32–34, 131
Mozart, Wolfgang Amadeus, 23
"Mr. D" (case example), 137–138
M response, 12, 13
MRI (magnetic resonance imaging), 28
"Mr. L" (case example), 138–141
"Mrs. Renfrew" (case study), 177–179
"Mrs. Vogel" (case study), 15–18
Murphy, Gardner, 12
Murray, Henry, 12
Music, 164

Narrative psychotherapy, 73
Narrative system, 55
Narrative themes, 93–94
Narrative thought, 43–45, 53–65
    children's play and origins of, 58–64
    and life story in ongoing consciousness, 57–58
    maximizing adaptive functions of, 64–65
    and role of imagery in human condition, 53–57
National Institute of Mental Health, 180
Nebuchadnezzar, 19
Negotiation metaphors, 121
New Yorker (magazine), 67
New York Psychoanalytic Society, 74
Nietzsche, Friedrich, 68
Night dreams, 176–177
Nondirective counseling, 72–73
Nonrational heuristic thinking, 47
Nonrepresentational visual art, 51
Nouveaux Essaix (Leibniz), 21
Novelty confrontation, 43
Nurius, P., 132

Obsessive–compulsive disorder (OCD), 123–124
Obstacles, overcoming, 149
OCD. See Obsessive–compulsive disorder
Old Testament, 19
Ongoing consciousness, 172–174
Openness trait, 169
Oppenheimer, Robert, 165
Ordered anxiety hierarchy, 110
Orgone boxes, 71
Out-of-awareness phenomena, 38

Pacini, R., 150
Pamuk, Orhan, 62
Paradigmatic mode, 43–45
Parataxic distortions, 101
Pavlov, Ivan, 75
"The Peddler" (Wordsworth), 22–23
Pennsylvania School of Social Work, 70, 72
Perls, Frederick, 71, 73
Persia, 19
Personal construct psychotherapy, 56, 79, 106, 118

Relaxation, 72, 75, 110, 112, 164, 170–172

Religious practices, 163–164

Repetition, 120

Repressive defensiveness, 169–170

Research, 74

Resistance, identification of, 95–96

Resource allocation stage, 154

Response propositions, 108, 117

Reyher, Joseph, 94

Risk taking, sensible, 148–149

"Robert" (case study), 62–64

Rogers, Carl, 5, 29, 70–73, 130

Role construct repertory list, 106

Role relationship model, 91

Role repertory method, 79

Romantic period, 22–24

Root-Bernstein, Michelle, 185

Root-Bernstein, Robert, 185

Rorschach, Hermann, 12

Rorschach inkblot, 5

Rosenberg, M., 133

Rubin, David, 57

Russell, Bertrand, 76, 77, 174

Ryle, Gilbert, 76

Safran, J. D., 103

Sales, tacit knowledge and, 150–151

Salovey, Peter, 158

Sarason, I. G., 108

Schachtel, E. G., 33

Schemas, 30, 53–54, 70, 131, 137, 152

Schiller, Friedrich, 22

Schonbar, Rosalea, 130

Schubert, Franz, 24

Schultz, J. H., 72

Schwartz, G. E., 112, 116

Scripts, 30, 124–128

Searle, John, 9, 28

Secondary thought process, 90

Segal, Zindel, 168

Self-conscious imagination, 20–21

Self-consciousness, 21

Self-disclosure, 184

Self-efficacy, 109–110

Self-esteem, 133

Self-guides, 131

Self-regulation principles, 142–143

Self-relevance, 132

Self-representations, 91–93, 127, 130–145

    case studies of, 136–141

    and self-system therapy, 142–145

    Singer's research/explorations of, 130–136

Self-system therapy (SST), 142–145

    cognitive therapy vs., 144

    treatment manual for, 159

Semantics, general, 76

Sensory image, 18, 54–55

Shakespeare, William, 20, 54–55, 179

Sheikh, A. A., 94, 164, 179

Sheikh, K. S., 179

Shenk, C., 169, 170

Shorr, Joseph, 94

Singer, Dorothy, 62

Singer, J. A., 127, 166

Singer, J. L., 6, 34, 38, 108, 127, 168

    and assessment of imagery, 116

    background of, 4–5

    childhood memories of, 10–11

    and enhancement of imagery, 118

    and imaginal thought, 169

    influences on career of, 12–13

    and intelligence, 146

    on William James, 27

    and positive imagery, 109, 111, 112

    self-awareness development in, 10

    and self-relevance study, 132

    and self-representation, 137

    at Villa Sorbelloni, 110

Skinner, B. F., 75, 107

Smith, M. L., 110

Social isolation, 174

Social learning therapy, 70

Social psychology, 26

Social Sciences Citation Index, 150

Socioculturally determined structures, 81, 83

Socrates, 147, 186

Spanos, Nicholas, 9

Spearman, C., 145

Specificity, image, 92, 94, 167–169

SST. See Self-system therapy

Stampfl, T. G., 115

Stanford-Binet test, 145

Stephen Dedalus (fictional character), 35–37

Sternberg, Robert, 56, 145–147, 149–151, 185

Stimulus propositions, 108
Storytelling, 91
Strategy formulation stage, 153–154
Strauman, T. J., 132, 134, 142, 168
Stream of consciousness, 24, 173
The Stream of Consciousness (Pope & Singer), 6
Stress inoculation, 115
Successful intelligence, 56, 145–159
    applications of, 152–154
    as basis for psychotherapeutic approach, 145–146
    case study of, 155–158
    components of, 147–152
Successful intelligence journals, 153
Sullivan, Harry Stack, 6, 70, 74, 93, 101, 131
Superego, 132
Superliminal (above-conscious-threshold) activity, 39
Survey of Mental Imagery, 116
Synectics, 184
Systematic desensitization, 110–111

Tacit knowledge, 150–152
Taft, Jessie, 70, 72
Tanar of Pellucidar (Burroughs), 12
Tauber, Edward, 183
Tchaikovsky, Pyotr, 23–24
Teasdale, John, 168
Technique(s)
    for psychotherapeutic situation, 85–88
    as term, 85
Thematic Apperception Test, 12–13
Thematic apperception tests, 5
Theory of mind, 25–26
Therapeutic alliance, 85
Thompson, Clara, 70, 74
Thorndike, Edward, 75
Thurstone, L. L., 146
Thurstone, T. C., 146
Time projection, 120
Tolman, Edward Chase, 5, 75, 76
"Tom" (case study), 166–167
Tomkins, Silvan, 12–13, 27, 29, 34, 38, 53, 112, 124, 142, 143, 166, 185
Tom Sawyer (Twain), 23, 62
Tower, R. B., 116
"Town imagery," 20

Training
    creative thought, 148–149
    meditative, 168
Transactional therapy, 78
Transference, 96–102, 181–183
    dream content emergence of, 98–100
    extramural, 101–102
    within psychotherapy session, 98
    in waking fantasy, 100–101
Treatment manuals, 180
Turk, D. C., 115
Twain, Mark, 23, 62
Twentyman, C. T., 175

Ulysses (Joyce), 35–37
Unconscious processes, 37–38
University of Pennsylvania, 5
Unwanted fantasy, turning off, 119–120

Van Egeren, L. F., 171
Velmans, Max, 9, 28
Verbalizer–Visualizer Questionnaire, 116
Verbal system, 49
Veterans Administration Clinic, 5, 12
Vieth, Angela, 142–144
Vivid imagery, 72, 116
Vividness of Visual Imagery Questionnaire, 116
Vogt, Oskar, 72, 95
Voluntary control, 50

Waking dream approach, 72
Waking fantasy, 100–101
Warren, C. S., 103
"Washers," 123
Watson, John, 75
Wechsler Intelligence Scales, 5, 145
Weiss, Joseph, 70, 78
Wertheimer, Max, 75
What Cheer, Iowa, 3, 4
Wilcoxon, L. A., 111
Wilkins, W., 111, 171
William Alanson White Institute, 5–6
Williams, Wendy, 151
Winnicott, Donald W., 70
Witkin, Herman, 83
Wittgenstein, Ludwig, 76

ABOUT THE AUTHOR

Jerome L. Singer, PhD, received his doctorate in 1950 in clinical psychology from the University of Pennsylvania. He is Professor Emeritus of Psychology at Yale University, where he served for many years as director of the graduate program in clinical psychology and also as director of graduate studies in psychology. Dr. Singer is codirector, with Dorothy G. Singer, of the Yale University Family Television Research and Consultation Center. He has authored more than 250 articles on thought processes, imagery, personality, and psychotherapy as well as on children's play and the effects of television. Dr. Singer has served as president of the Division of Personality and Social Psychology of the American Psychological Association and has also served terms as president of the Eastern Psychological Association and of the American Association for the Study of Mental Imagery. Dr. Singer has written or coedited more than 15 books, including *The Inner World of Daydreaming*, *The Power of Human Imagination*, *The Stream of Consciousness*, and *The Human Personality*. Currently he is coeditor of the journal *Imagination, Cognition and Personality*.